the post calvin

selected essays
2013–2016

the post calvin

selected essays
2013–2016

Josh deLacy
Will Montei
Debra Rienstra
Abby Zwart

Illustrations by Maria Smilde

First Printing: November 2016

ISBN 978-0-9983368-1-7

Available from Amazon.com and other retail outlets.
For bulk purchases, contact info@thepostcalvin.com.

http://thepostcalvin.com

for Professor Bill Vande Kopple

We are a collection of Calvin College graduates who couldn't stop writing when the classes were done. Here, we explore these restless post-diploma years in the best way we know how.

Editors
Josh deLacy
Will Montei
Debra Rienstra
Abby Zwart

Book Designer	*Copyeditors*	*Illustrator*
Josh deLacy	Catherine Kramer	Maria Smilde
	Geneva Langeland	
	Abby Zwart	
	Sadie Burgher	
	Anneke Kapteyn	
	Carolyn Muyskens	

Contributors

Alissa Anderson	Greg Kim	Jacob Schepers
Nard Choi	Andrew Knot	Calah Schlabach
Josh deLacy	Catherine Kramer	Elaine Schnabel
Ben DeVries	Jenn Langefeld	Maria Smilde
Melissa Dykhuis	Geneva Langeland	Andrew Steiner
Amy Frieson	Sabrina Lee	Libby Stille
David Greendonner	Matt Medendorp	Ryan Struyk
Gabe Gunnink	Rebekah Medendorp	Sarah Sundt
Lauren Harris	Nick Meekhof	Bethany Tap
Mary Margaret Healy	Paul Menn	Bart Tocci
Caroline Higgins	Will Montei	Katie Van Zanen
Laura Hubers	Stephen Mulder	Cassie Westrate
Matt Hubers	Andrew Orlebeke	Robert Zandstra
Griffin Paul Jackson	Katerina Parsons	Abby Zwart
Michael Kelly	Ben Rietema	Brad Zwiers

Contents

NINE TO FIVE

ODE TO THE MIDWEST

DEPARTURES

ALL'S FAIR IN LOVE

WHERE THE HEART IS

TO ACT JUSTLY

FEMINIST CONFESSIONS

GRAY MATTERS

BREAD AND BUTTER

List of Illustrations

Foreword

Debra Rienstra

I T's COMMON ENOUGH to tsk-tsk about young adults, or worry about them, or assemble statistics about them. Rarely, however, do we listen to them.

All the more reason to treasure *the post calvin*, a space created and sustained by recent graduates of Calvin College. In this space, we can all celebrate the power of writing, specifically the short essay, as a place for true speaking and deep listening. Anyone who cares about young people—anyone curious about human experience, actually—will find in these essays a window onto the passions, worries, and wisdom of twenty-somethings, freshly launched into adulthood. Plus, it's great writing, straight up.

A selection of *post calvin* essays in print honors the achievement of *the post calvin*'s first three years and, we hope, helps expand the circle of those who will come to this space for solace, provocation, and amusement. This print anthology, beautifully curated by Josh, Will, and Abby, with the help of the whole *post calvin* group, gives us something tangible to plop into a friend's hands with the admonition: "Read this!"

Life after college is what we might call unexplored territory in our public imagination. Yet it's a fascinating paradox of new responsibilities and new freedoms, a period of enormous upheaval and tentative settling down. Testing what you've been told. Trying one thing, laying it down, trying another.

In these essays, the best of our best excellent young writers recount their adventures, mishaps, ambitions, and joys. They review concerts and celebrate weirdness. They write a lot about change: getting married, having a baby, reconnecting with relatives, inviting old friends to move in with them, making new friends in new towns, and moving. Always moving.

Regret, nostalgia, kookiness, and prophetic pronouncements swirl together in a single essay. Wide-openness and wariness, earnestness and cynicism inhabit the same sentences. Doubt and faith, disillusionment and hope jostle together in their paragraphs.

I'm inspired by their exuberance and occasionally heartbroken by their longing. Maybe you will be too.

Debra Rienstra
Professor of English
Grand Rapids, Michigan
November 7, 2016

Preface

Josh deLacy

I DON'T OWN BEAUTIFUL books. I own books from clearance shelves, Barnes & Noble gift cards, rummage sales, and giveaways. An ashy Viggo Mortensen broods on a cover, and a tuxedoed Leonardo DiCaprio smirks at a spine. Oprah's sale-skyrocketing O plants itself front and center; an embossed *National Book Award Finalist* shouts louder than the title. Half a dozen sale-boosting reviews flood the first few pages, while publishers' advertisements drown the last. These are paper cookies fresh from the cutter. *Emma* is *Dracula* is *Beowulf* is efficiency, with identical layouts and fonts and colors. It means lower prices: $4.95 printed on a back cover or $2.99 penciled on an inside flap, and lower prices means I can fill my house with bookshelves and my bookshelves with books. Lower prices means more people can fall in love with Mr. Darcy, kill buggers with Ender, and save Middle Earth with Frodo. This is a good thing.

I don't own much that's beautiful. What do I have that wasn't created with cost as a primary concern? My jeans, mass-produced. My car came off an assembly line. My food grew on thousand-acre farms, and my wallet, shoes, contacts, deodorant—even my sleeping bag and rock climbing gear—all of it has come to me cookie-cutter, standardized for efficiency. What do I own that wasn't made in bulk? My haircut, I suppose.

It makes me see the appeal of farm-to-table culture: cucumbers and kale that are distinct and cared-for, in their own small way. Or the draw of live music, a small church, or microbrewed beer. It's all very fashionable, but it's also why people buy art.

I don't want to revive the arts and crafts movement, and God knows the world has enough macramé. I just want more things made with effectiveness, or beauty, or personality as a bigger end goal than efficiency. To know that something is the best it could be. Not a lot of things—I couldn't afford that—but a few things.

This book is not efficient. Making it was impractical, time-consuming, and not cost-effective at all. I can't say whether we succeeded in making something beautiful, but we intended to, and we obsessed over every detail except the printing and binding. That means the mistakes are all ours, but so, too, are the good parts.

I embraced that liberal arts cliché of learning how to learn and checked out two dozen books and two hundred websites about typography. I learned the difference between REAL SMALL CAPS and PSEUDO SMALL CAPS, *true italics* and *false italics*, good kerning and bad kerning. I can tell you that the font you're reading is Caslon, the favored font of the British Empire, and, ironically, the same one used for the first printed copies of the Declaration of Independence. I can tell you, more specifically, that you're reading a particular 1990 revival of that font called Adobe Caslon Pro, which contains no measly 52-charactered upper-case and lower-case alphabet, but a horde of ligatures, symbols, *Swashes*, & ornaments that add up to 2,721 different things we could print on this page.

Abby Zwart, Geneva Langeland, and Catherine Kramer proofread those things. They picked up misplaced commas and dropped off forgotten hyphens, cleaned up inconsistencies and buffed out double-spaces. They tidied and straightened every sentence in this book, and then the Calvin Center for Faith and Writing fellows floated in to finish the job of making these pages invisible. Like breath, referees, and sewer systems, you only notice grammar when it's bad.

Maria Smilde, our website's illustrator, reprised her role and perfected it. She translated the ideas in this book into images, just as the writers had translated those same ideas into essays. The illustrations in this book aren't the fuzzy result of some chain of idea → words → picture, with meaning obscured and lost at each step; the illustrations and essays stand here together, arm-in-arm.

All this to say: this anthology is more than its words.

But this doesn't diminish its words, and I like to think it accomplishes the opposite. Forty-five people contributed to this book, and their writing arrived personal and deliberate and inefficient. These eighty-eight essays from *the post calvin*'s first three years, eighty-eight picked from more than a thousand, follow no formulas or easy standardization. They present post-diploma life like it happens: confident and insecure, specific and abstract, self-absorbed and selfless. It's a conflicting, struggling, yearning mess, and the only through-lines I've found are honesty and a desire to make something beautiful from it all, however small or insignificant. We don't own much that's beautiful.

We crafted every part of this book we could, and now we pass it to you for the owning and the reading. Underline quotes and fold corners, spill coffee and stain pages. Read languidly, or sporadically, or however pleases you—I only ask that you do it

the post calvin

selected essays

2013–2016

Introduction

Abby Zwart

I F THERE'S ONE THING we've learned in three-plus years of curating a website featuring recent college graduates, it's that growing up looks different on everyone. As if that were any surprise. Almost anywhere you click on *the post calvin*, you'll find a piece with a coming-of-age undercurrent. *Where has the time gone?* we wonder. *Who was supposed to teach me about these adult responsibilities? Am I ever going to find a place where I belong?*

We've begun this collection of essays with a section called "Growing Pains" that plunges right into the current. Lauren and Caroline want the best of every age, every place, every thing. Rebekah and Matt watch the time slip by. Michael and Josh feel the ache that comes with growing out of a friend or a home or a dream of what your life could be.

You'll feel that current in other sections. We make grown-up choices, for better or worse, in "Two Roads Diverged." We squirm restlessly inside the size-too-small faith we've been raised with in "This I Believe." We're not altogether pleased with the adult world and the problems we've inherited in "To Act Justly" and "Feminist Confessions." And, of course, we're growing into love. In "All's Fair in Love," Will wonders about sex and

Catherine and Sarah are both newlyweds and Katie struggles with long distance.

It all starts to look a bit bleak. Post-grad, twenty-something, Millennial ennui has been the cliché of the century so far, and we've got a lot of haters in the older generations. We're too dependent on technology, they say. We can't work independently. We're spoiled and entitled. We don't love America. We hold up the line at coffee shops with our demands for single origin organic soy lattes. If only we'd wake up and smell the black coffee, they sigh.

But this anthology will also show you that we're not all angst and anxiety. Geneva celebrates a warm day on the farm and Nick learns to love Ohio in "Ode to the Midwest." Jake raises a potty-trained family and Greg's parents come to visit from Korea, both with much less stress than anticipated in "Where the Heart Is." And so many of us know wonderful, hilarious, inspiring people whom we've captured in "Portrait Gallery."

Yeah, we make a lot of mistakes. We quit our perfectly adequate jobs, or we drink too much, or we date a lot of people—often online, often badly. We can't help it. We've been thrust into a world with so many possibilities that it's almost paralyzing. As Professor Bill Vande Kopple, a great friend and confidant to many of us, used to say: "It's a tough world." He's not here to guide us anymore, but we're learning to strike out on our own. We're grading papers and going to grad school in "Classroom 101," traveling the world and meeting strangers in "Departures," and learning to live with the ugly in "Gray Matters."

And through it all, we're writing. Texts, emails, blog posts, to-do lists, tweets, essays, sales pitches, quizzes, bibliographies. Growing up looks different on everyone, but on *the post calvin*, at least we have that in common.

Growing Pains

I am a quilt of a person. Stitched together unknowingly by sunlit triumphs and unforeseen sorrows, the late-night conversations and early-morning prayers, and the sweat-browed determination and humble commitment of all those who came before me.

Stay Gold, Ponyboy

Lauren (Boersma) Harris

I REALIZED ONCE THAT I view the timeline of my life more like a tree than a line.

Each time the linear, everyday trunk of my life reaches a choice, the timeline splits into hypothetical branches. Paper or Plastic? Walk or Drive? Sushi or Takeout? Stay or Go? This series of choices mushrooms into a complex network of things my life *is* and things that it *could have been*.

If I decide to be a business major, I can no longer "be anything that I want to be." I am limited in my opportunities to become a gymnast, a nurse, or the next Jason Bourne. I fear making decisions because I fear that I will regret them; I fear climbing branches because I'm just taking one step farther away from the possibilities that are available before I make the choice. And, once I've finally gathered the courage to climb to a branch and I experience something wonderful, I cling to it with splintering fingernails long beyond the stunning season of its bloom.

Here's the thing. Robert Frost has a poem that you've probably heard if you've ever read *The Outsiders* (which you should) or you've ever been in a seventh grade literature class. He writes about nature, and how the green beauty of the world is preceded

7

by impermanent moments of gold. Every tree and branch has an instant of unique brilliance when it first buds and blossoms, but that brilliance is momentary. Soon, flowers and golden buds fall away to the dependable, familiar green that characterizes our everyday lives.

As Frost says, "Nothing gold can stay."

That's the trouble with me. I want everything to stay gold. I'm the crazy lady who picks a flower, rushes to Home Depot to buy fertilizer and Miracle-Gro, talks to the man behind the counter to find out the secret to agricultural eternal life, sanitizes my kitchen so that not a single floral disease will attack my precious plant, Googles the proper amount of sunlight, and rebuilds my kitchen to accommodate, never realizing that the flower actually died three days ago.

You can't hold on to every cup of coffee forever. If you don't drink it, it will get cold. If you keep trying to pretend that your daughter is still an infant, your experience as a parent chaperone on that next field trip is going to be a little awkward. If you lie crying on the floor outside your ex-boyfriend's apartment, dripping with snot and mascara while you continue to scream incoherent things about the way he smells like Old Spice, someone might mistake you for a crazy person.

It's okay when beautiful moments pass away. It just means that they were real. They were gold. We've all put a lightning bug in a jar, expecting it to light up our bedside table for the rest of forever, as long as we poke holes in the lid. But eventually, the light goes out. And we can't waste our lives trying to resuscitate dead lightning bugs.

Here's another thing. We can love those gold moments while they live, because when they live, they shine. Sometimes they flame out in a blaze of glory. Sometimes they glow and crackle and go out in a puff of smoke. Sometimes, if we're lucky, they're like that frozen moment when you jump off a swing and time seems to stop, like if you wanted to scratch your knee in midair it would be a very real possibility because you have years until your butt will hit the ground.

But eventually, all of our butts hit the ground. Summer vacation ends. We break up. J.K. Rowling stops writing Harry Potter books. The bath water gets cold. The ice cream scoop scrapes the bottom of the box. We realize that we're about to break curfew. We graduate from college.

Someday, we've got this promise of a glory land, a place where our forever will be golden. But in this life, as Frost writes, "Leaf subsides to leaf." We can only hold on to the eternal and know that the fleeting beautiful moments of this world are just tiny buds that flower and die on the tree of life. Maybe we can't climb to every branch on the tree while we putter around as the mere psychotic mortals that we are, but making some progress is better than standing, anxiety-ridden, at the bottom of the tree while everyone else works their way from branch to branch.

So what? So the world isn't perfect. So beautiful things don't last forever. So we can't just push the pause button when we feel like our life is right where we want it. Constant motion. Doesn't that make the adventure an adventure?

When one moment subsides, be assured that there will be another. Life is a bunch of golden moments, strung together, building a ladder to eternity that will crumble in the presence of something of which these moments are only crude caveman drawings. Life was built to be lived. So live it. And realize what you're doing. Don't let those golden moments pass you by—grab onto them with all your might, squeeze them between your teeth if you have to. But know when it's time to let them go.

Here's the last thing. Look backward with a happy heart. Look out for what's in front of you. And for now, climb that next branch and look forward to the resurrection day, when gold comes to stay.

Superlative Syndrome

Caroline Higgins

I AM REGULARLY TEASED for using too many superlative phrases. "This is the *best*," I will often proclaim. Another one of my favorites is "This is all I have ever wanted," which I have been known to use in a situation as daily and simple as reading a well-worn book with a warm cup of coffee. I realize that I can't keep telling multiple people, "You are my favorite person!" and I should probably stop referring to certain vacations, or even fun-filled weekend excursions, as "the best trip ever!" A friend once told me that I couldn't keep telling people that swimming out to the sandbar at the beach was "*so* much fun" because then, what will I say when we actually do something that is extraordinary?

But the truth is, it was so much fun, and all of my friends are my favorite in their own way. Sleeping in is my favorite. Waking up early is my favorite. Cooking healthy food is my favorite. Eating mac and cheese every day? Also my favorite.

Can't we love it all?

I am comforted by the fact that I am not the only one who has been faced with this problem. Kerouac, for example, was puzzled by the fact that he had too many ideas and passions. "I like too many things and get all confused and hung-up running from one falling star to another 'til I drop," he writes in *On the Road*. It is in this book that he also writes, "the only people for me are the mad ones ... desirous of everything at the same time."

I hate making decisions. Deciding what to watch on Netflix is impossible. I prefer to order last when eating at a restaurant in hopes that the pressure of everyone turning to me and the waiter's hand outstretched to retrieve my menu will force me into finally choosing between the vegetable pad thai and the fish tacos.

Do I embrace new adventures joyfully because I can't make decisions? Because I need a change? Or because there is a good chance that I will love it?

In early July, I spent a week in Alberta where my best friend and former roommate, Emily, had grown up. Ultimately, I was there to be a bridesmaid in her wedding.

The wedding was at her dairy farm, and everything about the experience was beautifully rustic. Remembering the way Emily had thrown herself into my family's New York life when she visited my hometown (despite the "I'm the only blonde person on the subway!" comment), I was excited to experience everything about the dairy farm where my best friend grew up.

So I let baby calves with rough tongues suck on my fingers before I unpacked and followed Emily up a dangerously rickety staircase to a hayloft. I listened eagerly to every detail about how Holsteins are bred and how often the government milk truck comes and when and how the oldest son of the family is going to inherit the farm—all while riding around muddy roads in a John Deere Gator.

I stopped caring about whether or not I was getting dust on my white shorts or cow manure on my shoes. I jumped at the opportunity to drive Emily's father's farm truck to pick up more wedding attendees and friends from the airport. After driving around the nearby downtown area with them for a while to purchase wedding gifts and such, I jokingly commented, "This city driving is exhausting! I need to get back to the farm!" A good friend called me out: "Caroline. You grew up twenty minutes from New York City. Stop pretending to be a farm girl."

Still, I could see the appeal of growing up in a place where you are awakened by your father getting up at 5:30 a.m. to milk the cows, spend your afternoons running through fields and around your mother's vegetable garden, and the evenings swinging on a big wooden swing that your grandfather built.

I loved the way the wedding party and relatives from afar congregated and camped on the farm, dozens of people arriving days before the wedding to contribute their hands and hearts. During the day, groomsmen climbed trees to hang twinkle lights and constructed the dance floor while aunts and cousins set tables and folded place-cards. At night someone inevitably built a campfire that was then encircled by everyone from small children to grandparents, us kids in our twenties being the last to linger over the smoking embers. The nights grew surprisingly cold, and one night the northern lights were just visible enough for the out-of-towners to stand in awe only to hear the locals say, "This is nothing."

After watching an incredible sunset from the end of Emily's gravel driveway, I was ready to buy a piece of land, raise a family down the road, and never look back. As I considered my options and prayed a two-word prayer I read once in a book by Annie Dillard ("Last forever!"), the photographer in me came once again to believe that everything and everyone is beautiful in the right lighting. But this—right now—is my favorite.

Quarter of a Century

Rebekah (Williamson) Medendorp

TODAY I AM twenty-five.

I like to think that I know myself well. After all, for the past 9,125 days I have been enfleshed in this one particular body and witnessed the world through the windows of these two particular eyes. I have spent a lot of time twiddling my thumbs and thumbing through my thoughts. As I tunnel deeper into the mines of memory, I discover moments and murmurs burrowed deeply into the caverns of my brain, unbeknownst to me.

I would like to believe that I know myself well, but I begin to wonder if this self is actually mine. This shell oscillates between compacting my world into a 5′6″ configuration of a body... to encapsulating an entire universe within itself.

Today I am twenty-five, but it has taken generations to assemble me for this day.

I am a quilt of a person. Stitched together unknowingly by sunlit triumphs and unforeseen sorrows, late-night conversations and early-morning prayers, and the sweat-browed determination and humble commitment of all those who came before me. I am a tangle of my mother, grandmother, and great-grandmother, one stitch of the bloodline sewing in as another unravels.

Today I am sixteen, and my soul quivers for adventure.

My brother overspent his monthly budget by calling me direct from Paris. As he congratulates me on surviving another year, I hear the whispers of conversation beyond him mingled with the clinking of glasses and sloshing of beverages. I hear the trickles of life shared in foreign pubs with old friends and new strangers.

My father's father was born in China to missionaries who believed they were barren. He was raised as an alien among citizens, and I wonder at the trickles of life he shared with strangers and friends in a world that was not his own. Did he quiver for the adventure?

Today I am five, and losing history.

I never knew my father's father. No, that's not quite true. I knew him the day he died. I was there. In the room of machines with their miniscule blinking colored lights and the low hum of robotic life that outlived the patient whose life it had, until recently, sustained. I was five and he was old and dying and death scared me but I wish I could go back and ask him to entrust me the wonders of his travels. I wish we could share whispers in rooms of clinking glass and sloshing beverages. I wish I could tell him that I have legends of him stitched into my skin and that I am so proud to be his.

Today I am twenty-one, and my body trembles from effort.

My mother called from Michigan, and I tell her about my chores. I tell her my hands still shake from chainsawing and that old blisters have skinned over to roughened palms. I need my mother to know I experience the earth under my fingernails just like her, and just like her dad.

I'll never be able to ask my mother's father if he wanted to be a sugar-beet farmer. Or ask if it was only what he did to feed his wife and five children. I am a byproduct of his existence on earth, and I crave the hardiness of calloused hands. Would he be proud? Where else can that joy spring from but a grandfather whose days were spent among the fields?

Today I am twenty-four and three-hundred-sixty-four days old.

Maybe I want to be fantastical, pristine, and delicious? Or maybe I want to be entrenched deeply in wisdom of grandparents who survived world wars.

In a time and culture when being twenty-five, unmarried, and professional is a deeply respected symbol of detachedness, I cling to the strands of blood and body that tether me to this hallowed ground.

I have lived a mere quarter of a century, but I am centuries old.

Playing Pretend

Michael Kelly

M̲Y̲ ̲C̲O̲U̲S̲I̲N̲ ̲R̲Y̲A̲N̲ and I used to play this game whenever our families got together for the holidays. The premise was elementary, as were we. We dreamt up this large, imaginary dog that was in his basement, waiting to chase us, but if we ran fast enough across the room and jumped onto a sofa or a chair, then we'd be safe. It was up to interpretation what the dog looked like. I pictured a white, shaggy dog, like a Komondor. I discovered later that my cousin could have been picturing any dog because this game he created was based off of a real phobia of his, which dampens the memory a little.

The fear, however, never outshined the fun of screaming and running through the basement, jumping on furniture, tripping, laughing, and enjoying this strange game that always had two winners.

I don't remember what age we grew too old for make-believe, but it was somewhere around middle school. The next logical transition was video games since they are basically still make-believe games, but more socially acceptable. Ryan is about two years older than me, so as we grew up he usually dictated how we spent our time. *Crash Bandicoot* was my favorite game, probably because I was younger and the main character looks like a stuffed animal. Ryan, however, loved *Golden Eye*, so that's what we played the most. He would try to teach me how to be James Bond, but I was more comfortably a sidekick. That said, I usually just sat and watched. But that was fine with me, because it still saved me from sitting at my parents' side listening to the adult conversations that bored me to death every holiday. We didn't have the time or patience to hear stories about grandma's sister's ex-husband who recently passed away or the rude phone call that Aunt Carroll got at her new temp job. Didn't any of them care that there were Russian space weapons to destroy?!

Ryan ended up beating the game without me. We only saw each other a couple days each year, so I wasn't hurt about it. What did hurt came later: quiet and unexpected.

It wasn't growing up, or growing apart; it was both, all at once.

Ryan hated school more than anything. He almost didn't finish high school because it was so excruciatingly boring to him. He didn't get anything out of reading books or writing papers. He wanted to build massive vehicles like monster trucks and semis, with a cold beer close by and a radio blasting '70s rock—and he appears to be living out that dream right now.

And then there's me, the guy who became so passionate about education that I not only went on to college after high school, but then also went on to a graduate school of education where I'm being educated about education every day.

We weren't opposites, Ryan and I. We were family. But that familial bond seems to have changed so drastically with us: from held hands to handcuffs.

I can't remember when or how, but one day Ryan decided that it was time to stop playing. He wanted to go upstairs and rejoin the rest of the family. I didn't understand. I was having so much fun. Maybe Ryan thought that since there were other children in the family now, they needed the basement space for their own fantastical adventures. Or maybe I did something that upset him.

It probably wasn't even a conscious decision, just a quick one out of boredom.

As I imagine Ryan running up the stairs before me, I imagine myself knowing that it was the last time we would hide away in his basement together. But what I couldn't imagine at that age was that it would be the last time we would play together, or laugh together. It was the last time that I would think, "At least we have each other." What I didn't know when I reached that final stair and saw Ryan sitting quietly, watching whatever football game was on TV, was that this was how we would spend every holiday after: watching the game, and watching the clock, from a few more feet apart.

Homeless

Josh deLacy

COURTESY OF A RACIST sixty-year-old neighbor who still lives with his mother; a virtually nonexistent housing inventory caused by Jeff Bezos, Mt. Rainier, and murky multi-family home regulations; the less-than-shining precedent set by other groups of male, twenty-something renters; and a healthy dose of my own selectivity and procrastination, I have been rendered, once again, homeless.

I'm typing this in Shari's, where I paid seven dollars for late-night wifi, warmth, and a place to charge my phone—plus bonus buffalo wings—after spending the evening in a library and showering at a gym. I'll spend tonight in the Shari's parking lot, probably in the back seat of my car, once I stop deluding myself that *this* time, sleeping shotgun will actually work out comfortably. I'll brush my teeth and change clothes at a coffeeshop tomorrow morning, and then I'll face another day of working from home without a home.

This might end next week. Or it might stretch deep into the following week, or even deeper into March or early April, depending on tomorrow's house showings, and depending on the success of my steamroll-the-landlord-with-the-most-goddamn-professional-emails-he's-ever-read strategy. In the meantime, I'm sharing a 10′ × 15′ storage unit with another homeless, male, twenty-something would-be-renter. We managed to stuff what was supposed to be a larger than necessary unit floor-to-ceiling with bookshelves and beds and couches and more bookshelves and a motorcycle. At least I'm saving money on rent, I suppose. Even accounting for the storage unit, coffeeshops, and midnight restaurants, I'll save a few hundred bucks this month.

I don't *need* to sleep in my car. Not really. I stay some nights with my parents as yet another reluctant victim of the boomerang generation, some nights with a friend who lives within driving distance of work meetings, and some nights with old friends from church. But it's freeing. And like leg day at the gym, or like a fourteen-hour all-night work session, tossing and turning in my sleeping bag feels like a masochistic form of fun.

It helps that this isn't real homelessness. There's an end in sight, even if landlords and leasing agents keep repainting the finish line farther and farther away. I'm not shackled by disability or addiction, or by a felony, or by the impossibility of supporting three kids with a minimum-wage job. My type of homelessness comes with a gym and clean clothes. It comes with a livable income, even by Seattle's standards. It's fake, I'll admit, and it feels a bit like slumming, but nights in my car reassure me.

They remind me I don't need my storage unit full of luxuries. After this last year of stability, in which I steadily collected possessions and paychecks in the same way, as a kid, I had once collected worthless glass bottles just to fill space and trick myself into thinking I had made something cool, I had started to worry. Had I gone suburban? Was I a suit? My dream of independence had melted, once I had it, and for want of a safety net and better beer, I had traded writing hours for working hours, late-night discussions for late-night productivity. And as I looked ahead, farther down that rapidly urbanizing road of health insurance, Roth IRAs, and the financially wise shift from renting to owning, I saw that trade getting even worse.

I still see it. I'm still worried. But this bout of homelessness has reignited another future, one that I thought my cul-de-sac had banned alongside bonfires and backyard barbeques. It's a future with a canopied pickup or a hatchback outfitted with a bed, cooking set, and a few suits for the occasional work meeting. It's a future in which I park under the stars and trade lawn mowing for writing, dish washing for rock climbing. It's a future that would even let me divert money away from rent and into savings, satisfying the *Is it practical?* part of my brain that nags louder every year. It's a future I can get excited about. I just need a few years to save up for it.

Shakespeare at the Y:
The Seven Stages of Male Nudity

Matt Medendorp

ALL THE WORLD's a men's YMCA locker room,
And all the men merely exercisers;
They have their exits and their entrances
And varied levels of clothing,
And one man in his time wears many towels.

His acts being seven ages. At first the newcomer,
Mewling and shy in his pre-changed glory.
He removes his coat in the locker room—no more.
Stashing it hurriedly, and spinning the lock.
Eyes downcast, face pink, self-muttering.

Then, the weeklong attender, with his gym bag
And shining morning face, creeping like a snail
Unwillingly to expose his bottom fully,
Instead holding a scratchy towel up as a shield.

And then a month later, all the bolder,
Checking over his shoulder with a woeful ballad
As he quickly drops his trow, bare cheeked
and bashful to return to shorted-safety again.

Then, the veteran of many months
Full of strange oaths and jested conversation.
Still sudden, and quick in nudity,
Absolutely no eye contact allowed.

And then, the naked shower walker,
Emboldened in his newfound freedom
Towel shouldered instead of waisted.
He steps his puddled feet upon the
scale, to learn the weight of his clothes.

The sixth age shifts
to the middle-aged dad, round in belly,
who might just skip the workout.
He eschews the towel, walking into the sauna nude.
Later he'll lounge, waist deep, in the hot tub
While daycare watches his children for free.

Last scene of all,
That ends this strange eventful history,
The naked and dancing octogenarian.
Carefree in his weirdly positive body dysmorphia.
Towel dropped, leg propped up upon the bench.
An imaginary breeze sways the baggage of age.
Almost forgetting, as he struts away from his kingdom,
That the rest of the world has a dress code.

Two Roads Diverged

Who knows where you might find yourself?
Maybe nowhere.

Almost Great

Bart Tocci

I REMEMBER THREE THINGS from high school physics: my super-nerd, super-sweetheart, super-pregnant teacher who took us outside one day to demonstrate friction by driving her car and slamming on the brakes, the fear of having a birth result from said experiment, and the idea of potential energy. The potential energy contained in a wrecking ball at its peak, about to swing to crush a building. The potential energy of a slingshot, pulled tight, ready to shoot a rock.

I took the escalator up three levels to Fenway Park's EMC club. The club is a large room where I would be networking, mostly with a French angel named Melanie. I passed former Red Sox icons remembered on the walls near the escalator, and my eyes rested on a black and white photo of a player named Tony Conigliaro.

Since starting my job at Tocci Building, I work closely with my uncle, who takes great pleasure in quizzing me on things that I have no business knowing—like lines from the 1957 TV show *Maverick*, or one scenario from a single *Three Stooges* episode (started in 1925, there are 190 of these), or the best player on the Boston Bruins roster circa 1970 (Derek Sanderson, duh).

"You know who Tony C. is, don't you?"

We were eating at a sports bar called *Tony C's*, with massive screens that take up an entire wall, and about a million beers on tap. I thought, *He's the guy who owns this bar, duh.*

"No I do not."

"How do you not know who Tony C. is?!"

If I knew then what I know now, I would have said, "Because Tony C. died when I was three years old."

Tony Conigliaro was a hometown kid from Revere—the only thing that makes us love players more is if they are from our city. In his first at-bat in Fenway, at age nineteen, he hit a homerun. He hit one hundred home runs by the time he was twenty-two, and he still holds the record for the youngest player to do that in the American League.

A month after he played in the all-star game in 1967, he was hit in the face with a fastball. His cheekbone was fractured, his jaw dislocated, and his retina was permanently damaged. After a year and a half break, he played four more seasons but was never able to regain the spark he had before the injury. He retired after his eyesight became worse.

Tony died in 1990 at the age of forty-five, after a heart attack and a stroke. People say that these were certainly complications from being hit by that pitch in '67.

I walked through the EMC club, made new friends, exchanged business cards, and ate food. I sat outside the club in the cool December night, looking down onto the half-lit Fenway Park. There were no people in the stands, no screaming fans, no yelling peanut vendors or loudspeakers. It was remarkably calming—almost somber, eerie, like sitting in a cemetery.

A group of three engineers sat next to me, and we talked about the things you're supposed to talk about at a networking event. What kind of company you are, what projects you do, where you perform work. When two of the three engineers left, Seth and I talked about what you're not supposed to talk about at a networking event. Why I moved from Chicago back home to Boston. Why he moved from California back home to Boston. Relationships, family, work. He was only a few years older than me, and he told me about raising two girls, being married, and living closer to parents. We talked about community and responsibility and the perils of growing up.

We *like* Tony C. because he was good, but we love him because he could have been great. We love him for his potential. *One hundred home runs by twenty-two?* He could have been the best player who ever lived. He was a slingshot, pulled tight then snapped; a wrecking ball just starting to gather speed before its cable broke. He's a tragic hero because so many people feel that his story of injustice is our story. "If only I hadn't thrown out my shoulder." "If only I had been chosen as the boss." "If only things had gone according to my plan."

Potential is what makes you appreciate an empty stadium in the dark. Fenway, packed full of people on a warm night in June, with the lights bright, grass green, cleanest dirt you've ever seen surrounding a pearl-white home plate. You know what it *could* be.

I Am Failing

Josh deLacy

"IT DOESN'T MATTER what you do," I will tell my children, "as long as you're the best at it."

I wish someone had bred that into me.

I wish someone had repeated it over and over, setting a hook deep in my gut to drag me forward from cradle to grave, a hook more unrelenting and irreversible than any inferiority complex or compulsive disorder. Friends and family wouldn't matter. Romantic love, either. I could forget fun, and health, and adventure. Morality would go out the window, too, unless, I had a shot at being the most moral person.

My entire life would be music, or writing, or exercise. No, even more specific than that. My entire life would be concert snare drum performance. Hiking in the Olympic Mountains. Critical interpretation of seventeenth century Polish poetry.

"It doesn't matter what you do, as long as you're the best at it."

I admire that line in the same way I'm jealous of orphans. No tethers. It's a freedom unrestrained by love or commitment. It's a freedom to dedicate fully, to don a monastic fervor and never remove it, to transcend humanity and become accomplishment incarnate. It's the freedom to choose Sam Hamilton's greatness:

"On one side you have warmth and companionship and sweet understanding, and on the other—cold, lonely greatness."

That line makes well-roundedness impossible and unnecessary. The elusively attainable "well-lived life" no longer matters. But achievement? Achievement becomes as instinctual and vital as breathing. I would strain toward success like plants in a woodshed, white and deformed and fully committed to my only option for life.

But instead, I'm a twenty-four-year-old millennial who can't make up his mind.

I know that the muscled, emotionally stable mountain climber who woos intelligent women, writes bestselling memoirs, and dispenses wisdom to a crowd of intimate friends won't ever materialize. There's a clog in that pipe dream; all that will leak through, at best, is a trickle. But I can't decide what that trickle should be.

When I hit a PR at the gym, I think of the stack of books I'm not reading. When I update my website, I remember all the writing I'm not doing. When I go home for a quiet dinner with my parents, I imagine friends laughing and drinking and hiking without me.

I'm a pendulum. A see-saw. A tetherball battered back and forth that never breaks free, never soars more than a few feet in any direction before a different urge snaps me back. Opportunity cost, "the loss of potential gain from other alternatives when one alternative is chosen," is the rope that keeps me stuck. Opportunity cost, "the benefit you could have received by taking an alternative action," keeps me swinging around a pole that is familiar, well-rounded, and unexceptional. And all the while, that rope keeps shrinking, wrapping itself tighter and tighter around mediocrity. Another year, another loop.

I'm not afraid of dying—no more than most people, anyway. Growing older, however, terrifies me. I might summit Denali, publish a story, take home $100k, and marry a beautiful woman, but all the while, my potential keeps shrinking. Another year, another loop.

Take away my choices. Trap me in a monastery. Throw me in a grad program. Exile me to Alaska. Someone make a choice for me, because I'm too afraid to do it myself. They say seven career changes is average these days, but some careers can't change. Some require a lifetime of dedication, and I don't want to rule those out. English professor? Corporate leader? Even short stints scare me. What will I miss if I spend a year in the oil fields, or two years in a master's program? It's not just job costs, but life costs. I want to watch my brother grow up, and I want to visit my parents on the weekend. I want the security of an office job and the freedom of a vagabond, the fame of authorship and the wholeness of loved ones and the excitement of traveling and the comfort of financial success. I'm searching for the perfect life, and I'm failing.

Worth It

Amy (Allen) Frieson

D ID YOU WATCH *Bill Nye the Science Guy?* I did, and not just in seventh-grade science class. *Bill Nye* came on after *Arthur* and before *Wishbone* when I was in fourth grade, all shows I watched to the extent that I'd recognize the episode that started the cycle over again. I could never make out that line about inertia in the opening theme song; every time, I heard "inertia is a property of Mallory." Mallory as in the glasses-wearing redhead of *The Baby-Sitters Club*. I Googled it just now, and so it's seventeen years later that I'm finally learning inertia is a property of matter.

I am not a scientist, but right now I'm thinking about inertia.

Inertia is the resistance of any physical object to any change in its state of motion. Inertia is why my sister's cat sometimes slams into my leg when he tries to scamper down our polished-hardwood hallway. It's why people collide with each other walking carelessly down the street and it's why taxis hit cyclists. It's why it's so much easier to stay sitting at your desk instead of getting up to file some papers. And it's why sometimes I keep eating chocolate all afternoon long—it's easier than stopping eating chocolate.

Just as inertia looks different on different people, there are different types of resistance as well. Lack of money is one. So, I don't buy more chocolate when I really want it because I'm resistant to spending money on it. Then all I can think about is the chocolate I'm not eating and I'm annoyed all day. Inertia's fault.

Or, I've gotten myself into a habit of climbing the stairs to the eighteenth floor once a day. My quads are stronger, I huff and puff less each time, and I feel good. Then I go away for a week and when I come back, it just seems like too much effort to take the stairs. Why would I do that? It's summer and I'm tired. Then two weeks later, when I do walk up to eighteen, it hurts. So that's it. Bye bye, stairs. Inertia, both times.

It's laziness, yes. It's easy to keep on the same track, to resist changes and conserve energy. It's also fear. It's safer to stay the same and avoid the possibility of failure.

Historically, I have been blasé about some big changes (transferring between colleges) and ridiculously terrified of small ones (going to a party with people I don't know very well). My inertia is capricious; it doesn't really make sense. But at some points I read that line from Mary Oliver about my wild and precious life.

And you know—there are things for which fighting inertia is just worth it:

Taking the stairs to the eighteenth floor once a day.

Skyping with that old roommate.

Cutting your hair.

Sending out your resumé again and again and again.

Spending the money on the wedding so your friends, your family, your community can be there to support you and to share in your lives.

Buying the chocolate.

Buying the shoes.

Not buying the shoes.

Saying no to the committee that looks great on your resumé but makes you overworked and miserable each month.

Saying yes to the late night at the beer garden with a couple you'd like to know better. Even on a Tuesday.

Yes. Sometimes no. But mostly yes.

Sheer, Stupid Inertia

Griffin Paul Jackson

I'm reading Thomas Merton's autobiography, *The Seven Storey Mountain*. He says lots of thoughtful things in it. Here's one of them from his pre-Christian school days:

"I had begun to get the idea that I was a Communist, although I wasn't quite sure what Communism was. There are a lot of people like that. They do no little harm by virtue of their sheer, stupid inertia, lost in between all camps, in the no-man's land of their own confusion. They are fair game for anybody."

And I think that's a terribly true sentiment because really, when you think about it, the way you came to where you are—intellectually, geographically, vocationally, spiritually—often has less to do with real deliberate thoughtfulness and more to do with sheer, stupid inertia.

This is not to say you didn't work hard or think for a long time or make important decisions along the way, but most of what got you to where you are is not genuine intentionality, but rather things like tradition, expectation, privilege, good/bad fortune, and a haphazard pursuit of the American Dream. Or sometimes it was because you got nudged down a course and just kept going.

Newton told us an object in motion will stay in motion. Like a bowling ball on a salt flat, it will keep going along in the same direction unless acted upon by an outside force. The same is true for us. We're always moving, and sometimes the pinball machine of life bumps us into new positions or relationships or ways of thinking, and that's normal. But if you don't pause once in a while to assess, to raise a finger to sense which way the wind is blowing you, who knows where you might find yourself? Maybe nowhere. Maybe somewhere that, if you'd spent even a moment thinking about it, you'd know you don't want to be.

I think about my own job and friends and life direction. I think about some of the things I think and some of the things I thought when I was younger. Sometimes I think, *Man, I'm still going down this road. I'm still doing the same things.* Or, *Thank heaven someone talked me out of that nonsense!*

Sometimes the continuity is good. Sometimes not. The present point is less about what direction you're going (though that, of course, matters a great deal), and more about whether it's a direction you chose or one that just happened to you.

It's this inertia that, if left unchecked, will make us convinced of things that, if caught early on, we could be talked out of with only the slightest bit of sense. It's this inertia that will keep us in a relationship that isn't good for us, or going after a relationship that obviously will never happen. It's this inertia that, very possibly, will find us waking up in ten years in a job we never really planned on, thinking, *How did I get here? This was supposed to be the thing that led to the next thing. This was supposed to be for the summer.*

I wouldn't change much about the years I spent in school or at my job, and I wouldn't trade my friends for anything, but I'm coming to realize that if I don't stop and think about what I'm doing, I could very well follow this same road until, fifty or sixty years from now, the car of my existence sputters off into a nursing home and I die.

Maybe that's not bad... if it's a good road.

But maybe it is, especially if I keep going because *This is what I've always done* or *What else would I do?* or *Hmm, I've never thought about that.* Then it's not anything deliberate moving me along, it's just time and momentum. It's that sheer, stupid inertia.

The Lord, I am certain, is faithful whether we follow a long, featureless, turn-less road, or one marked with lots of new jobs and new adventures and changing scenery. But he gave us neither minds of discernment nor hearts for adventure nor duties to "Go!" in order that we might simply stroll, meandering blindly, thoughtlessly down the same uncurving road forever. Dead things can't go upstream.

We ought not be hypercritical, hyper-sensitive, hyper-cautious about life. Sometimes you just need to commit to a path and go for a while. But life is also about readjustment.

Some of us find ourselves forever agreeing with whatever author we read most recently. Some of us are sticking to the script we wrote years ago or are hung up on the first thing that came along. Some of us are waiting, waiting, waiting for something better to just happen to us.

Don't.

At least, not without reading new books and editing old scripts and questioning, questioning, questioning.

Because when I wake up in ten or twenty years and ask myself, as I tend to, "How did I get here?" I want to have a better answer than sheer, stupid inertia.

This I Believe

Our stories spool inward, woven between ourselves and God.

Doubt

Will Montei

FOR YEARS, I HAVE SAID that I'm an excellent doubter and an okay Christian, always half-jokingly. But that description leaves the startling pain of doubt unrealized. Doubt, too, comes like a thief in the night. Skepticism, despite what I have always been led to believe, is not a choice. It creeps through open windows, crawls through the shadows, and thrusts itself upon you where you sit shivering by the fire. The initial stab keeps bleeding, and all there is to do is cup your hands beneath the wound and watch it drip through your fingers and pool on the floor. You cannot pick up the Bible with those hands, not if you want to keep its pages unstained.

One by one, things began leaving. First was *confidence*, the attic that held my faith. Rafters fell from the ceiling, and sunlight fell thick through the splinters and onto the surfaces of all the other things, drenching them. Slowly, beneath the heavy light, they soaked up sun until their wood frames bleached and their images faded. The first to go was *infinity*, a reflective globe. Anyone looking at it would see their self, unnaturally stretched outwards—but it had bathed in light for too long and collapsed in on itself, a glittering pile of dust. Then went *heaven*, the handbuilt dollhouse. It sat slumped against the wall. Then *spirits*. You could still find their delicate clothes ornamenting the tiny closets in the rooms of the dollhouse, but their bodies were gone. *God,* still present in the corner, the cradle that still swayed, but with each creak one wondered if the old wood might crack. There they were, suspended in light and fading. My own home collapsing, and nothing left but to watch in weary reserve.

For months after graduation when I lived in Wisconsin, I attended church alone. I liked sipping my coffee, not feeling pressured to sing along to the songs, and listening to the sermon with my own empty pew. It's an introvert's dream to be alone in worship. It was worship for me to wrestle with our young pastor's challenges, which were always well thought out, and so much more biblically rooted than most nearby evangelical churches. I liked that. I like when pastors never stop zealously reading and learning from their primary text.

It wasn't all solitude. I had my small group of elderly people, and I ate lunches with the twenty-somethings. I felt welcomed, and for the first time since Calvin, faithful.

Discomfort settled in anyways. The sermons became harder to stomach. Faith became a chore. The Bible was full of wretchedness that could only justify itself internally, paired with a beauty that can only glimmer briefly in its wake. Ask why God struck down the man who touched the Ark of the Covenant, and we are only allowed to say that God's infinite wisdom knows more, and that is entirely insufficient. If I am to suggest that it's an evil act, I'm a heretic. It's an evil act.

The first rafter falls.

One service, I sit in my usual spot, the music starts, and for the first time I cannot even listen to it. The words grind. I'm thinking of the girl I still love and my empty pew. I was standing, but the foreign lyrics and sorrow sink me into the seat. The sermon starts, where the pastor discusses Ecclesiastes and Job, about how God is greater than our pain. My gaze falls to my feet. For the first time in my life, I walk out of a church service, driving in silence back to my parents' apartment. The next day, when I get home from work, I collapse wordlessly in my mom's arms and sob into her shoulder. She doesn't ask for an explanation. She's crying too. She's familiar with grief.

All I want is God's touch, and maybe my mom's arms were God's, and her tears were his. But it was just me and my mom in her office. Touch is a fundamental love, and God's arms are in my thoughts constantly. If they could, even in a dream, wrap around me. Relief, relief, relief.

The spirits hang their clothes and leave.

In high school, my grades came home. I was never a good student. My parents sent me to motivation camps and outdoor trips to inspire me. My mom opens the letter that holds the product of that work with a glimmer of hope. Inside it are Ds and Fs. She starts crying. I don't know what to do, so I say sorry in the only way I know, and I hug her. She pushes me away and says, "no." She just stares at the floor with my grades in her hand, her eyes bright with tears—the disappointment of a parent who just wants her child to try. The disappointment of years filled with my repeated failure. I cannot imagine. That's how the evening ended, with her walking to her room and me feeling stranded in the kitchen. That is something like what doubt feels like—the failure, the search for comfort, the rejection of touch, the confused loneliness.

There's no home for the skeptic, not among the boldly faithful. When God doesn't feel tangible, the Word feels hollow, and being told to love the invisible doesn't make sense. Not among the callous atheists, who deny that there is any greater craving. But there is nothing childish about spirituality, and nothing inferior about thoughts that cannot rest without a Father. Not among the other soft doubters, whose only comfort is "me too." I cannot rest on a restless shoulder.

Come, loving touch. The rafters have fallen, the light has flooded, the memories have faded. Skepticism is lying on the floor of the attic, looking up in hope at a sky ragged through the rafters, listening for the sway of the cradle.

Loosening My Religion

Gabe Gunnink

MUCH OF MY LIFE can be viewed as a game of smuggling* my internal messes through conversations unnoticed. I wouldn't say it's my *favorite* game, but I'm pretty good at it and *love* winning! Last month, however, I found myself in a pickle. I was on a thrilling trans-Ohioan road trip with a dear friend when the conversation veered to religion. For how often I talk about religion in passing, I rarely talk about it in earnest. I was a competitive sales-speaker in high school; I like to present things in a polished manner, and honest assessments of personal faith aren't an easy sell.

But after my companion recounted an Odyssean epic of a faith story, I felt moved to share. As I opened my mouth, I realized I was about to put words to a trend I'd been observing in my faith life but that until this point had dozed cozily in my subconscious: "I don't care as much as I used to, and I'm kind of fine with it."

Given that I've actually gone to Costco to develop a photo of Leslie Knope for daily inspiration, a small identity crisis piggy-backed on this epiphany. I'm the kid who proof-reads text messages and stresses about where to insert his two magenta T-shirts in his colored-coded dresser drawer. (Before the reds or after the purples?!) How could I not care so much? The answer came easily: maybe I'm tired of caring.

I've never whined about growing up in such a committedly Christian area. I love the church I grew up in, I respect the thoughtfulness of the CRC, and I believe I'm a better person for them. But after years and years of hard pews and ham sandwiches and sleepy Sunday school sessions, can't a guy get a break?

Then at Calvin I found myself trying to attend chapel daily, go to Bible study weekly, and do devotionals nightly. But the push push push of constant spiritual striving exhausted more than it energized. College is framed as a time to grapple with one's beliefs, and I did. I was shaken by the suggestion that the Pentateuch was merely symbolism and doubt-stricken upon studying the convenient alterations to Mark's Gospel. Now, though, I'm not bothered. Can post-college be framed as a time to just chill out for a while spiritually and watch Netflix?

As I write these thoughts, I can picture my most admirably pious Calvin comrades narrowing their eyes and nodding along while quietly assessing how alarmed they should be. Knowing my audience, I also find myself wanting to stuff caveats between every other sentence. But more than that, I want to be honest: I've never taken a religion class that has interested me, my nightly devotionals rarely stick with me the next day, I don't even like thinking about going to evening church, and I'm done feeling bad about it. I will allow myself one caveat, though: I'm not saying that these things aren't valuable for others or that I won't find value in them someday, but right now, I don't.

I remember, somewhere in the jumble of Quest speeches and break-out sessions, a professor citing the classic Buechner quote on vocation: "The place God calls you to is the place where *your* deep gladness and the *world's* deep hunger meet." I think about that quote often and can't help but wonder: Is the world really that hungry for or am I made all that glad by me sitting at a table dragging myself through a devotional?

In a world of finite time, if I'm going to push push push, I want to push myself to teach my students better. Instead of a devotional, I want to lie on my couch and read an article on what ISIS is and why I should care. Instead of a Bible study, I want to help lead Calvin's LGBT+ workshop. Instead of saying a prayer, I want to appreciate the birds shimmering like a school of fish as I drive home on 28th Street. Instead of going to evening church, I want to sit in a plaza with my French host father and hear about his world travels or in a brunch place with a septuagenarian Atlantan and hear about his life as a gay Catholic or in a car with an Ohioan friend and hear about his faith story. I want to gladly blur the lines between being in and of this world.

I wouldn't call myself a pluralist or universalist or inclusivist because that would require thought. As far as I care, I'm the same labels I've always been; I'm just less concerned with them. I can't even claim to know if this laissez-faire attitude is helpful or harmful. My progressive, millennial self praises my waltz into informal worship while my type-A, descendent-of-Dutch-reformers self watches on with uncertain worry. But, to console the latter, I don't consider this a loss of religion, but a loosening.

I feel liberated, and I feel lazy. I want to be a better person more than I want to be a better Christian, and I sincerely hope that they're the same thing. I want to pull this all together and present it as a polished worldview, and, for once, I really want to find myself at a loss.

Saying a Sermon

Brad Zwiers

G0 AHEAD, PICK EACH sentence apart like taking petals from a flower, but you must know that once those petals float into the air they can never return to you. Not naturally, anyways.

You say them aloud and see what they do, whether they even sound like words. They might sound like words, or they might sound like a mouth full of pea soup trying to blow air. Or they might sound like an axe grabbing onto wood, grooved so deep that it won't release. Or they might sound like nothing, and as soon as you say them, they're gone and no one has heard a single word. They might not make a sound. They might be heard, but they might not make a sound, a *difference*.

Keep talking. Eventually, you assume, something will make sense. Pieces and parts of pieces will be put together, and the sense-making that has happened in your head will become public knowledge. Those listening will share your thoughts. They will borrow your paradigms (which were given to you) and understand your motivations. They will make eye contact and nod along. They will hear that mixture of air and muscle movement in your mouth that some call words and absorb them. Soak them in. Invite them into their world and let them bounce around for a while, colliding with other things and sparking a sense of wonder. Life will be real to them. God will be real to them.

But, crap, there's a yawn. And there's a conversation. About what? About you? About what you have said? What have you said? There is that feeling again: a very clear feeling of flower petals floating to the ground but never landing. The ground is there and you can see it, but the petals hover over the ground and never make contact and then a wind comes and carries them away.

"Just reach out and grab one!" you yell at them in your head. But just as you think that, something ridiculous slips into your mind, and it's this: you are still talking. More petals are being thrown into the air, more words that hopefully signify something are escaping out of you. And you reach out to grab them, to take them back in and inspect them and make sure they are right. Too late. They have caught onto the wind and you are helpless. They have been said.

You realize this, and cracks of lightning shatter your consciousness. No. No. No. I've said them. Made them and said them and then put them out there. For a second, you pause and look down at them again—those words you have pieced together—and still, you are speaking out loud. This will not do. This cannot last. And the inside of you begins to sweat and feel hot. Your feet twist unnaturally, or at least you feel they do. Still, you are forming words with your mouth and putting them into the world. Are they right or true or faithful? Who does this?

"God," you hope, "God." Out loud and in secret, your deepest fear—it might be you—crawls out through your skin and makes you shiver. "God," you hope, "God."

And then it's over and done. This time. At that moment exactly, something in you wants to scream with joy and frustration and fear all at once. Instead, you shake hands.

I Want a God Like NASA

Josh deLacy

I DON'T FEEL COMFORTABLE when people talk about God's perfect plan, probably because I don't believe in it. I believe in God's perfection, or at least I think I do. I don't really know what perfection means. Not fully anyway. As for the plan, I believe God has one in the same way Google has a plan to improve technology or NASA has a plan to explore space. It's too complex for me to understand, and it's full of opportunism and closed-door decisions that from the outside look like luck or inevitability, but there's a very real, laid-out plan powering the few pieces I *can* see. But a perfect plan? I can't believe in that, and it feels irreverent to try.

Abraham bargained with God over Sodom. Fifty righteous? Forty-five? Ten? Abraham argued, and God changed his mind. I can't write that off like God's disappearing acts with the Israelites, in which he abandons and returns like an abusive husband who spends half his life in prison. Those are slow shifts, and I can blame the Israelites. They deserved it. They changed. They changed again. Or I can blame the narrative perspective, or the lessons attached to the story as it was told, taught, told, written, translated, written, translated, translated, taught, summarized, taught, and then explained to me. But the Sodom argument happens in a single interaction. God came in with one decision, and he left with another.

And then there's the flood, the telling of which makes God look like an angsty teenager, flipping from *it was very good* to *I will wipe from the face of the earth every living creature*, and then flopping back to *never again, never again.* There's the Garden of Gethsemane, where Jesus prayed for the Father to change plans. *If it is possible,* Jesus asked, *let this cup pass from me.* The cup didn't pass, or at least I don't think it did, but I come away from that story seeing a malleable will. God asked God to change. There wasn't a break within the Trinity, but there was, however brief, a dissenting opinion. At times like that, God's plan looks more like wet clay than solid rock.

I find it hopeful. The idea of determinism scares me; there's already too much of that in the world for my liking. The control of genetics, of environment, of dopamine and serotonin and noradrenaline. I'm not looking for a divine buddy, or even for a relationship, but I want something more than helpless obedience. I want agency. And I think God does, too. I see that with the tree of knowledge, and I see it with the Israelites, and I see it whenever Jesus tells people to follow him. Tells, but does not force.

It's not all biblical, my problem with the idea of God's perfect plan. There are other reasons, too. More honest reasons. Part of me sees those non-biblical reasons as a weakness, and others would agree that it's just my own feelings and limitations, or my sin nature, or Satan himself tricking me into doubt. But in my mind, a perfect plan doesn't demand cruelty. And yet the Bible tells me Elisha sent bears to maul kids who made fun of him. "Baldhead," they said, and he killed them for it. God hardened Pharaoh's heart, and the Israelites massacred Philistines, and God slaughtered Uzzah for trying to protect the Ark of the Covenant, and if this is perfection, I'm selling perfection short. I'm selling God short.

And meanwhile, I read about another bombing. Another genocide, another rape, another abused kid. More cancer, more shootings, more suicide, and inevitably, someone steps forward—sometimes at the funeral, sometimes weeks later, sometimes years later—to smile, hug, and declare it all part of the Great Mystery. God's perfect plan. Not as if there were no other way, but as if this was the best way. He had to die. He had to die just like that, hanging in the garage at nineteen, or dead in a ditch for a week before anyone found his body. Perfection.

I'm getting angry. I have a lot of anger against a perfect God.

I'm learning to let go. A quiet church helps. So does reading, or talking with strangers, or listening to NPR. They show me new pieces of life, and through them, I think, pieces of God, or at least his shadow.

I was driving home during a conversation between Terry Gross and Tom Wainwright. Tom had spent three years in Mexico studying drug cartels, and he was telling Terry about the effects of drug legalization, of doctors who prescribe heroin to addicts, of governments that create safe spaces for drug use and paraphernalia disposal. It's not a good policy, he said, but it dried up the black market, and the number of new users dropped. Addiction rates dropped too.

"I don't think there's any good way of controlling the drug problem," Tom said, "because these are, for the most part, harmful drugs which aren't going to do people much good. But it seems to me that what I've seen is that the least bad way to control them is for governments to get more involved in the business themselves, because the choice that I think we face isn't really a choice between a world without drugs and a world with drugs."

If I extend that idea, maybe it takes power away from God. Maybe it's wrong, or arrogant, or sinful. But it makes it easier for me to value him. It's easier for me to accept a God who, even if not flawed himself, follows a flawed plan. No, not a flawed plan—not necessarily—but a not-perfect plan. A God who chooses the least bad option, and sometimes not even that. Sometimes just an option.

I don't say anything when I get one of those hugs, those "Great Mystery" hugs. The intention behind it is usually a good one, I think. But I can't say I don't bristle. I do bristle, and it takes time for my anger to fade. Time, a few conversations, and maybe a long drive, and then I find myself drifting back toward the God I see in the Bible, and the God I hope for. Not a God with a perfect plan, but a perfect God with a plan.

Gethsemani

Geneva Langeland

Amonk's day begins at 3:15 a.m.
At the Abbey of Gethsemani in New Haven, Kentucky, forty white-robed monks file into their narrow chapel hours before sunrise. This is Vigils, the first of eight daily prayer services, the monks' opportunity to bless the hemisphere while it sleeps. I slip into the back of the chapel, sweatshirted and bleary, ready to chant litanies and Psalms from the little booklet that materializes on a table before each service.

Monks know the Psalms like I know my own skin. These poems of agony and love spin slowly beneath their days, rotating through their liturgy every two weeks, bookended by hymn and prayer. How many years before each line is indelibly etched in the mind? How can I convince them to linger longer in mine?

It's spring break, and while my classmates slumber states away, I trace a cross—*forehead, sternum, shoulder, shoulder*—and sink into the first Psalm of the day. This is Gethsemani. This is peace.

The Abbey of Gethsemani has been in continuous operation since a handful of French Trappist monks set up shop in the

Kentucky hills in 1848. The men live by their hands, selling monk-made cheese, fudge, and the most bourbon-laced fruitcake I've ever sampled. Funds also roll in thanks to Thomas Merton, Gethsemani's famous son, whose bestselling 1948 autobiography, *The Seven Storey Mountain*, put the abbey on the map.

The operation is simple: a spare, white chapel flanked by a retreat house and the monks' quarters. Fields and forests unfurl for acres across the rolling hills. My group of six from Ann Arbor has joined the weekly complement of two dozen retreatants for a few days' respite. Here, settled, I'm free to do as I wish. No schedule, just the invitation to monastic rhythm. Time passes at its own pace, marked by bells but demanding little. Long minutes sink into a single cup of coffee. Prayer begins to come as easily as thought.

Many times and places in the abbey are reserved for silence, so we speak only when necessary. The mantle of silence is warm and weighty. Quiet sinks into my bones and stretches me, opens up spaces long constricted by noise and distraction. Untethered from screen and keyboard, my thoughts have slowed to a pleasant meander. The peace of this place releases the tension in the pit of my stomach. In its place, I find a smooth, warm stone of calm. I breathe at half-pace.

In the dining room, twenty-five people eat in comfortable silence. Most chairs face the garden windows, where cardinals and juncos hop over fresh-fallen snow and white hills rise to the horizon. My fellow retreatants sip soup and tea, and my heart swells with gratitude for their presence. Who knew what community of spirit could be built among people who never speak? We say all that's needed through smiles and held-open doors. Our stories spool inward, woven between ourselves and God. I find myself praying for strangers. We are solitary here, but not alone.

Between services, prayers, and chapters of *Mere Christianity*, I shuffle the retreat house halls like a convalescent, wrapped in a shawl, toting a mug of tea. Skip the shoes, shed the hurry. One evening, I slip onto the chapel porch and stand in my socks to watch fluffy flakes drift through the dark as the bell rings for Compline. This service draws down the monastic day at 7:30 p.m. Compline, alone of the eight services, remains the same from day to day, year to year. The monks know the liturgy by heart so we stand in darkness to sing our goodnight.

I Am Not Jesus

Matt Hubers

AT MY CHURCH, people call me Jesus. It began over a year ago when I, along with Laura and several others, were recruited to portray stories of Jesus for Sunday scripture readings. It was done in a series of tableaus, and being exceptional in the art of standing very still (and one of the few who could commit to every single Sunday) I was cast as Jesus. Every week during the course of Lent I stood in front of the congregation portraying Jesus. It was only in body—I never spoke—but people made the connection. From then on, everyone in the congregation knew me as Jesus.

The acceptance of my portrayal went quite far. Several parents needed to have the difficult "that's not really Jesus" talk with their young children. People would greet me as Jesus on Sundays. Some would cheer for Jesus on the church softball team (he's horrible at softball, by the way). The process embarrassed me. It was a large role to live up to. And few seemed to know my real name.

On the other hand, I enjoyed the status it gave me. All of a sudden I was being noticed at church. People would go out of their way to talk to me. As someone who had always arrived late and left early, this was an experience that made me feel like an important part of the worship experience. I was somebody. I was Jesus.

Our society today is one made up of individuals—and I love it. I love that everyone is unique and has a special story to tell. I love having the freedom to choose what is right for me—what to do, who to be, how to live. It's a way to make everyone feel special. We are separate, distinctively gifted, and all handcrafted by a creator to do different things. And being different we each get our own set of rules. I get to choose what is important to me. I get to decide between right and wrong. I get to *define* right and wrong. The world is relative, and it's relative to me. I am the center, the hero of my story.

A week ago at a softball game, a poorly thrown ball flew over the chain link fence and connected with Laura's pregnant stomach. Hard. She went down immediately, and as I ran to her all I could think of was a devastating sixteen-week premature birth. The pregnancy had been going so well, and one freakish accident was ending it. I pictured my wife going into labor right there on the grass. I tried not to think of how small our son would look in this, his twenty-fourth week of gestation. We hurried to the emergency room where Laura was propped in a bed and connected to monitors. They strapped something to her belly that would track the baby's heartbeat. For hours we sat and listened to that little heart beating. 150 BPM. Now 162—a little high—does that mean anything? Back down to 142—relax. Like a bad metronome my son's heartbeat rose and fell, and I just listened, helpless, waiting. They finally sent us home. No labor that night—just the sound of his tiny heart pumping away as strong as anything.

My son reminds me that I'm not Jesus. Not even close. Jesus healed the sick and drove out demons. He raised people from the dead. I am just another helpless, foolish piece of his creation. I am subject to both the beauty and cruelty of the world. I'm not the hero of my story. And I'm still coming to terms with that.

Melancholy Epiphany, Everyone!

Alissa (Goudswaard) Anderson

DID YOU KNOW the "Twelve Days of Christmas" are *not,* in fact, the twelve days leading up to Christmas? The whole thing was always a tad confusing to me... until I became an Episcopalian, and learned that Christmas is, in fact, a whole liturgical season! Great, right? It's a short one—twelve days, in fact—lasting from Christmas Day (or, well, Christmas Eve, because holy days run on the sundown schedule borrowed from our Jewish brothers and sisters) until Epiphany, on January 6. In a number of other Christian cultures, Epiphany is a Big Deal, but this is less so in the WASP-y corners of United States Christianity.

Epiphany celebrates the Incarnation of Jesus, including events of his childhood and his baptism. In Western Christianity, the feast of Epiphany principally commemorates the coming of the Magi to the Christ child (representing Jesus' physical manifestation to Gentiles). I know people with nativity sets who won't add in the Magi until Epiphany. Sometimes the Magi start on the other side of the room and travel a little closer each day.

I didn't really give the Magi much thought when I was younger. They were so foreign, so other. Besides, my preferred Christmas narrative is the one in Luke, and since the Magi only show up in

I shall miss the stars

Matthew's account, I can find myself skipping right over them if I'm not careful.

If I lose the Magi in the Bible, though, I find them again in more recent texts. I like T.S. Eliot's Magi, poetic license and all. I like that his poem about them is haunted and melancholy. It's been almost two weeks since Advent ended—away with the feasting and jollity, already. I'm all for feasting, really, and even a rollicking carol or five, even if I do prefer my music in a minor key. It's just that in the midst of the carols and the lights and the presents and the roasts, it's easy, for me at least, to forget what a fundamentally earth-shattering event the coming of Christ was. I think Eliot captured a little of this, with his magus who follows a star and returns to a life that is suddenly topsy-turvy.

Madeleine L'Engle, writing on the same theme, has a poem titled "One King's Epiphany" that begins and ends with the statement, "I shall miss the stars." She plays on the idea that the Magi were astrologers, studying the stars—but after the journey to the Christ, the revelation of truth, this magus finds such truth and wisdom have robbed him of his old way of life.

Epiphany is a time to think about what Christ's incarnation means, and this doesn't mean thinking about nativity sets and cute babies. (I mean, we have no idea—Jesus could've been a really ugly kid.) It means thinking about a completely other way of considering the world, of aligning values, and of acting in faith. It isn't an easy season, and it probably involves certain losses, certain kinds of dying. I can't say I like it, to be no longer at ease in my world. I will miss the stars.

Bringing Vince Carter
to Church

Brad Zwiers

I N THE MOST RECENT edition of *ESPN the Magazine* (September
30, 2013), Howard Bryant writes a short article on retirement in
professional sports. Many bastions of their respective sports are
quickly approaching the time to hang up their cleats or put down
the racket: Mariano Rivera and Derek Jeter in baseball, Venus
Williams and Roger Federer in tennis—the list could go on. But
so often when an athlete nears retirement, the public urges them
to stay in the game while simultaneously suggesting they retire.
As Bryant highlights in his article, many athletes hate this. They
don't want to quit playing—much of who they are is wrapped
up in what they do, and that competitive drive imbued in almost
every professional athlete cries out against the notion of retirement—of quitting. But they also don't want to limp toward the
end of their careers hobbled by the fact that their talent is rapidly
changing (read: decreasing).

I think a lot of this tension comes from the American obsession with performance. The public wants an aging athlete to keep
playing, but only if they can still perform. We'd rather not watch
someone disgrace themselves. Barry Sanders' retirement came
as a shock in part because it seemed he was still at the top of

his game: in 1998, the year he retired, he rushed for almost 1,500 yards. 1997? He ran for a career-high 2,053. He could still perform, and so we were annoyed when he announced his retirement. But as soon as a player cannot perform or it appears that way to us as fans, the public instantly begins to question their abilities and "The Retirement Question" becomes a conversation starter around the barbeque.

Rarely does a pro athlete age or retire well (looking at you Brett Favre). If one does, their "performance," measured by fans through statistics and/or entertainment value, drops. Take Vince Carter for example. He no longer posterizes tall lanky white men or causes Kenny "The Jet" Smith to invite everyone in the arena to go home, and so I'm sure there's pressure on him, because he's not performing as he once did, to retire. However, if you read NBA coverage from the past few years, you'll discover article after article praising Carter for his, wait for it, defense, court leadership, and overall basketball IQ. He's adapted how he plays the game to coincide with his age and environment, finding a team need and developing (or honing) the ability to fill it. He's not retired (yet), but he has retired the player he once was and moved forward.

Outside tight NBA circles, though, no one has taken much notice of Air Canada's late-career resurgence. It's easy to understand why: he's not performing anymore, no longer putting on a show. We have LeBron and Blake Griffin and Kevin Durant. We have new go-to's for our posters and other performers to entertain us.

Our society's obsession with performance shows up in the church, too. We celebrate conversion numbers, increased attendance, heightened programming, etc. We love to be part of a church that performs well. Let me be clear: this is not inherently a bad thing. A church does not have to hang on to a thread for years to be faithful. And yet, if we focus too intently on advancement or performance, we skew our understanding of what the church is meant to be and whose work is being done. If we get wrapped up in tangible signs of progress, we could unwittingly march into our own retirement. Because our performance *will* falter.

This, of course, is an inexact (and actually kind of absurd) connection to make. The church doesn't retire, and Christians don't retire from being Christians. Also, Vince Carter features prominently in the comparison. But maybe we have to learn to "retire" or age well in this time when Christianity is not as pervasive or conspicuous as it once was. Maybe if our performance drops, it's an opportunity to adapt and present a more authentic witness than waving around numbers or statistics. As Christians, we don't need to feel the pressure to perform or prove our worth, to be LeBron or Blake Griffin or Kevin Durant. That will run us into the ground. We've only, like Vinsanity, got to change our game and press on in faith.

Classroom 101

I wanted telepathic powers then, to beam a message into the minds of those kids: this is what you should remember.

Homecoming

Abby Zwart

I WENT TO MY high school's homecoming football game this Friday. It's a little hard to believe I graduated five years ago already. An overly sentimental person by nature, I had a lot of feels sitting there on the cold metal bleachers.

Football is not a game I understand particularly well, so I had a lot of time to reminisce about high school. As students filed past, I pictured myself in their shoes—wearing the week's themed outfit (rainbow or camouflage or black out) and trying to look cool and stay warm all at once. It was rarely successful. I remember football cheers. I remember frantic Monday mornings when you hadn't quite finished your homework because you went to the football game and then slept over at a friend's house and spent all of Saturday in pajamas watching movies. I remember sitting on the floor in the common area to eat lunch (we never had a cafeteria). I remember after school play practice and trying not to suffocate in the hairspray-filled dressing room. I remember the pop culture jokes we told so often that they stopped being funny (sorry, *Arrested Development*).

I feel a confession coming on. It's probably not cool, and I risk losing some of you who might thoroughly disagree.

I miss high school.

I miss the energy. The companionship. The routine. I miss the *rah rah* school spirit and the constant activity and the sense that I was always accomplishing something (seemingly) important. Camaraderie. Enthusiasm. A common goal.

Sure, I'm not remembering the bad stuff. That's the beauty of it, isn't it? All that drama, all the hurt feelings and vague text messages and failed tests fade into the fog of five years. I don't remember who went to the homecoming dance with whom, nor how hard the ACT was, nor whether I got nervous before my first forensics tournament.

Senior year, I had a teacher who liked to give us pep talks. One day, he laid down something that felt a little harsh. I don't remember the exact words, but the point of his speech has stuck with me ever since. He talked to us about perspective. He told us that in high school, everything feels important. Every joy, every nasty look, every minute activity. What he wanted us to know, though, is that it doesn't really matter. He told us we'd remember very little about what people wore or whether we got asked on a date or what grades we got. It was all well meant—based on his adult hindsight and experience—but I remember feeling like he just didn't get it.

But oh, was he ever right. As a high school teacher now, I feel a similar struggle for balance with my students. At some level, I have to indulge their complaints and drama, or they won't pay any attention to me. But every day there's a kid I want to grab by the shoulders and set straight with some real talk. Real talk: it doesn't matter that she Facebook messaged your ex-boyfriend from middle school. Real talk: you don't use chemistry in every-day life so it's okay if you don't get it. Real talk: not everyone is out to get you. I want to tell them that these things don't matter, that they should focus on the good stuff like making friends and learning to write and knowing how to laugh at themselves. But I know I have to let them figure that out on their own.

At halftime of the homecoming game, the couples of the homecoming court walk down the field in their suits and long dresses while the announcer reads off a long list of things they've accomplished in their four years. It's a hell of a lot. Was I this busy in high school? These kids are National Merit Scholars and volunteer at food pantries and are involved at church and have been on varsity sports teams for four years. They're in band *and* choir and they help organize the school blood drive. They spend their summers building hospitals in third world countries.

They stand there in their beautiful sparkly dresses and their crisp black ties and hear someone read a list of things they've accomplished. But a question nags at me: is this what they should really remember? Don't they want high school to be a sunny memory because of the happy times they spent making memories with friends instead of the hours they spent polishing their GPAs?

The quarterback of the football team was supposed to be on homecoming court, but he'd been badly injured in the previous week's game and was in the hospital undergoing several surgeries. A friend took his place on the court and walked the field holding an iPad where the quarterback waved and looked on. People cheered in that heartfelt way you do when someone has been brave, and I had to swallow around a lump in my throat.

I wanted telepathic powers then, to beam a message into the minds of those kids: *this is what you should remember.*

The Great Tassel Shift

Gabe Gunnink

O N MONDAY, A FRIEND who graduates this weekend asked me what the most difficult aspect of life after the Great Tassel Shift is. I had my answer immediately: the most challenging part of life beyond school is that it's not about you anymore. If you grew up in a developed nation with compulsory public education and moderate to strict child labor laws, chances are the first twenty-ish years of your life were entirely you-centric. Parents stowed your favorite sandwich in your lunchbox every morning, teachers dedicated tireless hours to Tetris-ing information into your brain, and politicians and pageant queens continually declared you "the future." It seems, however, that this future is brighter for them than for us. For while they have the privilege of retiring or settling into mediocre acting careers, we are yanked from our adolescent incubators and thrust suddenly into a working world that is thoroughly and disconcertingly not about us.

And there is no sphere of society in which this education-to-occupation whiplash is more drastic than in schools. As a new teacher, I'll admit I often envy my students. I watch them flit between classes like Hogwarts first-years, hear their accomplishments proclaimed in the daily announcements, and attend their plays, competitions, and concerts. I salivate like a leashed child at a Golden Corral, remembering the tasty buffet of classes and extracurriculars lined up for me at that age. But as a teacher, I'm no longer a Golden Corral customer, but an employee who must wipe down the soft serve machine every half-hour. It's frustrating to serve others when I still have such an appetite for personal betterment, and at times it has made my first year of teaching embittering.

But now, almost a year since graduation, the ache has diminished. This is partly because I've learned that investing in others and investing in myself are not mutually exclusive, but mostly because I've learned that if they were, the former would be a far more rewarding choice. For example, this spring I've volunteered as a coach for my school's track and field team, and on Saturday, after months of my training with the kids and learning their quirks, we arrived at our regional competition. Our school had recently been dragged up to Division I, and the new standards were high. Hulking Rockford throwers tossed shot puts like snowballs, and Okemos sprinters launched from starting blocks so instantaneously I suspected premonition. Meanwhile, our small stride (the collective noun I've invented for distance runners) quivered nervously.

One athlete in particular appeared burdened by her hopes of qualifying for the state meet in the 800-meter run. Entering with a seed time of 2:29 and a twelfth place ranking, she would need either a 2:20 or a second place finish to advance. The previous day after practice we had walked twice around the track together, visualizing her race and discussing strategy. So, by the time she finally toed the starting line, my hopes had so thoroughly meshed with hers that I teetered on the edge of my first panic attack.

The gun popped, and the clock ticked. And as I zipped back and forth across the infield, I witnessed one of the most poetic things I've ever seen: over the next couple minutes, she executed our plan to perfection, crossing the line in second place and a school record time of 2:20. Immediately, I sprinted to the finish and found my athlete crumpled like a pop can, every iota of her energy spent. I haven't felt happy or proud like I did in that moment for years.

Today, we had another track meet—an informal invitational that really doesn't matter. Unfortunately, I also had plans to attend my high school choir director's final concert tonight and could only stay at the meet for one relay. As I prepared to leave, I felt an odd pooling of emotion. I considered how I was about to miss a couple of my athletes' last races in a school uniform. Then I thought about my parents and grandparents coming to every single race, concert, and production of my childhood. Then I felt overwhelmingly loved. I took a final look at my little stride of runners huddled under blankets or foam-rolling their calves then turned toward my car.

At the end of the concert tonight, our director called up all the alumni in the audience to join the high school choir for the final two songs. The first was a folkloric romp replete with mandatory hoots and hollers, and it felt fantastic to be woven in with my past classmates under his direction again. The second was an arrangement of "The Lord Bless You and Keep You" sung at the end of every Chamber Chorale concert. Before we began, our director asked us to spread into the aisles and hold the hands of the choir members at our sides. As we sang the velvety words of the hymn, I watched our director and felt almost intimidated by the finality of thirty-eight years of teaching—continuously investing in the lives and voices of others—about to resolve in a single note. I watched his snowy blue eyes drift slowly over us with practiced satisfaction as we cascaded into the final "Amen" and, for the first time, thought I might have a small taste of what he was feeling.

Margin Notes on Gentleness

Lauren (Boersma) Harris

I'M A NINTH AND TENTH grade English teacher. I assign a lot of papers, which means I grade a lot of papers. (I know, I know. I signed up for this. Unless you signed up to be a rebarbative pest, please go away.) I teach approximately one hundred students.

Let me tell you something. One hundred papers is an insane amount to grade. It's inhumane. *I'm not complaining.* I'm stating a basic psychological human fact.

I'm also complaining.

Wednesday evening, I graded papers. Thursday evening, I graded papers. Friday night, I played violin for a wedding, and I slipped five essays into the outer lining of my case and snuck off to make margin notes in between wedding toasts. Saturday afternoon, I spent five hours at a coffee shop while, somewhere in the world, somebody baked an entire casserole, cleaned the house, and did seventeen loads of laundry. Saturday night, my boyfriend went out with his friends, my roommate went to a work party at the Gilmore mansion, and I spent my evening with a fraying knapsack and an immortal stack of essays in the 28th Street Denny's.

Grading stresses me out. My heart feels like it's in a door-less, windowless room that's slowly filling with water. My eyes get crusty. My head gets hazy. My body feels like someone has stabbed two violin pegs into the place where my shoulders meet the bottom of my neck, tightening all my muscles like strings near the point of breaking.

When I grade essays, one of the biggest psychological road-blocks I encounter is the unshakeable feeling that it's all futile. Nobody cares.

Friends say, "That sucks. See you next Tuesday!!"

Rebarbative pests say, "You signed up for this."

Students throw twenty-two minutes worth of margin notes into the recycling bin, if they're feeling environmentally friendly.

It makes me want to cry. It makes me want to quit my job. It makes me want to gather everyone I've ever disapproved of into one giant lecture hall, to stand behind a lectern and present an articulate, well-reasoned multi-media presentation of rage on every perceived injustice I've ever experienced.

I quiver on the edge of defeat. I snap at my friends. I whine to anyone who will listen. I pick at my boyfriend. I begin to hate most things in the world.

This particular Saturday night, in Denny's, my vanilla ice cream and characteristic joyful temperament were melting into a pud-dle of white-chocolate raspberry pancake balls and self-loathing.

My waitress was a young person around my age, with a gen-uine smile, square-frame glasses, and hair in shades of fuschia and teal.

"Are you ready to order?"

"Can I get you any more water?"

"Refill your hot chocolate?"

"Will that be all tonight?"

She tapped her fingers on the computer screen, waiting with my debit card in her left hand, and glanced down at the stack of orange-markered, poorly-stapled papers resting on the counter.

"Are you a teacher?" she asked me, smiling.

I gave some sort of half-crazed blink that indicated the accuracy of her assumption.

And then, this dear person with Buddy Holly glasses and My Little Pony hair said, "I think that's amazing."

And I said I think I want to buy you a summer home off the coast of Maine.

Aloud, I actually just sort of half choke-sobbed a word that may have been "thanks" or "shbuurr."

When I got my wisdom teeth out in high school, I reacted very poorly to anesthesia. Not in a physical, life-threatening way, but instead in a weirdly melancholy panic attack. I have a very vivid memory of sobbing in an elevator, touching things repeatedly and begging my mother to tell me whether or not they were real.

With her words Saturday night, that waitress had done the emotional equivalent of re-introducing me to what was real, but instead of my instability wearing off gradually, as the anesthesia had done, her words caused human gravity to return all at once.

I cried on the way home, and thanked God for the existence of this person. What an easy thing it is for us to affect other human beings. What a wonderfully and frighteningly easy thing to do. And also so difficult. I can write comments in the margins for years without altering a student's trajectory even a degree, but one off-handed comment in a Denny's altered my trajectory for a month, bare minimum.

Words are important.

I believe that, and I suppose it's one of the reasons I teach English in the first place.

I also suppose I became a teacher in hopes that the thousands of margin notes, probing questions, rebukes, and gentle reminders would pile up into a ramp that will lift a student just the tiniest bit closer to the height they aim for. (If I die young, you can read this line at my funeral. Side note: I'd prefer not to be buried in satin, or laid down on a bed of roses. Laying me down on a bed of Nutella and Disney vhs tapes will suffice.)

Sometimes, I wander around in that anesthetic fog of discouragement and feeble apathy, then I'm reminded by someone's gentle words that there are things that are real, that are tangible, that are worthwhile.

And I think that's amazing.

Lexington Minutemen

Bart Tocci

M Y HIGH SCHOOL HOCKEY letterman jacket is still hanging up in my closet. I tried it on while I was home for
Christmas, and it's still too big. As a freshman, I ordered it large
because I thought I would hit some sort of crazy growth spurt
and become a larger man. I hit a small growth spurt, and grew to
the extremely average height of 5′10″.

I figured that once I started lifting weights and drinking whey
protein shakes, I would put on thirty pounds. So I started lifting weights and drinking whey protein shakes and I put on zero
pounds. I just looked a little less skinny, which means that you
could see two fewer ribs.

Last week I put on the jacket and laughed, because I still
looked like a child in it. The thing wouldn't fit the Hulk. It didn't
matter though, because in high school it was a status symbol,
not a fashion statement. Its white sleeves and "Varsity" stitching
screamed, *I've made it. I'm one of these guys now.*

"You're gonna get so much play in those jackets!" (When I
say *play*, I don't mean using the jungle gym at the playground…
unless that's what people are calling it these days.) I still remem-

ber sitting in the locker room and listening to the seniors talk about the jackets.

"You guys are gonna have junior girls coming up to you and...." I'll spare you details here, but the team captain made wearing the jacket sound pretty appealing. "OC, remember? Remember that girl who [*did things she wasn't ready for with you, probably to gain acceptance or get attention or cover up some hurt at the expense of her emotional health?*] That was awesome!"

So we wore the jackets around. I had to unbutton it and wear a hooded sweatshirt under it just to make it not look idiotic. The first day I wore it, I expected some junior girls to try to make out with me in the hallways. Keyword: *some*. Fewer than three girls would be considered a failure. I was imagining myself fending off women, "No! NO! Not right now! You girl, LEAVE ME ALONE!" I would have to stuff the jacket in a locker until the very end of the day, when every female had left school grounds.

This did not happen. Maybe because this was real life and our team sucked and no one cared about hockey at our school.

When I started, the team had a storied tradition of sucking. The Lexington Minutemen hadn't made it to the state tournament in twenty-four years. (To give some reference here, all we needed was to win *half* of our games. Or tie all of them.)

We were going to change that. Our team wouldn't settle for failure; we'd shoot for mediocrity. Our goal was to complete the season with a .500 record and make it to the playoffs.

I started thinking of how we could boost excitement about our team. I thought about the film *Remember the Titans*. Denzel Washington has a line that I love: "In Greek mythology, the Titans were greater even than the gods. They ruled their universe with absolute power. That football field out there, that's our universe. Let's rule it like titans."

Chills.

That's *it*. I could give the same speech: "During the Revolutionary War, the Minutemen were… well, they were really poorly trained. They were no match for the British Redcoats, but what they *did* have… what they *were* known for… was being ready for battle in one minute… they were dressed so fast, and actually they ended up losing that battle on the Lexington Battle Green… but ah… let's put our equipment on in *one minute*!

Confused looks.

I looked at college football programs that were getting attention, and used them as my inspiration: The Florida State Seminole "chop," the Florida Gator "chomp," the Purdue Boilermakers "boiling things in the stands." All of these teams had some sort of action that got the crowd *into it*.

I made a list of the things that Minutemen had. Muskets, tricorn hats, gunpowder. Then I threw that list away and while making a powerpoint presentation thought, *That's it. The Lexington Power Point!*

We would get the fans to point, in unison, at the other team. The players would feel so insecure and accused that they would cower, giving us an easy lane to the net. I was never able to garner enough support to implement the Power Point, and failing to do so has been my greatest regret.

We didn't need the gimmicks though, because we had cheerleaders.

A bottle of Tommy Hilfiger cologne still rests on my dresser at home and reeks of high school. My cheerleader gave it to me. "Oh, sweet! Bart dated a cheerleader?! What a complete stereotypical high school brojock!" I didn't date her, but I was hers. (Seriously, I was assigned to her.)

The varsity hockey team was blessed with the JV cheerleaders. (The basketball team got the varsity cheerleaders, probably because it was safer to do flips and stuff on a court than on the ice.) Most of the JV cheerleaders had to cheer for multiple guys because there weren't enough girls willing to freeze their butts off in an ice rink for two hours.

They sat in the bleachers and did muffled clapping and stomping routines. (The clapping was muffled on account of the mittens.) Let me tell you, *nothing*, and I mean nothing, gets you more pumped up to play a hard-hitting, fast-paced, aggressive game of hockey than hearing this: "Bart—Go—Go—Tocci—*GO!*"

Boom, clap-clap, boom, clap!

"GUYS! Listen! THEY WANT ME TO GO! WE NOW HOLD THE KEYS TO VICTORY. I WILL *POWER POINT* YOU IN THE DIRECTION!"

They were sweethearts and they always told us good job, even when we lost by double digits.

At the end of the year, we had a banquet where we saw pictures and videos from the handful of games that we won. After that, the athletic director would come up and lecture about how sports aren't actually important, but having fun and being safe and being a huge pushover is important. We would give out awards, name next year's captains, and then exchange gifts with our cheerleaders.

Guys would go up to the podium, take a gift from the coach, meet their cheerleader and give her flowers and take a photo with her. She would give them a Snickers bar or a decorated hockey puck.

When it was my turn, there was joking from my teammates because word had spread that this gal had a crush on me. I shook hands with my coach, took a gift, gave my cheerleader—whom I had never actually spoken with—flowers, and then she gave me a candy bar, a puck, and the bottle of Tommy Hilfiger cologne. And I never talked to her again.

And yes, *of course* I wore the cologne. It would be rude not to.

$10,000 Razor Scooter

Mary Margaret Healy

I THINK MY DECISION to go to grad school was similar in a lot of ways to my mother's decision to buy a Razor scooter.

My mom says she always wanted a Razor scooter, and indeed, I remember her envying all the middle school prepubescents coasting around our block. But she's waited a long while to actually purchase one for herself. She's a big girl with a big girl job—the child's toy was not cost-prohibitive—but for whatever reason, she didn't decide to get one until right now. Specifically, a couple of months ago, when she saw one at a garage sale for a couple of dollars. She can't resist garage sales, and she couldn't resist that scooter sitting there, calling to her, saying, "This is the perfect time."

Maybe the scooter was right. The weather was nice this summer, my mom was trying to instill in herself and her granddaughter a love of a more active lifestyle, and in a lot of ways, she's the most carefree she's been in years. That certainly *sounds* like the perfect time to pick up a new scootering hobby.

But her used-new, sleek, fresh-out-of-the-'90s scooter came with more work than she thought it would. The wheels were rusted pretty badly, and in places the rubber had worn away lop-

sidedly so the actual scootering movement looks a little more like limping, and it will until she can figure out how best to clean the thing out. And once she does that, she'll learn what all my middle school friends learned years ago: scootering is more work than biking, more work than roller-blading, more work than walking wherever it is you wanted to go. It's actually very minimally fun, even when the wheels aren't effectively soldered to the chassis.

Hearing my mom talk lovingly about her scooter and all the great happiness it would bring her, my brothers and I all laughed like bullies in the cafeteria. We laughed because we remembered our mom talking about the scooter she wanted back when she didn't have one, and the hilarity of the whole situation hasn't changed much. But watching my mom talk about her scooter, I saw her sort of bashful smile, the way she staunchly refused to be amused by her dream, the way she really wanted this little relic to work for her, the way she visualized herself flying down our street, untethered by friction or feet. Watching her talk about her little Razor, I got worried that even if she did de-rust the wheels and manage to get the thing to stop listing awkwardly to the left, her heart would be broken by the realization that it's not the great liberator she's imagined all these years.

My two-year master's degree is not going to cost me only a couple dollars. But if its proverbial wheels are metaphorically rusted to the figurative chassis, I'm going to get a lot worse than a laugh out of my hypothetical children. And right now, as I sneak this blog post in past the piles of readings that strategically litter my dining room table, I feel like my whole life is listing awkwardly to the left. Did I really imagine that, after spending the next two years of my life trying to intimately understand and positively change the problems of the world, I was going to be zooming down the streets, the wind in my hair, using some sort of magic Social Worker Wand to zap the bad guys and super-charge social policy? When I told my family and friends that this is what I wanted, and some of them laughed and tried to tell me that I was crazy, were they foreseeing my broken heart and trying to protect me from it? I thought they were just being cafeteria bullies. Were they right?

I don't know if my mom still rides her scooter. I don't know if she ever really rode it after she bought it. But I know I'm going to be riding mine nonstop for at least two years, and I hope to God I don't regret the purchase.

Nine to Five

Safe in his will, guided by his spirit, I will soon find the work to which God calls me.

I Quit

Elaine Schnabel

I QUIT, AND IT was petulant. I disagreed with the way my manager dealt with me, so I responded out of proportion to reality and in proportion to how entitled I am. I wanted to be important immediately, skip the corporate ladder bullshit and be lauded for how smart I am. I wanted responsibility and autonomy, and when I didn't get it, I responded like a child who isn't allowed to stay up late with the adults. This was a tantrum that got out of hand, causing me to forget that my desires are not the most important thing in the world.

I quit, and it was far-seeing. I realized that even adjusting for the ups and downs of the beginning of a job, I knew and understood that The Company wasn't a good fit. My coworkers were not the kind of people who bring me joy or teach me how to be a better person. My work was unfulfilling and my paycheck an empty promise. Many people carry on the charade of being invested in useless endeavors, but I chose not to wed myself to a hopeless situation.

I quit, and it was God's plan for me. Just like it was God's plan for me to be out of work for a few months, he (in his great wisdom) gave me the opportunity to be frustrated by an underwhelming disappointment of a job. He called me to quit The Company, so I could explore the other options he has for me. Safe in his will, guided by his spirit, I will soon find the work to which God calls me.

I quit, and it was meaningless. The Company can find another drudge to upload documents and click "send" or "submit" all day. They will find someone more tractable, someone more reliable and less grasping. It's my loss, financially and professionally, if I don't understand that, if I don't realize how little I matter. I am replaceable. Worthless. An appendix that burst and was removed. Just an emptier cubicle, a few extra documents for the new hire to write.

I quit, and it was brave. Staying with The Company was a safe bet: I could have continued with the easy work, the long vacations, and the reliable pay. I went for what I wanted and what felt right rather than what was safe. I will apply to seminary, I will spend time writing, and I will seek out volunteer opportunities that feed my soul and do nothing for my bank account, my resumé, or my rationally-foreseeable future.

I quit, and it is lonely. No one would look at me while I cleaned out my desk. My coworkers did not say goodbye. "Do you have a minute?" my manager asked, the day after I gave my two weeks notice. I followed him to the office of the woman who hired me. She asked me what went wrong, and when I lied and said nice things instead of the truth she told me to turn in my keys and leave. ASAP. I went home to my cat and my couch and looked out the window at the leaves filling in the skeletal trees.

Training Collar

Alissa (Goudswaard) Anderson

I'M ONE MONTH INTO a year-long job/internship/"field ed" experience at a church here in NYC. It's great—I'm helping lead services and preaching and calling up newcomers and planning for a women's Bible study and helping with Sunday school. If you know me or have followed the things I've written for *the post calvin*, you know that I am a seminarian and an Episcopalian. You may also know, generally speaking, that Anglican clergy wear collars/clericals.

Well, at my field site, I wear a collar. It's a "seminarian collar"— it has a black stripe (a "racing stripe," according to my husband) to show I'm not all the way there yet. I understand the reasoning behind my wearing it—marking me as a member of the pastoral staff/clergy—and I'm perfectly happy to comply.

It's a uniform that I wear to do my job. But it's a uniform with baggage. People know that collar = priest. Seeing a twenty-something woman in a collar is something of an anomaly.

If I wear it on the street to and from work, I get noticed. Usually just in a neutral way: people do a double take, or their glance lingers. The thing is, I'm pretty nondescript most of the time: medium height, medium build, brown hair, no loud clothing or accessories. I still have to deal with the odd catcall, but generally I slip by unnoticed.

If others are aware of me, certainly I am also aware of myself. Even in anonymous mode, I have an inner struggle with how to deal with panhandlers. I could write out all my internal arguments for doing one thing or another, but the bottom line is that my usual MO is to walk quickly by without a second glance. When I'm wearing a collar, though, my inner dialogue goes haywire.

These experiences could belong to any newly-ordained collar-wearer, but I have another layer: I'm not ordained. I am and am not clergy. I am inhabiting, in a very physical way, a role that I'm still growing into. It is very much a liminal space—so, as a result, I expect to grow from it.

Now, let me be clear: I'm pro-collar. After months of sitting with my masters thesis material dealing with women's ordination in the Episcopal church, I believe there's a lot of rhetorical power in women wearing clericals, power that may lead to ordained women being more widely accepted and embraced.

I'm also pro-clarity, though, and most people—even the people to whom I'm ministering—can't interpret my collar. They don't entirely understand the difference between my role and the role of a deacon and the role of a priest. When someone calls me "reverend," I struggle with how to make the correction, or even how worthwhile it is to do so.

My husband has many suggestions for places I should wear my collar (brunch, family gatherings, The Cure in concert, etc). I ignore his suggestions, unless I'm running late straight from church, and even then it's easy enough to detach the collar and just look like I'm wearing a polyester dickie with a weird neckline.

I wonder sometimes, though, about how quick I am to snap off the collar as I leave church grounds. Yeah, it's my uniform, and I've left work. But it's a uniform with baggage—baggage that I'm living into, leaning into. The fact that I am cautious about the propriety of wearing the collar is healthy, as is my acknowledgement of its import. Perhaps, though, I need to balance caution with boldness, to embrace this transitory time and wear my transitional collar with pride.

Dr. Seuss, PhD

Melissa (Haegert) Dykhuis

Yesterday, April 12, 2014, I submitted my first first-author paper to a scientific journal, describing my work studying the Flora asteroid family. Today I rewrote that paper for my son, Matthew, describing its major findings in the voice of his favorite first author: Dr. Seuss.

Because every great scientific work should be written in anapestic tetrameter.

> A long time ago, just a few worlds away,
> A couple of asteroids had a bad day.
>
> The Belt that they lived in had always been roomy
> But on that bad day it got sort of BOOM-y.
>
> Rock 1 said "Look out!", Rock 2 said "Oh no!"
> And then those two rocks made a fireworks show.
>
> (Except, as we learn from our friend Mr. Nye,
> There isn't much noise when two big space rocks die.)
>
> And what was left over? Well, as you can guess,
> Rock 1 and Rock 2 made a bit of a mess.

They didn't clean up (per asteroid etiquette),
And the biggest Piece was the size of Connecticut.

8 Flora was that Piece's number and name,
Its asteroid family is called by the same.

The Floras spread out without pushing or shoving,
Gently nudged by the Sun, so warm and loving.

Sunlight's made of photons, and like little balls,
These photons can push things, both Big Things and Smalls.

We don't feel the push, because it's so tiny,
But Floras sit out a lot where the Sun's shiny.

The Sun's push was found by a guy named Yarkovsky,
And… there's just about nothing that rhymes with Yarkovsky.

Alas, because details can get kind of bore-y,
I'll take you back to our collision story.

A billion years came, and a billion years went,
Some Floras hit Earth, and each made a dent.

They could be a problem, and I'll tell you why:
There's a whole lot of Things here that don't want to die.

The Floras, you see, are so close and so big,
We want to make sure that we "zag" when they "zig."

So Earth hires folks to be smart like your Mommy,
To watch for their zigging and keep our skies balmy.

Hands

Abby Zwart

A BIRD IN HAND *is worth two in the bush. A firm hand. I have to
hand it to you. To have the upper hand. To be underhanded.*

What's the first thing you notice about someone? Their hair?
Their eyes? Clothing? Voice? The first thing I look at (well, after
your face, probably) is your hands. I love hands. I love how they
seem to reflect your career, what you've been doing lately, and
even your personality.

The man handing me a bunch of asparagus at the farmer's
market yesterday morning had big, rough, tanned hands with
dirt under the fingernails. I imagined them taking apart a trac-
tor, ripping back the husk of an ear of corn, scratching the ears
of a shaggy dog. The little curly-haired girl running out of the
Sunday school room with a picture of Daniel in the lion's den has
marker all over her hands. She's chosen purple for the lions, and
the Crayola violet is smeared between each finger. The squirmy
ninth grader who forgot to study for her English final bites her
fingernails and folds her hands repeatedly as if she's playing that
kid's rhyming game about the church and the steeple. A girl with
long pink false nails leftover from prom last weekend. A guitar
player with calluses on each tip. A teacher with dry erase marker

on the heel of her hand because it takes too long to find an eraser and she doesn't want to break the flow of the lesson.

Give me a hand. To have a hand in something. Sleight of hand. The matter at hand. Don't bite the hand that feeds you. Right hand man.

At work, my hands take a beating. They've become strong from gripping a scoop and pulling it through frozen mounds of chocolate and caramel and peanut butter then packing it onto a cone. I've given up trying to keep them clean, settling for a quick rinse in the sink when napkins start to stick to my palms. Instead of dirt under my fingernails, there are Oreo crumbs. I spend a good hour a day with my hands in the sink, washing dishes and trying to avoid the knives someone always insists on submerging in the soapy water. They're sore and cramped when I get home, like I've just been rock climbing. But despite the beating, I can't help but smile when I see a little set of fingers creep along the edge of the counter outside the ordering window. The owner of the fingers (how do the nails get so tiny?!) discovers the step stool we've set outside and a little face peeks over the edge, grinning.

Hand in. Hand off. Hand out. Hand over. Hands down. The hands of a clock. My hands are tied. Taking a handout. To know firsthand.

We have so many phrases in English that talk about hands. "Hand" can mean effort, position, relationship, possession, and yes, even the physical body part. Every meal prepared, every word typed or written, every pair of pants buttoned—our hands are so often utilized that they're almost overlooked. We wash them, moisturize, trim our fingernails, but how often do you stop to marvel at how your hands are made? Their dexterity is astounding, and their strength can be surprising. There are twenty-seven bones in the hand. Times two makes fifty-four. There are two hundred and nine bones in the average human body. That means twenty-six percent of the bones in your body are in your hands. Fearfully and wonderfully made, indeed.

Hands on. Hands off. To go hand in hand. Out of hand. On one hand, on the other. To know it like the back of your hand.

At church, we shake hands with our seat neighbors. We raise our hands during a powerful song. We hand the collection plate down the row. The pastor raises her hands in a blessing as we leave.

Jesus laid his hands on people to heal them. We are called to write the name of the Lord upon our hands. God will uphold us with a righteous right hand. Christ shows Thomas and the others his hands where the nails had pierced.

It turns out hands also mean health, faithfulness, protection, belief, peace, and love. Definitely love.

The Funeral Singer

Stephen Mulder

A SATURDAY IN NOVEMBER. I arrive about an hour and a half before the service and file up to the balcony. We're singing two pieces this afternoon: Moses Hogan's "We Shall Walk Through the Valley in Peace," which I know backward and forward but rarely can get through without choking up; and Lucy Hirt's arrangement of "Abide with Me," which I remember well enough to know that I should be nervous about tuning on the first verse.

Louise, eighty-nine, was a retired Christian school teacher with a generous spirit. Every Sunday afternoon, her house would be filled with the sound of family and guests. She dedicated her life to her family and her church. She knew death was coming, but she did not fear it. She was ready.

One of the eulogies is delivered by her granddaughter, who turns out to be someone I worked with at Calvin several years back. It's a lovely speech.

A Tuesday in December. I leave work a few hours early to catch some dinner and get to the church. It's just me, my father, and our pianist Carol this time, performing Henry Smart's setting of

Psalm 23 as a baritone-tenor duet. I still get stage fright pretty badly when it's just me and my dad, or really any situation where I'm so vocally exposed. But we've done this one before. I try, and mostly fail, to relax.

The service this time is for a man I actually know, just a little bit—I used to deliver his newspaper. Ken had a beautiful garden that surrounded the front corner of his house, with flowers for each of his children and grandchildren, and was often tending it when I came by with my press bag. A minister, he spent the last ten years of his life serving nursing home residents and hospital patients as a chaplain. He was seventy-one.

A Friday morning, just this month. The choir contains a mix of singers assembled by the director from his various groups, and we only have an hour to rehearse before the service begins. The piece we're singing is Franz Biebl's achingly beautiful "Ave Maria," which I've never sung before but heard many times. Fortunately, most of the singers already know it, and it comes together nicely.

Michael, sixty-four, was battling no illnesses and had shown no signs of slowing down, with more grandchildren on the way and new business ventures on the horizon. In some ways, his life was still just beginning. But on that one morning, his wife got out of bed, and he never did.

I estimate I've sung in at least ten funerals in my life, maybe a few more. When you've been in choirs all your life, it comes with the territory. Most were in memoriam of someone I didn't or only barely knew, to whom I was only tangentially connected. A fellow singer's mother. An old man at church. A high school principal. A friend of the director.

I have always considered it an honor to be asked to sing, and have always agreed to do so willingly and gratefully. Music is a powerful thing, able to comfort a broken heart, or provide a moment of rest to a weary soul, or create a lasting memory that provides joy or strength in the days to come. I want to be able to share that with others, if I can.

But funerals are never easy, they're rarely much fun, and although I've been singing in them for a long time now (including three in just the past half year), I never really get used to doing it. Concerts become routine. Going to festivals and conventions becomes routine. Leading evening worship services, admittedly, becomes routine.

Funerals do not. Each one is different. Each one leaves its mark.

I may not have known anything at all about the person in the casket before the service begins. But during the hour that follows I will get to know her. I will get to know her family. I will learn what she meant to her community and those that loved her. I will hear strain in her family's voices and see pain in their faces, and it will become all too easy to imagine myself in their place. I will be reminded of those that I have lost.

An hour and a half later, we will all go our separate ways. But her story will have become a part of me. And my song will be a part of her family and friends.

The service ends. I grab my coat and my backpack and make my way to the main lobby, where guests are gathering to decompress. I stand around awkwardly, trying to both look comfortable and avoid making eye contact with anyone at the same time.

I never really know what to do in these situations, but I try to make myself available for just a little while, just in case. Maybe someone from a past life recognized me and wanted to talk. Maybe someone will just want to talk, period.

I'm pretty sure I don't really know anyone here, so it's hard to imagine who would want to chat with me and even harder to imagine what I would say if they did. But it feels wrong, somehow, to leave so suddenly.

Most of these people I will never see again, and even if I do, we would not recognize one another. And yet we've shared something powerful and moving and meaningful. I feel compelled to just *be present* for a few more moments, to share this moment a little longer, even though I'm not sure at this point what it is exactly that I'm sharing, or who I'm sharing it with.

Ten minutes come and go. I've spoken to no one.

I turn and walk out the door.

Retail Resolve

Laura (Bardolph) Hubers

THE SUMMER BEFORE I started college, I got a job at Marshall Fields. I was officially hired in the children's department, but I ended up, for reasons I never understood, doing most of my shifts in the department next door: intimates.

I thought it was bad my first day in the department when a woman came in, lifted up her shirt, and said "I like this bra. Can you find me another one?"

Another time a woman came in and said, "I'm a size 38DDD. I'll try on anything you can find in that size."

I tried to look politely unsurprised as I did my best to find her a few options and sent her into the dressing room to get started. When I went to knock on her door a few minutes later with a couple more choices (feeling more than a little victorious for having won this particular scavenger hunt), she opened the door shirtless and asked, "Does this look supportive enough?"

I stammered a bit. She looked down at my own flat figure, sighed, snatched the bras from my hand, and slammed the door.

It was always terrible when a guy came in. Always. A couple times they hit on me while buying something lacy for their girl-friends. One time a wife sent her poor husband into the store three times over the course of one shift because she wanted a brown bra and he kept bringing home one that was the wrong shade of brown for the party she was attending. At which it was apparently crucial that she wore exactly the correct shade of brown bra.

But the worst—the day I vowed I would do anything it took to be able to move on and get a better job—came when I had about two weeks left of work before leaving for college.

And when I say leaving, I mean going a mile down the Beltline, but my manager didn't need to know that. I gently insinuated that I was going somewhere far enough away that, regrettably, I would be unable to continue working. Alas.

It was the beginning of a long shift and the phone rang. "Hello, is this the men's intimates department?" the guy on the other end asked.

"It's, um. Well, it's the intimates department. I can transfer you to the men's department, though."

"Oh, okay, well, do you know if they have any, like, really silky soft underwear?"

"You know, I'm really not familiar with their selection. They'll know over there. Just let me transf—"

"Because, I mean, I really like my underwear to be silky soft, and in baby blue or black. And I've tried women's underwear, but it's really kind of tight, you know?"

"Pl—Please just let me transfer you."

"Okay, but just in case they don't have anything for me, do you have anything like that?"

"You know, sir, I can check. But only if you let me transfer you first."

Five minutes later the phone rang again. It took quite the

effort of willpower to answer. I only did because another customer gave me a dirty look for letting it ring three times.

"They only had boxers," he said, as though this were a deeply offensive and embarrassing situation for a men's department to find itself in.

"I'm sorry to hear that." I was. I was very sorry that they couldn't take care of him. As a result he was calling me again. "Maybe if you tried, um—" I was too flustered. I couldn't think of the names of any other stores.

"So do you have anything that might work for me?"

"Well, I don't really… I mean, probably n—"

"No, I'm sure you have something nice and silky soft. Women's departments always do. "

"But…"

"And in baby blue or black, remember. I'll be in later today. So, what's your name?"

"…um." Another name. What is another name? WHY CAN'T I THINK OF ANY OTHER NAMES? "…Laura?"

"Great, Laura. I'm so glad you can help me. I will see you later today."

I think the woman working in the children's department that day thought I was ill; every time I saw a man approaching I ran to the bathroom and asked her to please just cover for me?

It was that summer that I made some resolutions that I have actually kept.

1 Go to college, work hard, graduate, and get a better job.
2 Be kind to everyone working retail. Everyone. Ever. Because just about everyone else is a pain in their butt.

Ode to the Midwest

When I'm vacationing far from home, I find familiar comfort seeing those blue blazes, knowing that if I just walked far enough, eventually I'd run into the same riverbanks and country roads back home in Grand Rapids.

A Muttering of Ducks

Geneva Langeland

THE OCTOBER SKY bends blue over the cornfields as I wind past faded barns and flame-edged trees. On the radio, mellow bluegrass trades places with static along each curve of the road. I'm driving south, leaving Ann Arbor behind for a day to visit my aunt and uncle on their farm in the tiny town of Tipton, Michigan. I've been in graduate school for more than a month now, and weariness is already creeping into my bones. I need some fresh air.

I've been visiting my family on this farm for as long as I can remember. My cousin Chelsea is two years my elder, two years younger than her sister Gillian, and we've always been close. When I was younger, my mom, sister, and I made the two-hour drive about once a year. When we pulled up the gravel driveway, Chelsea would fly out of the house and we'd fling ourselves out of the car and into each other's arms.

The small farmstead captivated my suburban imagination. It was a place of earthy smells and textures, goats to scratch and eggs to collect from warm nests. My sister and I played at being farm-girls, but Gillian and Chelsea were the true homesteaders. They were homeschoolers, 4-HERS, chicken lovers, rabbit breeders. We pitched tents in the backyard, and we ate gooseberries and played cards by flashlight late into the night. We donned long, flowing skirts and staged gypsy dances in the living room while our parents dutifully tossed pennies at our feet. We hunted for fossils in the nearby quarry, fed soggy dog food to whichever injured bird was recovering on the back porch, warmed our hands by the woodstove, washed the dinner dishes by hand. I loved every dusty, dewy, hay-scented moment.

Over the years, my aunt and uncle have added outbuildings, expanded their sprawling vegetable garden, adopted dogs, raised ducks and chickens, and cleared pastures for sheep and goats. Uncle Eric teaches high school science, but he pours every spare moment into the farm. My aunt—Mary to most, Tinker to some—homeschooled her daughters through high school. Now that the girls have grown and moved away, Tinker nurtures whatever people, plants, and animals come under her care.

Today, Gillian and Chelsea both live in West Michigan. Because I've been able to see Tinker and Eric when they visit their daughters, I haven't returned to the farm in probably five years. But it's an easy drive from Ann Arbor and the timing is finally right. Forty minutes after leaving the city, I pull into the gravel driveway of the big white farmhouse. Eric waves from the yard, where he's raking wood chips into next year's squash beds. I let myself through the back gate and am nearly tackled by two beefy, wriggling dogs. They festoon my sweatshirt with white hairs and I don't mind a bit.

The dogs rocket around the yard as Tinker walks me through five years of change. There's a new hothouse for peppers and winter spinach. They've added sweet potato beds beside the goat pasture. The barn rolls with a bumper crop of butternut squashes.

Their cantankerous black cat is gone. Tinker and I step into the henhouse and I automatically scan the nest boxes, but the morning's harvest has already been tallied and added to the wire basket hanging in the kitchen. I half expect Chelsea to come sprinting out of the house for a bear hug. Not today.

Tinker and I head into the pine-paneled kitchen for lunch. Surrounded by spice jars and mismatched green pottery, I brew tea and chop peppers while Tinker makes fresh guacamole for our taco salads. At the wooden dining table, we sip glasses of raw cow's milk and gaze through the picture window, watching a goat amble through the wooded hill pasture. Eric pops a bottle of home-brewed kombucha and we clink our glasses in a murmured toast.

After lunch, Tinker and I head out to the sun-soaked garden. We pick thumb-sized raspberries and listen to the ducks muttering in their pen. I fill a basket with crisp lettuce and Swiss chard. A raspberry finds its way into my mouth. I close my eyes, breathe deep, and finally feel my shoulders relax.

How the North Country Trail Taught Me to Love Ohio

Nick Meekhof

THOSE WHO KNOW me well understand that I am a fanatic proponent of the North Country Trail (NCT), the National Scenic Trail that traverses America's northern tier of states from North Dakota to Vermont. The East Coast has its Appalachian Trail, the West Coast its Pacific Crest, and the Rockies have the Continental Divide, but as a loyal Michigander who thinks our beautiful Midwest deserves to be showcased just as loudly, I was thrilled when I discovered the NCT.

I've always loved the idea of National Scenic Trails. They allow you to participate in something so much larger than your typical walk in the woods. I love knowing that the trail won't just loop back to the parking lot after a mile or two, that if I simply keep walking, I'll eventually hit either Lake Champlain or the North Dakota badlands 2,300 miles later. I love the notion that when I'm hiking through Fallasburg Park on a weeknight stroll, I'm on the same trail and engaging the same locomotive procedure as a backpacker in the Adirondacks or a lumberjack in Minnesota. And on the flipside, when I'm vacationing far from home, I find familiar comfort seeing those blue blazes, knowing that if I just walked far enough, eventually I'd run into the same riverbanks and country roads back home in Grand Rapids. I once applied for an internship in North Dakota to study agrochemical levels in the Sheyenne National Grassland. Ignoring peer inquiries on North Dakota's presumed lack of outdoor stimulation, I decided it'd be fine—because the North Country Trail was twenty minutes from Jamestown. If nothing else, I could backpack the Great Plains on the weekends.

But then there's Ohio.

I'll admit my dismay when I first discovered how deeply the NCT's route plunged into Ohio. Being called the *North Country Trail*, I figured trail developers would view Ohio as a bland-but-necessary connection between the pristine forests of Michigan and the rock-studded hills of the Alleghenies. Like a skipping stone over the Great Black Swamp, the NCT would hop around Toledo, Sandusky, and Cleveland on its way to Pennsylvania.

But that's not what the NCT does. It takes a severe downward gouge, nearly down to the Kentucky border in places, before coming up for air again in the prettier northern climes of Pennsylvania. *But why?* I wondered. *Who would want to hike that much of Ohio? That's so far out of the way!* Southern Ohio is *not* "north country," not by my definition. There is no reason this should be highlighted in the official showcase of America's northern beauty!

Naturally, Michiganders *hate* Ohio. Wolverines and Spartans sure know how to spar, but we set aside our differences when Ohio State visits the Mitt, because any school pretentious enough to include "The" in its name deserves to lose. Ohio is flat. Boring. Smoggy, smelly, and snooty. The cities sprawl into oblivion; legions of rusted warehouses and oily factories transition abruptly into very flat, very linear muck farms. There's a river in Ohio that caught fire, the pollution was so bad. Do I need to go on?

I do. The highways are busy, congested with traffic, and chock full of tolls. Cut the corner from Toledo to Pittsburgh, and you can easily shell out thirty bucks. Now, it used to be the case that you only had to pay Ohio tolls when entering the highway *within* the state. One could get away with driving through Ohio and never stepping foot on the soil (or paying tolls) by gassing up outside the border and never leaving the interstate. In the spirit of tradition, my friends and I would stop in Erie, Michigan for gas and food, then drive nonstop through Ohio while staring disgustedly out at the soggy farmland and smoggy industrial corridors. If you had to use the bathroom, you waited 'til Pennsylvania. Finally, we'd cross over into the Keystone State and breathe sighs of relief, having landed the road trip equivalent of a running jump over shit's creek.

Oh, how wrong I was. Ohio, I sincerely apologize.

This past spring, I had the opportunity to explore Hocking Hills, a rural slice of southern Ohio tucked away in the vast, interstate-less void covering three-eighths of Ohio's total landmass. 17,000 square miles of twisting back roads, rolling hills, dense National Forest, and labyrinthine trails through it all. Hocking Hills is one of the more popular gems, with steep sandstone gorges, thunderous waterfalls, wind-carved caves, and towering cliffs.

Even through pouring rain—a lens that mires a good impression like news of a dead relative—Hocking Hills proved to be spectacularly beautiful. Here, the North Country Trail meanders through a narrow slot canyon, clambers over boulders, squeezes through caves, and flirts with death on sandstone ledges hundreds of feet above the churning, turquoise waters of Queer Creek.

That name deserves an explanation. As you're hiking along the NCT, marveling at all the rugged beauty, seldom do your eyes return to the gurgling creek on your left as you walk downstream. But walk a little farther, and you'll do a double take. You are now walking *upstream*, but the creek is still to your left, gurgling along innocently. "Well isn't that *queer*," thought more than a few early settlers. So you backtrack a half mile, keeping your eyes trained on the creek, lest it change its flow the second you turn your back. And sure enough, as inconspicuous as a raven in the night, it turns out you'd actually been following *two* creeks toward each other, which merge and disappear discreetly through a crack in the sandstone wall.

And the beauty doesn't end with Hocking Hills. Southern Ohio is brimming with charming Trail Towns and backpacking corridors throughout its Appalachian foothills landscape. You can hike all over the Wayne National Forest, paddle primeval rivers, and explore a burgeoning craft beer scene, all within miles of the NCT.

This trail has taught me numerous times to take part in something bigger. And as 2016 marks the hundredth year of the National Park System, I am reminded that the NCT doesn't care about the trivial Michigan-Ohio rivalry; state lines are meaningless when the greater goal is connecting individuals with spectacular beauty through love of recreation.

Now I know why the North Country Trail divulges so thoroughly through the Buckeye State. Perhaps a better metaphor for its route might be that of an ice cream scooper, making sure to get the most out of a deliciously beautiful state.

From the Polar Vortex

David Greendonner

I SPENT MONDAY MORNING getting to know my street. I already knew I had to dig out my car because I didn't elect the snowbank it stopped astride the night before. After clearing out what I could see, I played the forward-reverse-forward-reverse game until it lurched diagonally into the middle of the road, where it was snow-seized again. I spun in place for five minutes before I remembered seeing my roommate escape from a similar bind. I got out, grabbed the rubber floor mats from the back seat, wedged them under my tires, and crawled free. I felt pretty cool.

Our road is L-shaped. I got rolling down the long arm without much trouble and made the elbow without drifting into any mailboxes or parked cars. The end was in sight. I gunned it up what looked to me like an incline about as threatening as what you might find on, say, the eighth hole of a miniature golf course, but it may as well have been a mountainside. I lost all traction and rolled back down. I backed up and tried again. And again. In my rearview mirror, I saw a man in a dark blue snowsuit shoveling the sidewalk back near the crook in the street. I didn't want him to come help. I decided I would flash my native-son status by performing my now-trusty floor mat trick as if I had been doing it successfully all my years. I stopped at the highest point on the hill I could, tucked the rubber mats in front of my wheels, and proceeded to melt their edges with impotent tire-spinning.

My best bet, I thought, was to turn around and try to make it out the street's other end. I backed up past several houses and swung into one whose driveway seemed relatively clear. I shifted into drive and didn't go anywhere. I stepped on the gas and didn't go anywhere. I looked out the passenger window at the blue-suited man shoveling, looked away, and revved stubbornly.

The garage door behind me started opening and a neighbor walked out. I rolled down my window. "I've got some cardboard we can put under your tires, and then maybe I can get this guy to come help me push you out," she said. I resisted the urge to endorse my floor mats.

We tore up a box and lined the ground with it. She called over to the shoveler. He wore a fur hat and his beard was frosted over. "Is no good day for driving, ah?" he said, as if he came from a place in Northern Europe that looked about like this in midsummer. I got back in the car.

Before I hit the gas, a little girl, bundled in pink, skipped out of the house. The three of them lined the bumper in my mirror. I started rocking the car forward, and they leaned in rhythm. When I caught the ground, I didn't stop until I made it off our street. I raised my hand high out the window and didn't look back.

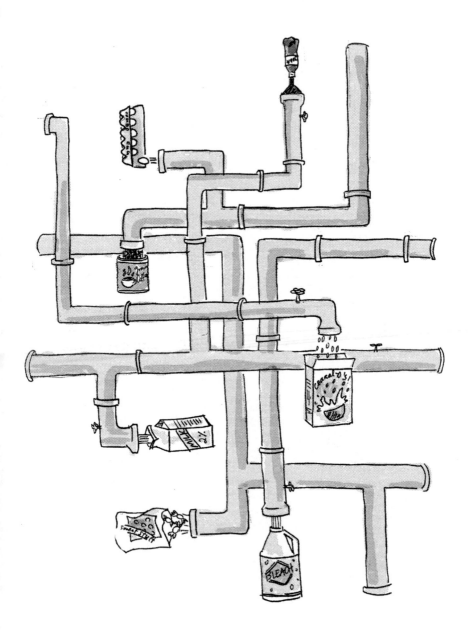

Body Burden

Geneva Langeland

IN THE SPRING of 1973, my mother was twelve years old with a cloud of dark hair. She was probably sitting in science class or running barefoot across the grassy backyard of her suburban Grand Rapids home, chasing one of her five siblings.

Half a state away, an employee at Michigan Chemical Corporation was mistakenly slinging some paper sacks of polybrominated biphenyl onto a truck bound for an agricultural feed-mixing plant. At the Farm Bureau Services facility, which served dozens of Michigan livestock farmers, employees would barely glance at the scrawled labels on the brown paper sacks before heaping them alongside bags of magnesium oxide, the product they'd expected to receive.

This was a devastating error. Magnesium oxide is a cattle feed additive meant to promote healthy milk production. Polybrominated byphenyl (PBB), a crumbly white compound that looks remarkably similar to magnesium oxide, is a flame retardant. A highly toxic one.

Thanks to a messy warehouse, scribbled labeling, and a general lack of supply chain oversight, an unknown quantity of PBB was tipped into batches of dairy cow feed instead of the magnesium oxide the workers thought they were adding. The first batch of contaminated feed reached only a handful of Michigan farmers. But clingy PBB molecules stuck to the mixers and sloughed off into each succeeding batch of cattle, hog, and chicken feed. Nobody at the plant noticed.

Across the state, farmers did. Stolid Dutchmen whose families had been farming for generations gaped as their previously healthy dairy cows withered. The herds' hides erupted in sores; they trembled, bled, aborted calves, refused to eat, went blind, and died. Neighbors shook their heads and whispered about plagues, about mismanagement, about abuse. Vets were baffled. But this was long before the age of instant information and online support groups. Each PBB-affected farmer thought this disaster belonged to him alone.

After months of agony and loss, the afflicted farmers began to find each other. With the help of university researchers, rural vets, and lawyers, they finally tracked down the source of their misery, the accidental intrusion of a brand-new chemical even its manufacturers barely understood.[1]

Finally, the system kicked in. Government agencies scrambled to set safety standards for flame retardant concentrations in Michigan's beef and milk. Herds were quarantined. Thousands of animals were shot and shoveled into massive burial pits near Kalkaska, Michigan. Devastated farmers accepted small settlements from Michigan Chemical and tried to rebuild their lives.

But the crisis wasn't confined to the livestock. Toxic, fat-soluble PBB molecules had spent months slipping into milk, meat, cheese, and eggs served on rural, suburban, and urban tables around the state. Entire farm families—highly exposed to their

---

1 Journalist Joyce Egginton tells the farmers' story in her fascinating book, *The Poisoning of Michigan*.

own toxic products—became riddled with cancer, skin lesions, dizziness, fatigue, and depression. If similar symptoms cropped up among the public, the patterns went undetected. However, a 1976 Michigan Department of Public Health study found that ninety-six percent of nursing mothers shopping at urban grocery stores had detectable PBB levels in their breast milk.

The media barely knew how to handle the story. Reporting loudly about the crisis would spell financial doom for Michigan's agricultural economy. Staying silent would leave millions of Michigan consumers in the dark about the shadows on their dinner table.

In the end, economics won. The story stayed low-key, barely reaching suburban residents like my grandmother, who continued pouring glasses of Michigan milk for her family. The toxic hitchhikers—designed to keep clothing and furniture from igniting in housefires, but capable of mimicking hormones and interfering with the body's cellular machinery—likely built up, sip by sip, in my mother's body. Even today, her cells could retain detectable levels of PBB. Thanks to the chemical's solubility in breast milk, mine could, too.

I'm not one of those people who stalk down the cereal aisle at Meijer, muttering darkly about synthetic chemicals in our food. I freely acknowledge that the post-WWII chemistry boom helped make my modern life possible; clean laundry, soft green lawns, the ability to microwave leftover pad thai in its plastic container—I owe all these luxuries and more to the ingenuity of people who threw a bunch of molecules into a superheated vat and waited to see what happened.

But chemical research is mind-bogglingly complicated and expensive, and the pressure to perform often forces manufacturers to throw new products on the market before they understand the true nature of what they've made. From the insecticides that might be destroying our nation's pollinating bees, to the cancer-causing BPA in the water bottles we're now forbidden to buy, to the DDT still detectable in Michigan's gull eggs, we've been forced again and again to confront one simple fact: *we have no idea what we're dealing with.*

A few paper sacks on the wrong truck inflicted environmental and physiological damage that Michiganders are still trying to sort out three generations later. God—what else are we doing to ourselves?

My inner environmental biologist panics at this point. *How many times must we realize ten, twenty, fifty years too late that something we invented is now coming back to burn us? How many billions of dollars will we spend cleaning up after herbicides, pesticides, pharmaceuticals, flame retardants, coolants, and plastics that once promised to improve our lives? How long before our big, tough planet builds up such a body burden of our molecular inventions that its water, its soil, its air, its living creatures are as doomed as Michigan's dairy cows?*

But whispers of hope keep these fears at a reasonable volume. In all likelihood, my mother's cells will never be forced to reckon with their polybrominated inhabitants. The natural world is blessedly resilient. Organic produce and metal water bottles exist. And as long as we bumbling humans keep making messes, good people will always be there, trying to clean them up.

The Shirt of Your Back

Rebekah (Williamson) Medendorp

THE FADED AUTUMN leaves reflected a dappled luminance as if the sun himself had sprinkled extra rays upon the rolling Pennsylvania forests. Each curve in the road brought a new glimmer of yellow, a visual scent of setting amber as I drove east in search of Lancaster.

I've driven this route once before, but that time had been in early summer and the hills were bright green and wholly alive. That first drive was darkened by a consistent eight hour downpour and wracked nerves of crinkled MapQuest printouts that never include construction reroutes.

This trip is faint, dry, and thankfully guided by my phone.

Ellie and I fashioned a tradition of yearly visit swaps after we lived as roommates during a semester encamped in the Oregon mountains. This year it's my turn. I made a pit stop in Ann Arbor to snag my dad's car. By snag I mean beg because there is no prayer in heaven or hell that would give my '99 Taurus the stamina to survive a drive to Pennsylvania.

As I drive, I prepare myself for the plunge into ineluctable kindness of Lancaster folk. Mennonites have a near-sickening habit of friendliness and "give-you-the-shirt-off-my-back-which,-incidentally,-I-hand-wove-yesterday" style of hospitality. They welcome guests in with soft smiles and fresh food. Ellie's family, the Shenks, continue to entice me into their home with something baking in the oven.

Last visit was peach cobbler. Delicious peach cobbler with bubbled juices of a neighbor's backyard peaches and the perfect flakiness of a cobbler top. This year I can smell apple crisp as I pull into the driveway alongside their honest yellow farmhouse. The sweet aroma wafts through the air and my nose drags me out of the car and to the front door. Jedidiah, Ellie's father, opens the door and welcomes me in with a hearty shake of his calloused carpenter's hand.

Dinner consists of the apple crisp I smelled. The apples are hand-picked and the crisp hand-mixed from Grandma Shenk's special recipe. Seriously, that's dinner, and it is fantastically tasty. As we munch hungrily on our crisps in the living room, whose broad wooden floor boards were crafted in place by the Shenks themselves, Mr. Shenk gifts us all with the surprise of cinnamon rolls for dessert. Hand-mixed and rolled with the added blessing of fresh handmade icing of his own creation. I am not making this up.

As Ellie finishes up a scarf for her coworker, Mrs. Shenk and I chat about family updates. She and I are very close. As we gab, I engage my personal tradition of testing the authenticity of the Shenks' Mennoniteness.

"That's a lovely chair. Is it new?"

"Oh no, that's been in Jedidiah's family since the Civil War. His great-great-great-grandfather constructed it from an oak that had been struck by lightning."

"This candle smells divine. Yankee Candle?"

"Oh no, I made that last week. I had a spare afternoon and whipped up a few dozen candles. I just love creating new scents."

"Well, of course, who doesn't!" *I don't. How the hell do you even create a new scent?*

"Hmm. That wood-stove sure is keeping me toasty."

"That old thing? Ah, Jedidiah threw that together on a whim during our honeymoon in his backyard forge."

Mother of Pearl! Are you *#@%!^ serious!

"By the way Bekah, I love your hat. What size needles did you use?"

Classic Mennonite assumption that I knit my own hat.

"You know, actually, this particular hat was a gift." *A gift I bought myself from The Gap because I don't have spare afternoons to knit myself outfits.* "I'll have to ask about needle size next time, completely slipped my mind."

During the drive back to Michigan, warm and cozy in my new Shenk hand-woven cardigan, I reflected on the art of craftsmanship.

I have friends who brew their own beer. My dad brews his own blog. My mom's garden rivals that of the Babylonians. In his spare time, my brother constructs a composite four-seater retractable airplane in his friend's garage.

Up until now my craftsmanship has been limited to drinking my friends' beer, sipping my dad's blog, and consuming my mom's vegetables. I want to do something more than eat!

Incidentally, I am in the process of carving my own spoons.

Departures

We helped each other learn the past tense. We cooked together. We walked together. We were together, trying to figure out the beautiful, capricious Italia.

Tongue Ties

Sabrina Lee

Between the cobblestones and the hills, nothing is level here in Perugia, Italy, and although I've wandered through almost all of the piazzas, vias, and alleys of the historical center, I still haven't found a right angle. Nothing is flat. Nothing is straight. Nothing is easy in Italy, say two fellow Americans who have come here several times before to study Italian. My first afternoon here I wandered the same three streets for an hour trying to find the apartment I would move into in a few days. (I swear half of the streets in Perugia aren't even mapped.) When it was time to move in, my landlady told me that something had happened: she had rented my apartment to someone else, an accident that had never happened to her before. However, she offered me another apartment for the same price, and I accepted. At that time, I was just happy to have somewhere to sleep and shower, but now I've realized that my move from Via Cartolari to Via del Poeta landed me in a less-savory neighborhood. No worries—I've only had my butt grabbed once. However, I can't help but wonder how much less my apartment should really cost.

Not knowing much Italian also adds another difficult twist to Perugia's unexplained idiosyncrasies, and I find myself circling around unknown words, using roundabout ways to ask how to say something as simple as "rain"[1]—*what is it called when there's water in the sky?* Or "cry"[2]—*what is it called when there's water in the eyes?* It's a strange feeling realizing that you have no idea how to ask: *what happened?*[3] Or, more importantly: *where's the bathroom?*[4] Or, even: *what's your name?*[5]

During my Italian language placement test, I sat next to a Polish man, and we smiled and said "ciao." We eventually figured out our names and nationalities. And that was it. I couldn't ask him what he did for work. I couldn't ask him why he was studying Italian. I couldn't ask him what "tedesco"[6] meant on the section of the information sheet where we had to check little boxes next to the languages we knew. So we sat, quietly sweating next to each other in an elaborately painted, non-air-conditioned lecture hall, our own little Tower of Babel.

I thought that "language barrier" said it all. Without a common tongue, two people can only greet each other—if that—intersecting for a mere moment. Then, they must go their own ways. The shared path is shut. There is no outlet. There is no progress. The tower is abandoned, I learned in Sunday school.

And, yet, this month, my close friends were not the Americans or Australians or New Zealanders or Canadians; they were not the Anglophones. Instead, they were Turkish, Korean, German, and Kurdish. For the most part, we spoke Italian. In fact, my Korean friend told me that it was easier to understand my Italian because I spoke too quickly in English. Even when I did speak

1 piovere
2 piangere
3 Che è successo?
4 Dov'è il bagno?
5 Come ti chiami?
6 German

English, I was limited by my friends' vocabularies, and that was okay. It was more than okay, actually, for I'm still not sure how much any of us have in common, and had we all fluently spoken the same language, I'm afraid our babbling would have called attention to our differences and would have separated us. By not speaking easily or perfectly, however, we grew closer. We ate gelato on the palazzo steps and pizza on the main drag. We helped each other learn the past tense. We cooked together. We walked together. We were together, working to figure out the beautiful, capricious Italia.

Twice, I went to mass at the Cattedrale di San Lorenzo. I didn't understand what the priest said, and I couldn't sing along with the congregation, but my heart recognized the rhythms of the Nicene Creed and the Lord's Prayer, and my ears picked up enough of the Italian words to make me forget the English ones. During those moments, I stood with my brothers and sisters in faith, speechless and understanding. We stood together, and as I lost my English words and as their Italian ones trilled over my head, our differences were pared away.

One night, my friend Emir and I sat on one of the many city walls, trying to slurp up quickly melting gelato. I had only been studying at the university for a week, so while Emir spoke Italian slowly and clearly enough for me to understand him, my responses were limited to short questions, longer stories being beyond my working vocabulary. He mainly told me about growing up in Turkey. I mainly listened. But as we were looking out at the lights over the valley, he asked me: *Credi in Deo?*[7] *Sì, io credo in Deo,* I paused, struck by the direct question, *e tu?*[8] *Sì,* he

7 Do you believe in God?
8 Yes, I believe in God, and you?

responded. I didn't press him in whom, exactly, he believed, and he let the silence sparkle a bit. We left it at that, both having affirmed: *io credo in Deo*. Never mind that I am Christian and he is Muslim, for in that linguistic moment, we believed the same thing, the limitations of language drawing us together as we sat on the same wall and under Abraham's same starry sky.

Are You Living Abroad as Authentically as I Am?

Katerina Parsons

Wow, so great to meet you. How long have you been in the country? Three whole months? That's incredible. I remember those days. I remember being so overwhelmed and lost three months in. I can promise you—it gets better! How long have I been here? Almost a year, actually. Well, okay, six months. But coming up on a year.

Are you just *turisteando* then? You might not know that word. It's slang for "being a tourist!" So funny. Anyway, tourism is so great here. I'm sure you've seen the ruins, the cathedral.... Oh, you work here? Really? Let me guess, you're an English teacher? No? You must work at an orphanage then. Funny thing, I read this article online about orphanages: did you know most of the kids aren't even orphans? You think you're rescuing them from the streets, but really.... No? Oh, development work. Hmm. Development work can be so helpful when it's *sustainable*. Have you read the literature on sustainable development? Give me your email, I'd *love* to send you some sites.

So, how's the language coming? Haha, yeah, I remember when I first got here, it was pretty hard. Well *relajate, vos*. Have you learned that tense yet? It's not one they teach you in school. It

135

took me ages to pick up. But don't worry too much, people won't expect you to use it.

What an adorable headband. I have one similar, but I bought it in the mountains out west, where a group of indigenous women have a microbusiness handweaving them. Most of the textiles you buy in any old souvenir shop are actually made in the next country over—or even in China! It feels good to know the source of your purchases, you know? But your headband is cute too.

Well, what are you doing right now? We could go grab something to eat if you'd like. There's this street stand that's just to die for around the corner. I'm friends with the guy, so he'll let us eat cheap. I do have to warn you, the flavor is pretty strong, so if you're not a big fan of local food, this place is not for you.

I'd love to keep catching up. It's so rare to find another *gringa* here—especially where I'm living. Not a lot of white people can handle my neighborhood, I guess. It's a little rustic, you know, but charming, when you really get to know it. Maybe, if you're up for it, you could come visit sometime. But I totally get it if you don't want to. Like I said, not a lot of *gringos*.

I just want to be a resource for you and help you out however I can. I know you must have so many things going through your head right now. I remember when I got here, it felt like the first time in my life that I didn't belong somewhere, that my surroundings weren't created with me in mind. I felt out of place, like I had to justify my existence here by burrowing deep into my best estimation of authenticity, wanting to belong to this place, but more than that, wanting it to belong to me.

I'm so glad those days have passed. I get it now. I get the culture. I totally get poverty. If you want I can explain it to you—it's not so hard once you have it figured out. Oh, sure, another time then. *¡Nos vemos!* That means, "see you later."

Grocery Shopping in Austria

Andrew Knot

Austrian law mandates that, with a few exceptions, super-markets remain closed on Sundays. Raised according to oldschool, Dutch-American Sabbath observance—bike-riding is okay, football-watching is reluctantly winked at, but any practice of commerce, tithes excluded, is very much frowned upon—I could have taken this as a comfort, a federally ordained slice of familiarity.

Instead, I stood there quaking in the checkout line. I'd been in Austria, my home for the next two years, for four days and had lived, to that point, almost exclusively on kebab and sausage from streetside stands.

It was early Saturday evening, and I'd slipped in the door of my local Billa—short for *Billiger Laden*, or Cheap Shop—ten minutes before closing. Immediately I felt like I should apologize. This is probably because 1. Contrary to American cultural commandment, in Austria the customer is pretty much always wrong, and 2. There's an exponentially positive correlation between the feeling of anonymity and guilty self-awareness. And I, the alien within their gates, was feeling particularly anonymous.

I had scrambled for the essentials—cheap pasta, cold beer, a handful of produce—and had picked up a *Milka* chocolate bar from where the tabloids and gossip magazines would have been at home. By the time I reached the *Kasse*—checkout aisle—an expanding queue of Saturday evening shoppers had grown restless. Behind me stood a frail-seeming Austrian woman, who I later learned was only adhering to Austrian cultural commandment when she demanded the opening of second register.

"Zweite Kasse, bitte!"

I shivered.

Had I been less desperate, I might have stayed home. Instead, I pocketed the spare change on my desk—€9.83!—and set out for the grocery store. Desperate for what, exactly? Cheap pasta, cold beer, sure, but mostly for proof that I existed in this new place, that I wasn't hiding.

In a week I'd be teaching foreign faces in a foreign building in a foreign country. Until then I was a stranger in a place that would be home, or at least was supposed to be but definitely wasn't yet. I knew no one and had little to do. So I walked around, cloaking myself in pedestrian anonymity, occasionally completing one or another task in my checklist of expat to-dos.

On the first day I registered with the city government. I shuffled into the city hall and submitted a form declaring my occupation, religion, and residency. On the second day I opened a bank account; a jovial banker, whom I now remember fondly as Austria's lone apostle for customer service, gave me a cappuccino before I signed on the dotted line. On the third day I bought a cell phone, a gray Nokia pay-as-you-go brick. It came with a wallet size plastic card listing my phone number, a PIN code, and the long-distance calling rates.

In a post-fall world, I realized, the Genesis story begins with bureaucracy and proceeds through the impatient checkout line of an Austrian supermarket. And there I was, evening on the fourth day.

Per the frail-seeming woman's sharp request, they opened a second register, which made me next in line. I stepped forward, knees trembling, and fumbled my items onto the conveyer belt, where they were scanned and rung up before I could decide whether to respond to the cashier's greeting in the formal or the informal.

In Austria, you are the bagger. This is a country that shares a language and a complicated sibling relationship with Germany, home of the Albrecht brothers, founders of Aldi. It's up to you to greet, bag, and pay before the frail-seeming woman behind you sighs and asks for a *zweite Kasse*. Austria is a Catholic country, and sometimes these rituals feel like the rushed litany of a Latin Mass might to an outsider—routine, yes, monotonous, perhaps, but replete with meaning that's only partially understood.

"Grüß Gott," (God's greetings).

Three seconds too late, I returned the cashier's benediction in the formal. I then struggled to collect my items by hand, briefly contemplated which of my purchases I could most easily part with—beer or green peppers?—and finally caved to the cashier's stern suggestion that I just buy a bag. I fished around my pockets for a loose euro coin, but was interrupted by a tap on my shoulder, a frail-seeming hand extending me a euro. Sheepish, I took the coin, bought a bag, and gathered my groceries.

I took the long way home, walking along the river. The sun barely hung over the hills but cast a ribbon of gold light on the gray Danube. And there was morning the next day.

A Selfie Stick Could Just Save Your Life (Not Really)

Ben Rietema

To this point in my life, I have borne a slight rancor towards the "selfie." While I understand the impulse—to somehow capture a picture of your own face from arm's length while including the background—the result is usually disastrous, leaving me looking like a disgruntled frog with God-knows-what in the background. I go into a selfie thinking I look somewhat decent and leave with crippling insecurity and the need to take ten more of the exact same picture—just to, you know, get the best angle, lighting, and hair sway.

Now I'm not against the casual, occasional face shot; such an action is simply the only one possible at times. If you're alone on a deserted island and your last recourse besides somehow contriving a five-second timer on a shaky, this-is-probably-going-to-fall-into-the-water-and-have-me-yelling-"SHIT"-repeatedly balance on a tree root is to take a selfie, then by all means, proceed. It's better than not having the picture at all.

But the extent, *the extent* that people have taken this to is simply ridiculous. The fact that a selfie stick has been invented and that people actually use it shows that maybe we have taken this too far. All that is really required for a very decent picture of you (with the background!) is to ask someone who looks respectable to take a picture.

Cameras, after all, are not very complex pieces of machinery—unless you get a technological troglodyte who, when you hand them your camera, looks like you've just handed them a gasping fish and asked them to gut it.

However, instead of a pleasant exchange between people or a fish disembowelment, we have an environment where people wander around with selfie sticks taking innumerable pictures of themselves. I would like to say that's an exaggeration, but it's not, and I swear on all that's holy that I have had to skirt around people who—while surrounded by landscapes God Almighty crafted from the living bones of the earth—spend their whole time staring at a four inch reflection of themselves.

Anyways, this is all relevant information that looks irrelevant, and I was not thinking about the selfie at the moment we begin my story. Rather, I was considering how long it would take to tempt some driver to accept a lovable if scruffy individual into their passenger seat.

Yes, I had a thumb outstretched toward the open road, a hobby for both the poor individual, the adventurer, and, of course, the poor adventurer. My destitute backpacking butt was stationed in Port Campbell, midway along The Great Ocean Road, a gorgeous stretch of highway that winds along the coast of southern Australia.

After a short wait, a van packed with an Asian family rolled to a stop—mom and dad in the front, two elementary age girls in the middle, two high school guy hooligans in the back. I must admit that I was surprised, both because families usually leave you in a cloud of carbon monoxide as they blaze down the road, and because they seemed to have little room in their car for anything but a few sandwiches.

As I chucked my bag into the back of the van and dove into the backseat, I found, however, that I was dead wrong—these were college students on a semester abroad to Adelaide. On a weekend whim, they had decided to drive eighteen hundred kilometers to Melbourne and back for the weekend, which—while not the most brilliant idea—earns my admiration for sheer audacity. It was just coincidence really that they looked and acted like a disorganized and clueless family.

They dutifully shoved over their collected backpacks, food, and other sundry crap to make room and gratefully accepted me in. I think they were just as excited to pick up a hitchhiker as I was to get a ride this quickly, as they peppered me with questions after I jumped in the back.

Soon enough, it was time for a confession.

"Ahh yes," a guy next to me with a newsboy hat and dark sunglasses said, "We hit a kangaroo yesterday night...." He laughed. "The front part of our car is... not so good."

Five minutes later, when we stopped near the Twelve Apostles (a gorgeous collection of massive limestone stacks off the coast), I took a look at the busted front bumper and the distinct smear of dirt and kangaroo blood.

"Can you notice?"

"Uhh," I laughed. "Yes."

"Then I should make a call later," Dom, the most classily-dressed of the crew, said nervously and then grinned.

We soon arrived at the Apostles, and sure enough, the group had pulled out a worn selfie stick, and were now ready to start an inescapable torrent of selfie shots. I offered to save them, to take the iPhone away from them, and take a decent photo—a real classic white person shot where everyone has to stand around with swiftly fading smiles while I take seventeen identical pictures. But they refused.

Instead, they wanted me to join them in the picture, which either means that they were very kind or they had never seen someone with so much hair and wanted to show their friends back home what they picked up. I have no doubt that my face is now on a Facebook page somewhere on the Internet with the tag the "American Yeti Hippie," shoved in alongside the photo of "the kangaroo we hit."

Thus, I found myself under the "selfie stick gun," and I will admit I felt conflicted. My principles—my principles, mind you!—were at stake. But as I grew aware of the laughter and the true smiles around me, I realized, for all my crafted tirades about how selfie sticks would singlehandedly ruin photography and maybe humanity, that I might have been a bit harsh.

As the iPhone shutter clicked, I began to embrace the absurdity of the situation. More and more tourists stopped and stared at us, and I grinned—I mean, what the hell? If we were taking fifty pictures then who was I to have such a self-righteous stick shoved up my butt?

Later, after we had arrived at my drop-off point at Apollo Bay, I asked if I could take a picture with them. We scrambled out of the car and after ten minutes of directing the impromptu family to the desired picture spot, we were ready for the photo. Viva, the mother of the group, handed me the selfie stick, and I stared at it. If I were a man of principle, I would have shouted, "GET THIS DEVIL STICK AWAY FROM ME" and thrown it into a tree.

But instead I connected it with my cell phone and prepared to use the unwieldy device. It was strange; it was cumbersome, but I like to imagine that somewhere God smiled, simply because he's a cheeky son of a gun. I snapped away and grinned, a real smile, an action that showed, *Yes, right now I am doing this and maybe, just maybe, I might actually be enjoying it.*

Reverse Culture Baffle

Elaine Schnabel

AFTER TWO YEARS in Korea of watching buses and taxis swerve from lane to lane to sidewalk to two wheels and back unscathed—in my last hours in the country—my bus finally got hit by a taxi. Feeling accomplished, I started my journey back home to Amurica. Appropriately, given the bus-taxi augury, the trip was not the smoothest I've ever experienced: a five-hour delay to start things off catatonically, fourteen hours in my least favorite airport, and ten hours of a small boy screaming and kicking my seat on our way over the Pacific. But I arrived, albeit bleary-eyed and greasy-haired, in Chicago.

Once at baggage claim, I began looking for a likely someone from whom I could borrow a cell phone to warn my parents of my arrival in the country. I once used about six different Thai people's phones on a bus from Bangkok to Chiang Mai trying to call a missionary's number. I spoke not a bit of Thai, no one else spoke English, and the missionary had accidentally given me the wrong number. Calling my parents here in the States, I figured, would be no problem.

The first person I asked was a taller woman whose husband stood next to her. She gave my greasy face and toothpaste-stained pink shirt a once-over and strained grimace, but no phone.

"I don't loan my cell out to strangers."

After five more people declined, I began to wonder if I looked even more unwashed that I realized. Finally I got a hesitant yes from a girl about my age who had clearly spent four, not forty, hours in the clouds, judging by her shiny hair and makeup.

"Only if I dial the number for you," Shiny-hair said, frowning at me.

"Anything. Thanks so much. I probably couldn't even work a phone like that." She tapped the number I gave into her iPhone, but held it back.

"Do you mind switching places with me?" she asked.

"Sure." I did, baffled, and she handed me the phone.

"I've heard people run off with these things," she explained.

"I should have given you my passport for collateral," I offered, but Shiny-hair shrugged it away, gesturing to her power position over not only my passport, but my violin, wallet, and computer. I made a mental note not to rob her.

The experts call where I'm at right now "reverse culture shock," but I've never really believed in culture shock to begin with. In my two years working for a Korean university, there have been plenty of times I've wanted to scream at my boss, but nothing that shocked me. In one memorable department meeting, she laughingly announced (uncontested) she was likely to contract cancer from all the stress foreign teachers gave her. Baffling, such moments undoubtedly are, but shocking? Not really. Everyone has their opinions after all, and every country has its idiosyncrasies. Perhaps it's misnamed. Culture Baffle, it ought to be called.

I was Reverse Culturally Baffled last week walking through my sister's trim, manicured neighborhood. The playground sign near her house advised Indiana suburbia: *NO guns or hunting allowed.*

"Do people use guns around here?" I asked my sister. Cornfields waved around us. A retention pond and a neat row of houses sat serenely under the open sky.

"Yup," my sister said. "One of the girls in my Bible study jogs with a gun strapped to her back."

On Yeongdo, my island in Korea known as one of the slummiest areas in the city, I frequently went for midnight walks. As a monolingual English-speaker, I was in competition for the scariest thing around—the other competitors being bus drivers and the pack of undersized wild dogs that sometimes patrolled the university. I'm not even sure the police had guns.

Coming home is great. Dinner with my parents, tennis in the park, grass and space and stars at night, driving myself where I want, and being able to ask for directions or make the tired worker at the bank laugh instead of look terrified that she might have to try to speak English. But it's also baffling. Guns remind me of the safety of Korea. Begging half the passengers from my plane for thirty seconds on their cell phone reminded me of that bus ride across Thailand.

On that ride I was scared to leave my seat. What if someone stole something out of my bag? What if I got off at the rest stop and the driver forgot me? I didn't belong on that bus. I read my Kindle and watched the rice paddies go by as the Thais chattered around me. Flip-flops, ratty purses, cheap manicures. Prepaid cell phones with dusty rubber keys. How in the world would I ever get anyone to lend me their cell phone? Easy. When I asked, everyone obliged. Willing verging on eager, dialing the number for me when it didn't work the first time. The man across the aisle from me woke me up around midnight so that I didn't miss my stop.

Maybe for Reverse Culture Baffle, like jet lag, it takes a day to adjust for every time zone through which you travel. Give me three more days, Amurica, and I'm sure it'll be good to see you.

How to Move to a New City in Seven (Not-So-Easy) Steps

Ryan Struyk

MY FIRST BREAKDOWN came about seventy-two hours after I moved to New York City.

I had just graduated from Calvin less than a week earlier, abandoning a community I loved in pursuit of adventure—in the form of a risky, low-paying temporary internship in the most spectacular, ruthless city on earth.

Mumbling "what have I done" over and over to myself in my closet-sized Queens apartment with my suitcase only half unpacked on the floor is not exactly my proudest life moment.

I've changed cities a whopping four times in the last eighteen months—parachuting into everywhere from East Coast metropolises like Washington, D.C. and New York City to the rural west of Boise, Idaho.

Here's what I wish someone had told me when I stepped off that first plane.

1 *Name The Loss.* Change on this scale becomes a substantial threat of instability and uncertainty. But when we make major life changes, we don't resist the change itself, per se. We resist loss. There's plenty to lose: friends, family, and a place to belong—not

to mention the little, unexpected things that constantly remind us we don't belong, like having reiterate that you want a "soda" every time you try to order a "pop." The often overlooked first step is just to name these losses—big and small—and give ourselves permission to grieve them.

2 *Take Lots of Initiative.* When we move to a new place, our lives have been turned upside down. So it's difficult—but imperative—to take a step back and realize that everyone else's life has stayed almost exactly the same. Some people will make an intentional effort to make you feel welcome in their city, but those people will be few and far between. Latch onto them. Say yes to everything. For the rest of the people you want to meet, take a deep breath and make the invitations yourself. I didn't really get to know some of my favorite people in Boise until my last month there—just because I never said "let's grab drinks."

3 *Don't Rush to Conclusions.* In that same vein, let's take a step back and remember that relationships take time. Settling into a new job, a new church, or a new neighborhood takes time. We aren't going to be best friends with anyone in a month. Or maybe even six months. We aren't going to feel at home in our new jobs during our second week. And we can't replace lifelong friends from our most formative years in a matter of weeks.

4 *Find a Church.* How does God usually show his faithfulness and comfort in our lives? Friends, family, familiarity, and belonging. But there isn't much familiarity or belonging when we move to a new place. Most importantly, church grounds us in our true, unchanging identities in the midst of a topsy-turvy season of life. It doesn't have to be your dream congregation with exactly

the right music and perfect coffee. Some of my most meaning-ful moments in Washington and in Boise happened on Sunday mornings and with the people I found there.

5 *Make Some Small Immediate Habits.* Here's another way to find some immediate stability: fall into a few habits. This will give us some familiarity. Maybe it's learning the barista's name at your new favorite coffee shop. For me in New York, it was running the exact same route after work. In Boise, it was finding a half hour to wander around Barnes & Noble. Find something tangible that you can own and go to for stability.

6 *No "New City, New Me" Resolutions.* One of my biggest mistakes when I moved to New York was trying to kick all of my bad hab-its during the first week. I thought this was a fresh start for me: I was going to eat healthier and go on Facebook less. Turns out some of those "bad habits" were major ways for me to stabilize, and trying to kick them made the move much more tumultuous than it should have been.

7 *Keep In Touch Back Home.* Although it may seem like it at times, moving to a new place does not mean our old friends cease to exist. People who have walked through our most formative years are not "fallback friends." Yes, these relationships will look differ-ent. When I moved to Washington, some friendships actually got much stronger through the distance. Others fell by the wayside. But spend some of that initiative reaching out to friends and family back home—they are not as immersed in the change as you are.

Riding in Buses with Strangers

Andrew Knot

T HERE ARE THE unabashed lovers. They sit one seat in front of you and carry on like Europeans. Kisses on the nose, forehead, cheekbone, upper and lower lip. Nuzzling. Giggling. You realize they're your countrymen, United States tourists, when the exchange of their tender, sweet, occasionally nationally and geographically based appellations, in all their Yankee splendor, reaches such a crescendo that you're privileged to overhear.

You're my Hungarian meadow, tan and rolling underneath a setting sun.

You're my Danube, blue and worthy of musical adaptation.

This is enough to permanently rattle all of your nearly cemented conclusions about national identity and PDA. Perhaps it's not as distinctly European as you thought. Maybe even Americans, with their big lawns and streets, will sacrifice their treasured personal space for some cuddle time. Your interior monologue continues to stage this debate with itself, weighing past experience against the spectacle of the lovers one seat in front of you. Of course PDA exists in the United States, but never had you seen it to the extent that you do in Europe. The Austrians, for example. It's safe to say that the assumed Viennese escalator riding posture

positions the shorter partner of the pair on the top step and his or her partner one step below. From there said couple can canoodle. You saw this, week in and week out for the entirety of your semester abroad and cling to it as proof of your hypothesis. But maybe you were at this point in your life lonelier and therefore took more notice of it. You tell yourself to resist the urge to turn every observation into a sweeping socio—

At this point a backpack frees itself from the overhead compartment and comes crashing to the bus floor inches from your right foot. There is a moment of intense silence as your traveling companions look around for a passenger whom they can shame with accusatory glances. At last an older, stodgy, bald man arises from his seat, gives you an understanding, not-quite-apologetic nod, and grabs the fallen rucksack and puts it between his feet.

You do not know which language this bald-headed man with the gruff but kind-looking face speaks. He might speak English. You know that English is the only language with which you could manage a response, one that's subtle, reassuring, and with aplomb. At this moment you are met with multiple emotions. First, awe at the full complexity of language. Second, sympathy for those living outside of the geographical reach of their mother tongues. Finally, and most permanently, intense hopelessness for the progress of your German. Then you sigh.

Less than two hours into the trip, advertised as three hours, and you've hit traffic. Far off in the distance you see wind turbines, which you assume are across the border in Austria because, well you don't really know, but Austria is richer than Hungary and can afford such alternative energy technologies.

I'm lost in the Old Glory of your blue, star-spangled eyes.

You overhear this and are proud of your homeland and the

whimsy of its lovers. It almost feels like you've shared a moment with the couple. She's seated on his lap with her arms around his neck. Occasionally you make eye contact with her.

There are the British frat boys. You don't know whether or not the British uni system has Greek life. You don't yourself know much about Greek life because you went to a small, denominational liberal arts school where Greek letters are reserved for seminary students, wannabe seminary students, and, you know, *the* Alpha and Omega.

On the bus, the frat boys really aren't that bad. Before getting on the bus they were roughhousing—chest bumping, falling over, calling each other "mate"—in the metro station and you expected the worst from the bus ride. So far, however, you haven't heard much from them; they are sitting somewhere behind you.

There is the Eastern European woman sitting next to you. She is in her mid-thirties, you estimate, and is preoccupied with a Nokia phone that looks like the grown-up version of your youngest sister's Hello Kitty plaything. So far she has made four calls, each one of them longer than the last. You are confident she isn't Hungarian because you know four words in Hungarian and you're pretty sure you haven't heard her say one.

More traffic up ahead by the turbines. You are nearing hour four of the trip and have just crossed the border. This irritates you, and you aren't alone. The frustrated sighs from the back are becoming audible. With each abrupt stop you hear luggage shuffling around overhead. The stodgy, old, bald man with the gruff-but-kind face hears it too. Then he looks at you. You don't know how to respond, so you smile.

Eventually the traffic disperses. Out the window to your left you see two cars in a wreck. Standing next to the cars are two women: one in a headscarf and the other in jeans.

We all know whose fault that was.

You smirk, knowing that came from the British frat boys. Then you remember your thought about the difficulty of living away from your native tongue. You feel bad.

Fifteen minutes before you arrive, your Eastern European neighbor takes a pickle out of a paper bag and starts eating it. That's strange, you think, but it looks good. You resolve that six hours in a bus are probably enough to change the way you think about anything.

And that is how you got from Budapest to Vienna.

All's Fair in Love

There is a time of day when everyone is beautiful. Low light, slanted sun. Hair, skin, and eyes glow. At some point, the golden hour started to last all day. No matter the hour, my eyes started finding you first.

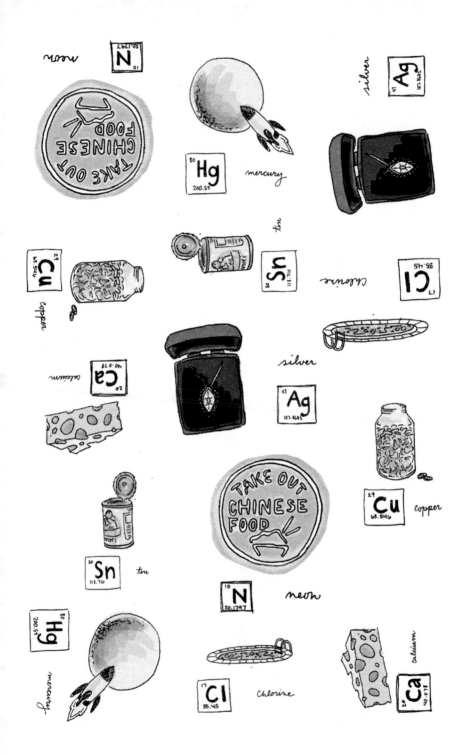

The Elements of a Relationship / Love Is Periodic

Caroline Higgins

Neon

I KNOW YOU DON'T like the city and sometimes this makes me like it more. I can't help it. I'm enamored with the eight million people and the eight million stories I will never know. The buzzing sign advertising Chinese takeout at 3 a.m. The exhaling buses. The pigeons. The noise.

Calcium

I don't know why I ever tried to make it work with you because you don't like cheese and that's crazy. However, it did work well when we went to that cheap Italian restaurant where they served breadsticks with a small plastic cup of cheese sauce and a small plastic cup of marinara sauce. More for me.

Copper

Sometimes when I'm cleaning, I just throw away pennies. It occurred to me recently that you would never do that. You are so methodical. You probably have a location reserved for spare change found on the floor. Or perhaps you never find pennies on the floor at all because you have a special place to put your change when you empty your pockets at the end of the day. Maybe it's a old, metal coffee can that you took from your grandfather's barn. That must be it.

Oxygen
For most of my twenties I've been trying to find someone who makes me feel the way I did when I was nineteen on a tram in the Tampa airport and I couldn't breathe because when the doors opened I would (finally) see you again.

Mercury
We both knew it could never happen. In a different world, yes. On another planet, totally. I was half-expecting it when you asked me if I wanted to run away with you. But there were no space ships involved, so I said no.

Chlorine
Thank you for always being the one who books our hotel rooms and for always remembering to check if there is a hot tub.

Gold
There is a time of day when everyone is beautiful. Low light, slanted sun. Hair, skin, and eyes glow. At some point, the golden hour started to last all day. No matter the hour, my eyes started finding you first.

Helium
If you haven't gotten the hint by now, propose to me in a hot air balloon.

Lead

You wrote the majority of your letters to me in pencil. This worries me, because it means I can only unfold and refold them so many times before they begin to fade. Already, the grey has begun to rub onto my fingers. The truth is I'm not yet ready for them, nor you, to disappear completely.

Platinum

I can't remember why it was that you had no money when we were dating. Remember when I bought you a J.Crew sweater and then you bought me a slice of pizza and I wasn't even mad? I promise this wasn't the reason we didn't work out. I really never minded paying.

Carbon

Carbon has been called "the tramp of the elements" because it bonds with everything. Maybe she just loves to be in love.

Silver

When you asked me why I got teary-eyed opening the necklace you got me for my birthday, I explained that you were the first man to buy me jewelry. "Really?" you said. "Really."

Tin

Do you remember when we ate Chef Boyardee ravioli cold, out of the can, at 1 a.m. on January first? You got out of bed and brought it from the kitchen triumphantly, with two forks. I was skeptical at first, but it was undeniably delicious. This will always be my favorite memory of us.

Iron

There is a verse in the Bible that explains how men (and women, I assume) should sharpen one another as iron sharpens iron. This means that we make each other better, we build each other up, we bring out the best in each other, and we keep each other accountable. But what happens when that person you go to—the person who makes you feel like the truest version of yourself—leaves? What happens then?

Untold Stories

Katie Van Zanen

I REMEMBER OUR UNLIKELY beginnings: a particular gleam of sunlight on the plaza outside Wrigley Field, the thunderstorm that cracked the sky the night we sat for hours in his old Toyota in the church parking lot where he asked if he could hold my hand. That was two Junes ago. We have not gone back to Chicago, and rarely have I been close enough to reach his fingers.

When I have told him about my solitary days, in blue bubbles of text or fragmented phone conversations or occasional video chat, I have recounted rarities. I have failed to share the sensations that have become, already, so familiar that I do not consciously recognize them. I realized, the other day, that I can identify the peculiar smell of Boston bus exhaust. I can hear it coming long before it rounds the bend; I can guess its proximity from flickers in the window of the west-facing house at the bottom of the hill. Sometimes, when I step jerkily toward a vacant seat, I see people I recognize. I couldn't tell you when I'd seen them first, nor definitively where. I can only say that this particular, unextraordinary face is familiar. This particular, unextraordinary stranger now makes up my world.

I do not, I cannot, describe for him each face I see. I do not pause to speak of the dusty glow that purples the Boston skyline on nights I walk up Fairview in the dark. Perhaps I am too embarrassed, or perhaps I simply forget, to tell him that the streetlights lit up the underside of autumn's oldest leaves one evening and I can still picture them splayed bright against the darkness. The less lovely moments, too—I do not say that I marked a finger with ink putting the cap back on the pens he bought me. I do not tell him that a woman left a teal scarf on her bus seat one morning. I noticed it when I stood to get off, but I didn't know what to do. When I turned to cross the street I saw someone else stand and pick it up before the bus exhaled and moved away.

When he is here, at last, I will omit these same snippets from the accounts of my day. I will come through the door and announce the errands I have done, and I know I will fail to describe the woman whose long fingers held her necklace as we waited at the cvs checkout. I will recount happenstances: things that made me laugh, or made me angry, or slowed me down. The pale moments of stillness will remain caught in my throat, because they seem unimportant, or because they seem desperately and inarticulably important, and remind me so beautifully, so cruelly, that "we live alone in the house of the heart."

"We are utterly open with no one, in the end," writes Brian Doyle, "not mother or father, not wife or husband, not lover, not child, not friend." It seems odd to speak of the limits of human intimacy when anticipating our reunion; to record for the world the untold stories which are themselves just fragments of a billowing moment already passed away, to promise that I will fail again to share them fully. It may be unromantic to say that their quiet ache will be unsoothed by his boyish laughter or the solid warmth of his chest. I can never quite explain the importance of an abandoned scarf, but I will try. And soon he will be here. He will ask to hold my hand, and I will try again.

To Know and Be Known

Will Montei

I FIRST HAD SEX when I was eighteen years old. It was very unromantic. We had to be quiet and careful because her parents were rustling around in the downstairs kitchen. My thoughts were flushed with the moment, doing my best to appreciate what was happening. Of course I didn't know what I was doing. I was young and still so shy with this girl. Earlier that day we had run into each other in the halls of our high school, my cheeks flushed just from the sight of her wide, brown eyes. That night, I was looking into them and wondering *Where do I touch? Where do you want to be touched?* Such a primal thing, but still a lot for a boy to grasp. Movies always made it seem ravishing, like you simply forgot about your surroundings and lost yourself in the glory of the other person's body. And my peers played it down, like sex was the natural course of things. "It's just sex." That phrase, along with everything else I expected, fell to pieces when I looked into her eyes, gazing up at me in all her nakedness, and wondered what was happening behind them.

When we finished, with my expectations of sex forever defeated, we went back downstairs and drank tea with her mom, and I was not a virgin. As sensitive as I tend to be, that change didn't bother me. What bothered me was that even after something so intimate, my insecurities had heightened. I knew less of her then than I did before.

I didn't love her. I probably thought I did at the time but was just scared to say it. Lush that I am, I often told girls that I loved them after only a couple weeks into dating, which never failed to freak them out. So I didn't say it, but I felt more deeply for her than I had for anyone else previously. Truthfully, our relationship could best be described as puppy love. I was always slightly awkward around her, never saying things the way I meant to say them. We got around that by doing a lot of kissing.

She was the kind of girl who preferred the company of boys over girls, often found saying things like "girls are so dramatic!" So I heard a lot about the guys she hung out with. They often got confused about boundaries. They also gave her grief for dating a "good Christian boy," which made her angry, but always self-consciously. "Do they think I'm going to change or something?" she would say, which would undoubtedly shame me into silence beside her. Sex became my affirmation in the face of all that insecurity. Whatever happened, wherever else, it was only the two of us on that bed. And, just like our conversations, it was always something full of uncertainty. All the excitement and tension and imagination that led to each encounter always boiled down to two bodies, warm, sweaty, all tangled up, but still, just two bodies.

We had sex a few more times over our two-month relationship, and when she broke up with me I didn't have sex again for seven years. I wanted to, obviously. And I didn't want to. I was worried I would do what I usually do; that is, become deeply attached, even more so because of the mystery that develops between two minds that encounter each other like that. I wanted to wait until marriage before I dealt with it again. But time dragged, and I couldn't hold on to love.

I think it was the damn loneliness that brought me into bed with two other women at the end of those seven years. Just to be held, to be wanted.

Each time, a familiar sensation of hollowness settled over me—that seven-year-old feeling of defeat. Shame, and no self-respect to fight it. I can still feel their eyes wandering over me so uncertainly. Am I still that eighteen-year-old boy, blundering into something he doesn't understand?

Yes, of course I am. I am older, wiser, and the same. I can't look at my past, both distant and near, and say otherwise. I still desperately want sex and all its disappointments. But I want it with someone I love. If only I had left sex alone, where instead of this burden that needs redemption, it was still something hopeful.

What is beautiful about sex after all this? But of course, the moment I ask that question, I can see it: we are together and I look into her eyes, my wife, and instead of feeling insecure, I will know her, looking up at me in all her nakedness, and she will know me.

Then, all of our insecurities will be splayed out together. We will be naked inside and out, clinging to each other in longing and understanding. And if none of this happens, and I grow old with no one but my friends and family to love, at least that loneliness is a better one.

I Watched *Christian Mingle* so You Don't Have To

Alissa (Goudswaard) Anderson

MY HUSBAND REGRETTED sending me this Facebook message on Friday: "off topic—in my Netflix browsing last night I discovered that that *Christian Mingle* movie is on there now."

He regretted it because that evening, after knocking out another Blue Apron dinner, you'd better believe I made him watch it with me. And it was at least as terrible as I thought it would be. It's so over-the-top. The plot and acting ability are Lifetime-movie caliber. (And not the good Lifetime movies, either, but the ones you put on when you just want to zone out and not use your brain.)

The plot goes something like this: Gwyneth is a high-powered thirty-something marketing exec who has everything—except a man. She keeps seeing TV ads for Christian Mingle, so despite being only marginally religious, making a profile seems like an awesome idea to her. She finds someone and tries to fit in with his obnoxious family and friends by going to a Bible study, dressing like a grandma, and saying long, awkward prayers. Her farce is ultimately revealed (on a mission trip in Mexico, of course), and they break up, but it's for the best because NOW SHE CAN WORK ON HER RELATIONSHIP WITH GOD.

The film distributors put it this way: "In an honest realization, she sees her superficial life for what it really is, and she's driven to create a personal relationship with God. In the end, He delivers on the true desires of her heart: 'life-changing' love." Super heart-warming and inspirational, right? I think you get the picture.

It's a romantic comedy that is not really romantic and isn't funny, either. The main characters have no chemistry (possibly owing to the love interest's rather ambiguous sexuality). Even the best actors couldn't deliver this script believably. The Christianese made me squirm, but not quite as much as the uncomfortable white-saviors-in-Mexico facet.

I think the highlight of the movie for me was when the judgy, annoying Christians went out to Steak and Cake after church, not because of any plot point or transcendent acting, but because Steak and Cake is exactly what it sounds like. The table held a platter full of grilled steaks and two full cakes (chocolate and carrot) on cake stands, served together. Because who wouldn't want a nice big sizzler with a side of Death by Chocolate?

You might be wondering why I would waste an evening watching something I knew would be terrible. I have a history of watching terrible Christian movies with my husband (*God's Not Dead*, the *Left Behind* reboot, etc.). I always know they will be bad, and they always are.

My time at Calvin taught me that Christian art is good art, that the vocational call of Christian artists is to create the best art they can. Good art speaks to the spirit. *Christian Mingle* is not good art.

It's not even all that Christian, if you ask me. Now, I don't want to discount anyone's experience—it's entirely possible that some people watching were uplifted in their faith—but I saw an uninspiring relationship and a lot of ignorant, judgmental people. The most Spirit I saw was in the (rather dumpy) charismatic strip-mall church where Gwyneth finds God on her own.

But I watch it anyway. Maybe it's some weird masochism on my part. Maybe I'm looking for that part of evangelical Christianity that I miss. Maybe part of me taking my faith seriously enough to take it lightly—to laugh at it, even—involves sitting through train wrecks of poorly done moralistic movies.

I think Jesus would watch *Christian Mingle* with me and would snort and groan and make snarky commentary in all the right places—and then he would go out and love the people who thought it was a good idea to turn a Christian dating site into a movie plot just as much as he loves people who agonize over beautiful, transcendent works of art.

That said, don't watch this—or, watch at your own risk. It's an hour and forty-three minutes of your life you can never get back, and you could do a lot in that time, like make cupcakes, or read a couple hundred pages of a fluffy summer novel, or deep clean the tile grout in your bathroom—all superior options. Don't worry; I'll take this one for the team.

Holy Matrimony, Batman!

Lauren (Boersma) Harris

L AST SATURDAY, I found myself in an unfamiliar room watching a parade of thirteen perfect strangers; a hundred more
strangers surrounded me, weeping into their blue-cushioned
chairs.

Ahhhh, weddings.

I would dare to say I'm more comfortable at a marriage cer-
emony than most people are shopping for groceries. I am one
of the youngest of twenty-eight cousins. Forty-two if you count
spouses. Forty-three if you count the wedding next July. I knew
how to order a nohito at the open bar by the age of eight. I know
that if there's open reception seating, you should seat yourself
as close to the bride's parents as humanly possible and if you
"gain a brother instead of losing a sister," all you'll really gain is
a reputation for plagiarizing maid of honor toasts. My closet is
a ghost town of half-empty, beribboned bubble containers and
bags of potpourri.

I've been to thirty-three weddings and counting.

And despite the fact that I've seen more brides walk down the
aisle than I've had candles on a birthday cake, I adore weddings.

And I believe in marriage wholeheartedly, because I believe
in true love.

NOW HOLD ON.

Don't do what I would probably do in your situation and close this book because you saw the words "true" and "love" in immediate succession. Put your hands where I can see them!

Let's make a list of things I DON'T believe in: love at first sight, destiny, soulmates, boundless romantic love, and people who think that picking through trail mix is wrong.

Even though I respect these beliefs, I don't share them. But I believe in true love. Because I think I've found it.

STOP.

TURN OFF THE CELINE DION.

PUT AWAY THE SCENTED CANDLES AND SHOVE THAT DANG CORK BACK IN THAT BOTTLE OF CHAMPAGNE.

It isn't what you think.

If you commonly frequent the website www.pinterest.com, you're more than likely expecting the phrase "I've found true love" to be followed by one of five things:

A   a picture of Ryan Gosling.

B   a lovely illustration of a bottle of wine.

C   a picture of a cat with Zooey Deschanel eyes accompanied by a meaningful caption that says something like "I CAN HAZ UR LUV, PLZ?"

D   a 465-pin wedding album that has been justified by a recent engagement.

E   a picture of Ryan Gosling.

Now, let's give Ryan Gosling the benefit of the doubt and assume he's a very nice man. Let's give red wine the benefit of the doubt and assume it's delicious. Let's give cats the benefit of the doubt and admit that it is *relatively* possible that they might not be soul-sucking demon spawn. Let's give people with wedding albums the benefit of the doubt and admit that when planning a wedding someday, it might be handy to come back to a list of personally selected nuptial preferences (and it's certainly more economical than buying a bunch of wedding books).

But let's be honest with ourselves and admit that none of these really fall under our true definition of love. The English language is sadly hamstrung by its lexical limitations when it comes to the word "love"; we only have one term while some languages, like Sanskrit, have over ninety. So we do what we can to differentiate by adding adjectives to the mix: "romantic," "brotherly," "motherly," "true."

The word "true" is synonymous with words like "real," "genuine," "valid," "authentic," "sincere," "devoted," "constant," and "faithful." Let's use some of those adjectives. Real love. Genuine love. A love that is valid. Authentic love. Love that is sincere. Devoted love. Constant love. Faithful love.

So, yeah. I've found true love.

It's two in the morning and my stomach feels like a vacuum cleaner in reverse. The three-week-old Thai noodles that tasted so good several hours ago are now punching me repeatedly in the throat. The floor is frigid, my neck is cramping, and something smells like musty Band-Aids. As I'm considering what it might be like to call my mother and beg her to make the twelve-hour drive to my duplex, one of my roommates is suddenly on the floor next to me, holding my hand and talking to me while my cheek squeaks against the porcelain of the toilet. She's taking a break from writing a paper, she says. Yeah, it's due tomorrow, but she's still got time! Her hand squeezes mine a little tighter.

I'm ten years old and I'm stuck in the uppermost branches of the pine tree in my front yard. The slow, creeping numbness in all my fingers and toes, the fluffy enormity of my snow pants and down jacket, and the seven-foot snow bank to my right make the hope of escape all but impossible. But the branches beneath me begin to tremble as my dad picks his way through them. Pine needles dig into his gray snowsuit and stab through his red and blue hat. Dirty wintergreen snow falls in my face as his arms reach through cracks the size of sidewalk lines and anchor themselves to mine. It's days before I remember that my father is claustrophobic.

It's day four of the backpacking trip. I'm sitting underneath a single blue tarp with my co-counselor and ten teenaged girls. I watch our fourteenth match sputter and die; our propane tank is only good for tossing angrily at the heavens. We can't hear each other over the sound of the rain, so we can only stare at one another's faces, a mixture of dirt, sweat, and unseasoned defeat, as we eat raw potato soup by the spoonful. I go to bed and all of my bones ache. My sleeping bag is wet. I'm sleeping directly on top of a root. But I awake the next morning to whispers and giggles. As I poke my bleary head out of my tent, I'm greeted by eleven beautiful pairs of hands holding a still-warm plate with the first two chocolate chip pancakes.

"This is how we know what love is: Jesus Christ laid down his life for us. And we ought to lay down our lives for our brothers and sisters" (1 John 3:16)

That's how we know what true love is. Just as Jesus Christ loved and gave himself up for the church, so should a man love and give himself up for his wife. So ought a man love and give himself up for his brother, his neighbor, his aunt, his mother, the annoying coworker that gossips too much, the girl who told him it was over, and his best friend since second grade who never calls anymore.

We've got to stop limiting ourselves to thinking of love as some cheap animated slow dance and remember that he *laid down his life for his friends.* And that is what I love so much about the thirty-three weddings I've been to: people pledging to lay down their lives for one another. Forever. It's not weddings that I find beautiful; it's marriage. And marriage isn't the only way to experience true love; it's just one of the few public commitments to do so. It's the idea of a life lived in purposeful service to someone else that makes my heart swell to bursting.

Yeah, maybe sign me up someday. And maybe not. I won't deny myself the giving or receiving of true love just because I haven't made a pledge in front of hundreds of people. True love is just as present in daily testimony as in holy matrimony. Do you take humanity to be your neighbor, to have and to hold from this day forward, for better or for worse, for richer, for poorer, in sickness and in health, to love and to cherish; from this day forward until death do us part?

I do.

Triathlove

Gabe Gunnink

HAVING NOW PASSED through Calvin College without snag-
ging a significant other to speak of, I realize that the task
of acquiring one becomes more complicated. With all of the
engagement pictures and relationship upgrades overrunning
Facebook, it often seems it would be easier to strap on a Velcro
suit and skydive through the summer Grand Rapids air without
accruing a single cottonwood seed than it would be to graduate
from Calvin without accruing a lover of some label.

But despite the unlikelihood, I and many others have con-
quered the odds and accomplished this feat, and, believe it or not,
some of us are not too distraught! However, the reality remains
that any future soulmate searches will need to be conducted with
a bit more ingenuity. So, if you also find yourself sufficiently lov-
erless, I have a scouting report just for you.

In addition to being romantically unaffiliated at the moment,
I am also an avid athlete and have spent the past few summers
training for triathlons. There is something fantastically bizarre
and wonderful about a herd of spandexed bodies splashing, ped-
aling, and lurching themselves along for hours on end while others spend their Saturday mornings reading, idling at the beach,

and not vomiting. But before you dismiss the concept entirely, let me say that triathlons are the single best venues I've discovered for finding potential partners, and let me tell you why.

First, when surveying a field of triathletes for objects of affection, it becomes clear that almost all options are meticulously healthy and supremely fit, thin enough to slice through the heavy July air and strong enough to punch through adversarial waves. There is even a Clydesdale category for men and an Athena category for women meeting certain height and weight requirements if you prefer a more robust, muscled frame. Also, as previously mentioned, triathlons are one of the few public settings where near-nudity is encouraged, so little will be left to the imagination.

Second, all triathletes are conveniently marked with information that would be helpful in evaluating or pursuing a potential courtship. When a triathlete arrives to the venue in the morning, he promptly reports to a race official who takes one of those extra-fat art class markers and labels the competitor's right calf with his age and event ("T" for triathlon and "D" for duathlon, which comprises only biking and running). These markings will immediately signal if a given athlete is within an acceptable age range and whether or not he can swim, if buoyancy is something you're into.

In addition to this information, each triathlete is also labeled with a race identification number on her upper arm that will be used to record her results. This means that when milling about the awards area after the race, all you need to do is memorize the ID number of someone who catches your eye, type it into the results website later that day, and watch in wonder as that person's name and city of residence unfold clandestinely before your eyes. From there, romance is just a brief Facebook stalk away from reality. Finding a new mate becomes as simple as selecting the correct variety of bell pepper on the self-checkout touchscreen at Meijer!

But before I objectify my fellow triathletes (and, I suppose, myself) any further, I would like to note that triathletes prove to be quite a chummy bunch. Something about almost drowning each other and then slowly frying in the unyielding summer heat together fosters a mutual respect and camaraderie that leads to ample fellowship after the race. It also helps that most competitors are so thoroughly exhausted upon completing their races that they have little choice but to languish in the finish area and talk to various passersby, making post-triathlon chats perfect opportunities to approach a particularly promising and immobile finisher. What's more? You don't even need to worry about what to say! Simply ask your admiree how his race went, how he trains, and where he works out so that you can plan an encounter at a later date... or perhaps for a first date.

Finally, if you have been convinced that triathletes are the most attractive, accessible, and amiable romantic prospects on the planet but now feel intimidated by their seeming perfection, worry not! Instead, simply stand at the end of a triathlon racecourse and watch the bedraggled string of competitors hobble, flop, and fling themselves through the giant inflatable arch marking the finish line. Something about witnessing an otherwise elegant woman drooling on herself or a normally pleasant man elbow his way past a septuagenarian competitor can prove very soothing and remind you that even the most sculpted and respectable individuals are still human.

So, dust off your old road bike, strap on some new tennis shoes, and buy some arm floaties if you need to! There is still plenty of time to prepare for your summer triathlon and secure the love of your life. And if you're happily single, contentedly wed, or in a similarly vulgar sentimental state, I suppose you can come along too. Opening up the arteries, making a few new friends, and being reminded that we are all beautifully and frustratingly human are things that we can all use now and again, no matter the numbers on our calves or who's waiting for us at the finish line.

Newlyweds

Sarah (VanderMolen) Sundt

THE HONEYMOON WAS OVER, and the two whole weeks since we had been married felt like a vacation. Every grown-up thing we needed to worry about was negated with one simple mantra: *After the honeymoon.* Changing my name? Installing new cabinets? Starting on thank-you notes? We can wait to think about all of that until *after the honeymoon.*

Well, now that the honeymoon was over, I had assumed that grown-up mode would kick in instantaneously. Instead, I reverted to the typical mindset I had when we had been dating long-distance for four out of our total of seven years together. I turned to Mike and said, "So when's the next time we'll see each other?"

He looked at me like I had lost my marbles. Because we're now living together. Forever. And we're hardly ever *not* going to be seeing each other.

That transition between dating and marriage has been longer than I thought it would be. I keep saying things like, "Last night we ran home to get some things—sorry, we ran to mom and dad's to get some things. Old habits." Or I keep looking up at my new husband doing the dishes in our kitchen, and I think, *You're seriously still here?*

I feel like I'm playing house. I have this steady stream of commentary for everyday activities. *It's dinnertime. There's no food on the stove. Oh, that's right, because I have to make it. How fun and cute! I'm actually going to cook dinner in my own kitchen! Maybe I'll wear my apron and everything. It's like it's actually real life!*

With marriage has come the inevitable marriage-y questions, which—don't get me wrong—are fun to answer because it means I get to talk about myself. But I do feel like my answers are underwhelming.

"Have you learned any strange things you never knew about Mike?" my older sister asks.

"Not much," I say, "although I did learn that he refuses to use anything but fabric Band-Aids."

"Have you had your first big fight yet?" asks my uncle.

"No," Mike replies. "But we've never really *fought* a ton. We argue or have disagreements, but it's not like we scream at each other." On my part, I didn't foresee any throwing of pots and pans, but, then again, student loans haven't been taken out yet, so I don't think we've necessarily seen the real, stressful, ugly side of marriage yet.

And speaking of the real side of marriage, the most common question people ask us is, "Does it feel weird to be married?"

To be honest, I'm not sure. It still feels like a vacation. I had been on summer vacation since my first year of teaching ended, so everything—and I mean *everything*—had been wedding mode for three solid weeks. The wedding day, opening presents, setting up your apartment, going on your honeymoon: it all felt like we had stepped out of real life into this alternate reality where you are the center of everyone's attention and you're constantly happy.

The first time I really felt married was the Monday after the

Fourth of July, when real life seemed to kick in. I was starting summer school that morning. I woke up late and didn't have time for breakfast. Mike and I had to coordinate cars. In addition, Professor Vande Kopple's funeral was that afternoon, and I was very much on edge. I called Mike after work to ask him to make me a peanut butter sandwich that I could swing by to pick up on the way to the funeral. I also asked him what he had done that morning. "Well, I practiced bass a bit and figured out some stuff for our insurance, but I haven't exactly put on pants yet."

Ah, sweet mystery of life, at last I've found you.

Through Fire, I Do Wander

Michael Kelly

Aᴮᴼᵁᵀ ᵀᵂᴼ ᵂᴱᴱᴷˢ after I moved to Boston, my friend and I began authoring an online document together. We had a grand vision. This document would be a new platform for story sharing. It would be a sacred space of truth and honesty, but it would also be playfully sarcastic to give it some edge. It would be about love, belonging, rejection, despair: all of the trending topics of the twenty-somethings. After a surprising amount of thought, I finally decided on a name for this soon-to-be-coveted guide to romantic success:

"What Tinder Taught Us"

Yes, Tinder: the infamous smartphone application that markets itself only as a "connection maker," but if you ask the users, they'll give you the real rundown.

Tinder is used exclusively for chatting, dating, and/or sex. First, you "like" or "dislike" someone based on how attractive that person's pictures are to you. If they "like" you back, then you receive the gift of chatting, where the real chaos ensues.

At this point, you may be thinking:

Okay... but I still don't really understand the appeal....

You're not alone. The popularity of Tinder—referred to as *The*

Tinder Effect—is becoming a contemporary topic of study and debate because of its mystery (I encourage you to check it out). While I won't pretend that I'm an exception to the research-based theories of why this application has become uniquely successful, I can say that from the beginning of my online dating endeavors, I've always had a different motivation.

I wanted an adventure.

Taking risks, meeting strangers, sharing meals, stealing kisses, cutting ties, breaking hearts—it was a new world for me, and I was its Columbus. And finally, with the help of a friend, I created a place to write of our journeys in this online dating world: a coauthored document of Tinder tips.

After only a few moments of reflection, the advice began pouring out.

Some of it was funny:

Lesson 1: Always assume that people you're meeting will cross-dress. That way, you might still stand a chance—however small—at looking more fabulous than they do.

Some of it was unsettling:

Lesson 9: If a guy says he doesn't read and you're a writer, don't make fun of him. Turns out, he does read, but only *Guns and Ammo*....

And some of it was crucial:

Lesson 17: Once the overly aggressive, Pokémon-themed pickup lines start to come out—i.e. I'm gonna catch you in my Masterball and never let you go—you've gone too far. Put down the phone, and walk away slowly.

But all of it was ours, for better or for worse.

It's safe to say that our document turned out to be more for the benefit of the writers than the readers. As you might also deduce, our tip sheet leans more towards satiric inside jokes than heartfelt self-help. We generally don't start adding to this document after we've met people who stir up an addictive nervousness in us, making us feel unworthy of their attention. Instead, we write with a quickly disappearing bottle of Moscato at our side, uncontrollably cackling as we review our latest travesties of dates.

But even still—despite all of my whining—I can't erase the invaluable experiences that my online endeavors have awarded me. My first date, my first heartbreak, my first relationship, and my first breakup all resulted from dating applications. In fact, my current Tinder pursuits have elicited dreamlike rewards: a Puerto Rican hip-hop dancer, a late night walk on the south side of a new city, a meal beginning with ginger-tequila shaved ice and ending with green apple cotton candy covered in Pop Rocks, and a disco-themed dance party performance of *A Midsummer Night's Dream*.

(Okay, so maybe I'm the only person who has dreams like that.)

The point is that I got what I was looking for: a journey out of the monotony of the ordinary toward somewhere that's almost fantastical, but more wonderful because it's real.

The question still remains, I guess. What has Tinder taught me?

To be honest, not too much. But it helped me to take a risk. To fight against complacency. To turn fear into hilarity. And to strive for something better.

To keep in stride with what I've learned, I'll end with this request: come out on a date with me! Let's do it for the story. Meet me at the Shakespeare disco.

(I'll be in the hot pink pants.)

Tossed Salad and Scrambled Yawns

Catherine Kramer

I'VE BEEN MARRIED for two months, so I know pretty much everything there is to know about my husband.

Everything except for, you know, what he's like in the morning.

Here's the thing: I hate mornings. Every member of my family will tell you this, *ad nauseam*. Seriously. If you tell them how delightful you find me (oh, how sweet of you!), they will simply reply with, "Have you seen her in the morning?!" as if my preference for some peace and quiet is an inexcusable offense. Want me to be pleasant before eight in the morning? Here's a hint: Don't talk to me. If you must speak, don't look to me to respond to what you said, and for the love, do not ask me a single question. This will be your downfall, every time. And mine too, because you'll judge me by my angry grunts and rude stray syllables for years to come.

But take heart! None of you have to live with me. I've got a permanent roomie and he thinks I'm all that and a bag of chips, yes, *even in the morning*. Shocking, I know. Our secret to success centers mainly on the fact that when he gets up, I stay in bed. When he takes a shower, I stay in bed. When he gets ready for work, makes our lunches, and gets out the cereal for breakfast, I stay in bed.

At least, I assume these are things he does in the morning, because by the time I finally heave myself out bed and into work clothes, grunting without ceasing, all of these things are already done.

But on his birthday, the day after our two month anniversary, I decided this morning routine should look a bit different. In fact, I had a brilliant beyond brilliant idea: twenty-four years of life + twenty-four hours in a day = one whole day of celebration— starting with breakfast in bed.

Early that morning, I snuck out of bed to get his breakfast ready, and somehow managed to walk into our room just as his alarm was going off.

"HAPPY BIRTHDAY!" I shouted, throwing the lights on. And boy, was he ever surprised! Not only was his alarm beeping, and the lights were on, and there was a plate of breakfast in front of him, but there I was, fully awake, and seemingly *happy*, all before 7 a.m. Yes, the element of surprise was on my side.

"What is this?" he said, still shocked, looking down at his plate of tossed salad and scrambled eggs.

Now, you might not serve your spouse tossed salad and scrambled eggs as a birthday breakfast, but you also probably do not watch as much *Frasier* as we do. (For those of you who are unfamiliar with the aforementioned television show, "Tossed Salad and Scrambled Eggs" is the theme song of NBC's classic sitcom *Frasier*. Both the show and the song are perfection. If you don't believe me, just ask its eleven seasons and thirty-seven Emmys.)

So when he asked what it was, I knew he could figure it out on his own. But it took a while.

"You... you made me tossed salad and scrambled eggs?" he said. Groggily.

"YES!" I exclaimed. Loudly.

He proceeded to push the food around his plate, nibbling a bit.

"Were you surprised? Did you even know I wasn't in bed anymore? Could you hear me in the kitchen?" I asked, breaking my own cardinal rule of mornings THREE TIMES OVER.

He mumbled muted responses, still eating slowly, while I continued gabbing away, as if mornings weren't the bane of my existence.

But when he looked right at me, brow furrowed, I stopped. "Can... can I take a shower?" he asked.

"But what about your breakfast?"

"It's great, I just... I can't eat it right now. Can I eat it after my shower?"

What is it with this guy and showers? I thought to myself. Other thoughts included *THIS IS NOT HOW BREAKFAST IN BED WORKS* and, thankfully, *It's his dang birthday, you should probably let him do what he wants.*

So he showered. When he emerged, he was much more like the husband I was accustomed to: cheery, with functioning motor skills and the ability to form complete sentences on the first try. Up to this point, I've never really spent time with him before his shower. Turns out, he's as dysfunctional as me in the morning without it! Well, not quite. But enough that breakfast in bed is pretty much out of the question in our newly-formed family.

Where the Heart Is

Your fears—of new responsibilities and discrepant self-exposure—have no place in the presence of people who embody deepest love for you.

Fieldnotes from
the Potty Chair

Jacob Schepers

"WE CAN POTTY train him. We have the technology. We have the capability to make this family's first diaper-less child. Liam will be that child. Better than he was before. Better... stronger... *cleaner.*"

That's the hope, at least. It's been a week since we've hunkered down on this whole potty training deal, finally going cold turkey and kissing those diapers goodbye (figuratively, of course, very, very figuratively. I can't stress this enough). Sure, this undertaking's not quite as advanced as rebuilding the Six Million Dollar Man—though that price tag might just be in the ballpark for the cost of diapers *hardy-har-har dad joke.* Nonetheless, it still involves a surgical precision in meticulous planning, a propping up that quickly gives way to a potty training freefall. Chaos. Leaky, naked chaos.

Dealing with said chaos involves a precarious mixture of determination and exasperation. Murphy's Law is in full force here, and I'm torn between Simba's brazen declaration, "I laugh in the face of danger" and Nietzsche's harrowing assertion, "And when you gaze long into an abyss, the abyss also gazes into you." So, yeah... if you haven't guessed already, I've been staring at the hypnotic swirling of a toilet bowl far too often for far too long.

Potty training is as much a learned behavior as it is one of the more abstract concepts Liam has had to tackle yet. Ay, there's the rub: Liam, like many tykes in the toddler/preschool bracket, is lousy with conceptualizing and on guard against demands that he knows he can best. On this desert island, Liam's decided to enact an alliance of one to be a Survivor—"outwit, outplay, outlast." Free will's a pain in the butt, though you better believe that the butt in question is going to be diaper-free by the time Liam first steps through the doors of his preschool in the fall.

He'll get there, right? Geometry holds that the shortest distance between two points is a straight line, and, hey, time flies like an arrow after all. But if I've learned anything this past week, it's that potty training is anything but an exact science. (Though I have seen more than my share of parabolas in action....) It's only fair that guiding Liam through this shift in the potty paradigm means that I too must be willing to adapt. I've had to master the duck-and-weave (figuratively *and literally* this time). And so coaxing and pleading have suspended, upended, overturned, and replaced logic. Simple rationalization seems less effective than blatant bribery; an enticing reward bowl of M&M's works wonders. But that's the endgame. Getting on to that blasted potty seat is another story altogether.

Enter the undies. Enter the realm of magical thinking. It's almost as if an education centered on stories has prepared me for this after all. Supposedly, the trick is to get a child to tell you when he or she has to use the potty, which means my auto-looped questions of "Do you have to go the bathroom?" better come with some enticements.

So when Liam donned his first pair of undies, I treated him to a far-fetched tale of a global diaper shortage, a halt in the production of Huggies Pull-Ups for big kids like him. Now, it's not that I condone white lies to kids: it's that I condone selective truths. At least, that's what I tell myself when I'm lying shell-shocked in my own fetal position. And as Liam admires his new digs emblazoned with the likes of Thomas the Tank Engine and Lighting McQueen, I have to concoct more stories. I can't tell him that he has to keep his undies dry because Daddy doesn't want to do a dozen single-article laundry loads every day. That's just asking for trouble. So I turn to the stories and faux rationale:

"Hey, bud, did you know we have to keep Thomas dry? That's because he only runs on train food like coal. We don't want to make him sad, right?"

[Thirty minutes later]

"Ugh. Okay, take two, let's keep Lightning McQueen squeaky clean. We don't want him to get dirty and break his engine! Let's help him win the race by telling me when you have to go potty!"

[Fifteen minutes later]

"You did it! Good job, kiddo! Wash your hands and grab your candy. Look how happy Lightning is!"

[Five minutes later]

"Oh, you have to go potty again? You didn't get it all out last time? Okay, here we go."

[Five seconds later]

"You have to go?! We just put Lightning on again! Oh, you just like the M&M? No, no, don't cry, I'll hold up my end of the bargain.... No, 'bargain.' It's like a deal. A deal. Never mind, let's go potty."

Needless to say, it's quite a tangled web. I lose track of this invented impromptu toilet mythos pretty quickly. And Liam is surprisingly adroit at catch any contradictions or inconsistencies. Regardless of my lapses, he soaks up this instructional nonsense. He's more leak-proof than the cotton fibers covering his rear. So I go on playing the court jester unapologetically; it seems to be working. He'll get there. We'll get there. Together. And an added perk: I'm gathering up enough embarrassing stories for later use when he's sixteen.

Above and Below

Will Montei

THERE ARE NO MOUNTAINS in Wisconsin, but rather, rolling hills of cornfields and forests that stretch toward the horizon like a rumpled blanket. This leaves a vast, unencumbered sky that's allowed to speak its emotions plainly. So a clear sky might resemble a still ocean held over your head, and clouds might become great, floating mountains lumbering toward some unknown place. I'm reminded of this as I stare out the window in the back seat of my parents' truck watching the landscape's folds and creases pass by. Above and below, everything is stretching and flattening, letting out a contented sigh. My parents' voices from the front seats lull me into a comfortable nap.

We are driving the long, familiar path to Cedar Campus. Cedar first and foremost recalls to me a particular smell, one of wood, dust, mildew, and air fresh off the shores of Lake Huron all mingled together into one. I thought that I might be overwhelmed to breathe it in again after eight years away. But as I carry our bags up to our small room in the dimly lit lodge, no such feeling comes. Instead, it's as if the scent never left, having never fully exhaled it from my lungs.

The rooms of my brother's and sister's families are just a few floor creaks down the hall. Their rooms have cribs set up for their children with books and toys strewn about the floor, which reminds me just how long the eight years apart from Cedar have been. My immediate family may no longer share a room, but at night I can hear the excited chatter of my nieces and nephew through the doors as their parents whisper them to sleep.

One morning I wake up to my three-year-old niece's face inches away from mine. "Wake up, Uncle Will" she whispers, barely pronouncing the L's. Her dimpled fingers cling to the bed frame. She giggles when I tousle her hair and mutter "g'morning" before she scuttles out of the room with a toothy grin. I'm reminded again of how a child's eyes reflect the existence of God. By the time I finally lift myself out of bed, falling from the top bunk with a *thunk*, she is already downstairs eating cereal and asking to be pushed on the swing.

My mom refers to Cedar as a "thin place." She means that whatever barrier keeps humans at a distance from the Spirit is measurably smaller. This isn't just true of Cedar's programmed Bible studies and gatherings, but also of the in-between moments— bleary breakfasts in the old dining hall, walking along the boardwalk to grab a sweet from the Hunny Pot, glancing up between the pages of your book to see Lake Huron spread out before you, with all that water sitting still like the sky has wrapped down past the horizon and settled on land. Immense and quiet, not unlike the Spirit. At Cedar, divinity sprouts from the ground up.

Later, after the kids are all asleep and the sun melts pink into the waters, the no-longer-kids sit by the fireplace and talk. My brother, my sister, their spouses, my mom, my dad, all in one place for the first time in years. We laugh until we cry when my sister shares about the time she discovered Mom and Dad had been watering a fake plant for weeks. My brother's laugh is the loudest. We talk late into the night until our eyelids droop and we stumble back to our rooms. I am well rested before I even crawl beneath my sheets. They smell the same as they did when I was as old as my nieces and nephews.

The end of the week finds my mom and me visiting Grandma Shirley before I fly back to Seattle. Like waking a child from a nap, my mom kneels by Grandma where she's asleep in a chair, taking her hand in hers, running her fingers along the veins and liver spots of her forearm.

"Hi, mamma," my mom coos.

"Well, hello," says her mom.

Grandma looks at my mom and me as if we are strangers, which I suppose we are on some level. She tolerates us a little helplessly, distracted by the People magazine in her hands and all the objects around the room she's forgotten the names of. When she makes eye contact, her expression is searching. I can see her thoughts running into wall after wall as she tries to remember, remember, remember. But there are no memories left.

"Do you know who I am?" says my mom.

"I'm not so sure," says her mom.

"I'm your daughter. Ellen. Does that name mean anything to you?"

"Would you stop it?"

"I'm sorry," says my mom, patting grandma's leg, "is this making you uncomfortable?"

"I'm not going to say yes. But I'm not going to say... I'm not going to say something else, either."

"That's okay. That's okay. I'm your daughter. Did you know that? You were a great mom. You always loved me so well."

She can't remember the faces and names of the family who love her so dearly. Can't remember tucking my mom in when she was little. Can't remember her own husband. But there's still a soul stirring in there, wandering in circles through an endless fog. I'm left wondering if there could be a place thin enough to let loose that fog.

Someday, someone I love may be holding my hand and tracing my forearm, pleading for me to look into their eyes and remember, remember, remember. And I hope in that moment that all these faded memories leave the same words on my lips that my grandma spoke to my mom.

"Well, I like to love you."

Miracle Drug

Ben DeVries

2:28 a.m.
Arrival

THE GATE TO the emergency care lot lifts, and the car, its faulty timing belt cricket-creaking beneath the hood, tools in. Jes sits forward in the passenger seat and raises her eyebrows.

"Didn't feel like stopping?"

For a moment, the digits of the car radio appear, reflected, in the lens of her glasses. She grins and leans back.

"Don't be sorry. It's just that's what you did last time. Walking is fine. Walking doesn't hurt."

The headlights sweep blindly over a brick wall as the car pulls into a spot. Jes, bundled in her Carhartt and mittens, eases herself out and stands breathing in the cold.

Back a ways, at the carport where an on-call valet waits outside the sliding doors to the hospital, a pair of ambulances roll up and back into the docks. Lights on but no sirens.

2:35 a.m.
ROMI

They do an impromptu triage in the lobby.

"So, you're feeling some pain in your arm?"

"Arm and shoulder. And jaw a little bit."

"Are they tingly?"

"No."

"But it's constant."

"No. No. Well, maybe. It's been on and off. Tonight was really bad, though."

"She couldn't sleep."

"Hmm."

The nurse taps her chin. After a moment she says she'll take Jes's vitals and look into getting her a bed. It's been busy, though, so busy, so she'll have to wait till one frees up.

"Ben," Jes says, turning, "did you get your visitor's sticker?"

3:10 to 3:30 a.m.
Good Patient

There are rules to being a good patient, and Jes knows them. In her room, she takes off her shirt upon request. She puts on the gown. She's cold, but she lies quietly in bed and doesn't make a fuss, though when a nurse comes by to ask whether she'd like a blanket, Jes says yes, please, thank you—all very politely—and drapes it over her legs. She folds her hands. She waits. She smiles. She waits.

3:30 to 7:10 a.m.
Pharmakon

There are other rules too, in addition to these. Sit tight. Speak clearly. Press CALL if you need anything. Know your medication (Trivora, prednisone, plaquenil, Tylenol). Have insurance. Don't get frustrated when you have to repeat yourself. Don't get frustrated when you don't see anyone for a while. Be polite. Don't fiddle with anything. Bonus points if you know which arm is better for drawing blood. Stay in bed. The remote to the TV is over there if you need it. The bathroom's down the hall, but CALL for that too. Be pleasant. Don't fight the nurses. Don't fight the doctors. Suck it up, if you can. Be patient.

Be patient.

That last one is hard. Still, it comes with the territory of one further rule, which is to trust in the miracle of medicine. Trust, trust, trust.

In fact, "trust in the miracle of medicine" might not even be a rule at all but the premise that all those other rules assume, the rock upon which this church is built. Else, why would anyone so agreeably submit to needle-jabs, boredom, radiation, poison?

4:45 a.m.
Okay
They might have to run a CT scan. Once the labs come back, they'll know if they need to.

"Check out that everything's okay with your heart," says the doctor. "Okay?"

He waits and then says okay? again.

"Okay," says Jes, and she smiles.

5:10 a.m.
Flirt
A nurse comes by to administer a belated EKG, and she asks Jes if she wants to be alone for it since the nurse will have to lift the front of her gown.

"No," she says, and when the nurse turns away, she looks sideways and wiggles her eyebrows in a way that's supposed to be suggestive. Under the circumstances, however, it comes off as more seismographic than anything: a measure of uncertain, moving ground beneath.

6:30 a.m.

CT

"How did it go?"

It went fine. It was weird. The dye made her feel like she'd peed her pants.

"You didn't, right?"

Of course not.

"Did they say when the results would get back?"

Soon, but they didn't say when.

"Oh."

A pause.

"Well, do you want your phone? Do you want your book?"

Jes leans back into the bed and shuts her eyes.

7:20 a.m.

Homeward

Walgreens hasn't filled her prescription yet, and Jes shifts uncomfortably in the passenger seat as the car squeaks out of the drive-thru and onto the road. Traffic isn't bad. At the McDonald's near the corner of Neil and Kirby, a queue of cars and SUVs coils slowly around the back of the building.

A stack of stapled paper lies in Jes's lap. On the top page are home-care instructions for pleurisy.

"You'll go back to pick it up?" she says.

Then she says, "Thanks."

She wipes at a smudge on the glass with the thumb of her mitten and then grimaces and starts plucking at her seatbelt, trying gently to reposition her shoulder.

"Can't imagine sleeping like this," she grumbles. "They didn't do anything."

But they did. They did do something. They said what it wasn't, and they said what it wasn't with such confidence that negation became a sort of charm—an amulet that you can hang around your neck and that's far better for your chest than some old bottle of anti-inflammatories that'll be waiting for you at the pharmacist's an hour from now.

Jes sits back in her seat, resigned. Ahead, the stoplight turns. The car swings slowly from Neil onto Windsor, and beyond the overpass, the apartment complex comes into view, the brick gone shadowy-cool against the pale yellow of the sky.

Semi-Charmed Life

Jacob Schepers

STEP INTO MY HOME, and you'll likely be greeted by the songs of your childhood.

Yes, the magic of Disney has comfortably set up shop in the Schepers household. It is a Pandora's box of imagination, entertainment, and—of course—some ingenious, diabolically clever marketing. And much like the Greek myth alluded to just a moment before, Disney is something of an ur-text for our culture. It's something of a rite of passage, at least for many of us, and I'm now revisiting that journey and seeing it anew by introducing these touchstones to my kids.

To be honest, it's a pretty good gig.

Sure, I can be choosy. I'll shy away, for now, from showing the boys Disney's darker ware: the sin, guilt, and ecclesiastical corruption of *The Hunchback of Notre Dame*; the racist undertones of *Peter Pan*; the colonialist overtones of *Pocahontas*; and the occult insanity, the how-did-they-ever-get-away-with-this of *Fantasia*'s "Night on Bald Mountain," complete with demons, mostly-nude sprites, and Satan himself, all set to the tune of Mussorgsky. Long story short, it's a daunting task of filtering Disney's legacy of a not-so-great history of cultural insensitivity and laughable take on the G: General Audiences billing from the MPAA.

All that said, it's still a pretty good gig.

Chock it up to the teachable moments. From the tricky navigating of *Robin Hood*'s steal-from-the-rich-to-give-to-the-poor ethics to *Mulan*'s richly complex investigations into feminism and queerness, not to mention the family drama and strife of the archetypal "evil" stepmothers and the Claudius-inspired *Hamlet*-esque Uncle Scar, I've found multiple opportunities to answer Liam and Oliver's pressing questions with as much grace as I can muster. Revisiting such storylines, in fact, has allowed me to view Disney films through a much less black-and-white lens ("Steamboat Willie" aside, you literalists you). Rather, for all of Disney's problematic depictions of feminism, cultural appropriation, etc., I do what I can to instill the lessons I consider necessary for children (two boys, no less) in today's politically nuanced and ideologically infused climate.

Am I overthinking all this? You bet I am. But what else can I do when it comes to curbing the obviously magical and influential takeaways of such stories? Speaking as someone who, once upon a time, did not seek to question the trickier aspects of Disney-fied life, the hypersexualization of characters like Ariel or Jasmine, the racial characterizations of *Aladdin*, the Sinophobic elements of *Fantasia*'s dancing mushrooms, or *Snow White*'s Dopey and his flagrantly offensive impression during the Dwarfs' "Silly Song" sequence, all beg the question of why I would want to expose my kids to all this in the first place.

So why do it?

It boils down to reckoning with Disney's effective attempt to carve out this world as simultaneously more magical and more fraught than we often give it credit for. A child's world begins in black and white, an analog that carries some truth to why infants may be especially drawn to stark dichromatic images, but the world can quickly eat away at that burgeoning absolutist morality. To be fair, I'm talking about all this while my boys are only five and almost-three years old. So much of this goes over their heads. That's to be expected.

But what's the bottom line for the parent(s) of these kids?

I've no good answer, but instead a mere anecdote.

Liam and Oliver are drawn, as they should be, to Disney princesses and other female characters. When it comes to Disney's most complex and developed characters, leave it to the "princesses" (loosely conceived) to show what real power, real change can look like. Appropriately enough, our Disney phase began—as I imagine is the case for many younger children—with *Frozen*. From Elsa and Anna's true love that flies in the face of previous attempts to define true love via heteronormative romances, we've ventured into the bookishness of Belle, the heroism of Mulan, the singular Lilo. And all the while our boys remain entranced.

So, the anecdote:

While grocery shopping a week or two ago, Charis and the boys were avidly discussing Disney favorites, when a woman stops the three of them to ask, "Oh, do they have an older sister?" Charis explained that, no, they did not. To which the fellow shopper says, "Oh, well, they seem to know an awful lot about Disney princesses."

And that's a story that I imagine has been told a million times over. You have boys? They should like Aladdin, or Simba, or Hercules, or [insert male character here].

The kicker is that all of this fascination with Disney film-lore has coincided with our teaching Liam how to ride a bike with training wheels. We found a bike he fell in love with and, you guessed it, it's pink and princess-emblazoned. He does not yet realize that this is not what is "expected" of him, and more power to him for it. So when I'm out on the sidewalk coaching him and teaching him and encouraging him in whatever way I can, it never leaves my mind that, for everything he's learning, for every way he's training his body to move in motion and coordinate itself, he's just a kid having fun on a bike he loves because he can look down at his handlebars and see the characters he's fascinated by cheering him on as well.

And if I can help these little ones on the right track, even as they're learning to ride a bike, my greatest hope is that, with a little coaching, the Disney lessons that enthrall them now can be questioned later, an exercise in challenging norms and expectations which may someday seem as natural as riding a bike.

When My Parents Visit

Greg Kim

THERE'S AN INEVITABLE collide of two worlds when your parents visit. I say this as a Korean child whose parents came to Calvin for the first time to attend my graduation.

They live in Uganda, and we Skyped a few weeks before their flight. My father loves to travel and told me to start planning a trip to Niagara Falls. *We'll drive all night if we have to!* My mother just asked me the usual: *Any food you want me to bring?* I told them I'd probably be busy with exams and that we had plenty of food.

After our conversation, I quickly became nervous thinking about when they would come to Michigan. I imagined them meeting my Calvin friends and professors and struggling to understand quick bursts of American conversational English. They'd gasp at the dishes stacked in the sink in my apartment, and my mom would chide me about how I hadn't bought any fresh kimchi for so long.

Because I spent most of my school years away from my parents, I've come to hold the moments when I meet and part with my parents with an overbearing sentimentality.

The first that I can remember was when my parents dropped me off at boarding school in Kenya for the first time. I was twelve, and our blue Toyota Land Cruiser, carrying my parents, disappeared behind wisps of brown dust as it did a final hop over the hill next to my sixth grade dorm. I remember standing still, looking over that hill, and waiting to see if it would reappear through the curtain of dust. It didn't. All of a sudden, a realization smacked me in the head: *I had to do my laundry, cooking, dishes, and cleaning all by myself! How was I going to do all of this without Mom and Dad?*

It turned out I didn't have to do most of those things; the school did them for me. For the next seven years, I attended boarding school in Kenya while my parents worked in Uganda. After that, I spent four years at Calvin, living and studying on a different continent than my parents. This persistent geographical separation allowed me to developed two separate lives: one with my friends and one with my parents. I'd briefly have "overlapping" moments at airports and bus stations, but my parents rarely met any of my friends.

In time, I came to believe that a perfect union of my two identities in one person, and at one time and place, was impossible. That's why I dreaded my parents visiting me. They'd lock me in a paradoxical space where I had to hold two irreconcilable yet naturally expressive selves. I would have all my friends and loved ones in one place, but I would have no place for me.

I think that's really the source of my fear when my parents come to visit. On the surface, it's a fear that when they leave, there will be another thing I have to do on my own. Deep down, it's the fear that what I had done and become on my own while they'd been away had turned me into a complete fraud.

They arrived in Grand Rapids on Tuesday, May 20. I had just come back to my apartment from writing my final exam.

My brother suddenly burst through our screen door with luggage in both hands. "They're here." I went outside, and my dad was only a few yards away. I immediately saw that he was still limping from his Achilles tendon injury earlier in the year. We hugged and then I hugged my mom, who was right behind him.

That's the moment we met. But, in my memory, their visit is not distilled into overly sentimental snapshots of our meeting and parting moments. Instead, I remember that my mom and I prepared supper together that night. While we ate, my dad kept asking how we'd get ourselves to Niagara Falls. By the end of the evening, my mom began preparing a batch of kimchi so big it lasted us for two months.

In the next few weeks, my parents met my friends and teachers, and they understood each other just fine. We didn't end up visiting Niagara Falls, but we did see the Sleeping Bear Dunes and spent a few nights at a cottage on the lake.

I remember it all with a feeling of a relaxed warmth, much like an evening in the early Michigan summer. I suppose it's the feeling you get when you realize your fears—of new responsibilities and discrepant self-exposure—have no place in the presence of people who embody deepest love for you.

To Act Justly

Take time to inspire hope, in whatever small way you can, because the world has enough despair in it already.

I'm scared she gonna die

Josh deLacy

I DON'T DO ANYTHING for the man who bangs on the church door and tells me about his probation and court date in Bremerton an hour and a half away and the company that let him go after thirty years to save themselves a retirement plan and the chronic pain in his shoulder and the botched knee surgery and that he just needs eight dollars and ten cents for the ferry or else they'll throw him back in jail over a lousy eight dollars and ten cents and could I please, please, I know you're good guy, please just give me eight dollars and ten cents for the ferry?

I don't do anything for the woman who calls St. Luke's to ask if we have a rental assistance program or something like that?

We don't. I'm sorry.

I'm in a real bad spot, real bad. I got three kids and no husband, and they're gonna kick us onto the streets Saturday if I can't pay rent.

I'm sorry. We do all our community giving through REACH.

I tried the reach, I tried everywhere. No one's got money and I'm in a real bad spot.

I wish I could do something.

My babies need a home and they're gonna be on the streets in three days if I don't get help.

I'm sorry.

I don't do anything for the hundreds of Seattle homeless living under I-5 or the one napping on a worn-out cardboard box next to Rhein Haus, where six bucks gets me a disappointing IPA.

I don't do anything for the Makah tribe that huddles in the rains of Neah Bay, exiled into the far corner of the country where they live in secondhand jeans and forty-nine percent unemployment, where fifty-nine percent of their homes are considered substandard, and where drug addiction and alcoholism are more common than college degrees.

I don't do anything for Kenny the neighborhood homeless man who asks for empty cans and bottles so he can take them to Family Fare for Michigan's ten cent refunds. He tells me stories I don't believe about his kid, his ten-year-old kid, who he just found out today is goin' to school with a hole in his pants. Right on the butt, babe. The butt! He's only got two pairs of pants and one's got a big ol' hole right here. His underpants all showin' and everything.

That's rough, man.

He getting picked on every day for those pants and his underpants pokin' out, and I don't got money to get him new ones. He comes home and tells me, 'the kids are makin' fun a me again', and I want to laugh, you know, because it's funny, only it's not.

I have a few bottles, but I can't give you any money.

I don't sponsor Haitian kids or fill UTO boxes or buy Girl Scout cookies or round up my purchase to the nearest dollar. I carry my bag of groceries past the Santa Claus who has rung his bell outside Safeway through hours of soggy Washington winter, and I don't do anything for the starving kids in Africa or the sex slaves in Europe or the prisoners in North Korea.

I write a check to my church. I send twenty bucks to missionary friends in Romania.

You got a dollar, buddy?

Save the whales.

ALS.

Plant a tree.

Got a dollar?

I'm sorry.

I'm sorry.

I'm so sorry.

I'm traveling through all fifty states and taking pictures and collecting stories because everyone has value, you know, but most people don't take the time to listen to them so could you fund my Kickstarter?

I don't.

I don't do anything.

Is there a connection between money and faith? hangs on a piece of butcher paper in the basement of my church, along with a one-to-five scale and three dozen dotted stickers placed by parishioners at the annual meeting. The dots make an even spread across the scale. Like smallpox.

I don't do anything when Kenny bangs on my door in the middle of the night. You in there? You guys in there?

I stay upstairs.

My kid's sick, babe. She got a fever and cryin' and I don't got money to get her medicine or nothin' and I'm scared she gonna die. I'm scared she gonna die, babe.

I don't do anything.

I promise I never ask another thing, babe. Help a brother. You gotta help my kid.

I don't.

Brothers in Christ!

I'm sorry.

NPR runs a pledge drive.

Wikipedia asks for three dollars.

I don't do anything.

I'm scared she gonna die, babe.

I take forty bucks out of my checking account and a new sweater appears in my closet.

Eight dollars and ten cents. Please, guy, that's all I'm asking. That's all I'm asking.

Crazy

Libby Stille

"HEY, MISS, WHAT time is it?"

Crap. I had sat down next to the crazy person on the bus. I knew because of a slight intonation that I had heard plenty of times on buses—a vocal shakiness unearned by years—and the way he looked—jeans and a jacket; long black hair pulled into a ponytail under a stocking cap; weathered, rough skin.

The 825 bus route was supposed to be safe, full of silent commuters taking it to their jobs in fancy skyscrapers downtown. It wasn't the 10, where you could expect crazy and a half all day long.

But here was Crazy. Maybe he would be quiet crazy, not make-best-friends-with-strangers crazy.

"Seven forty."

"Thank you."

I opened my book.

Soon he started to chat with the bus driver. "Hey, what suburb are we in?"

The driver didn't hear him. "The 825."

The man asked again.

Still didn't catch it. "2014."

I wanted to answer, but I did not want to engage Crazy. I opened my book.

After a third try, the driver finally said we were in Northeast. Poor guy. He looked new, freshly minted. The MetroTransit gods probably gave him the 825 route because of the usual lack of crazy.

Then Crazy heard the faint electronic strains of music—it was probably coming through someone's headphones, I figured. "Hey, miss, is that your phone?" I shook my head, my eyes still glued to the page. "Hey, miss, is that your phone?" More vehement shaking. "Excuse me, miss, is that your phone?"

The middle-aged, pleasantly plump woman across from us answered. "No, it's not." I breathed a sigh of relief.

"Hey, I like to listen to music, too—Ray Charles," Crazy said. "She give me money when I'm in nee-eed," he sang in a voice not much different than his speaking voice: quavering, raspy, and toneless. "Yeah, she's a fine girl, a friend indeed."

Please don't ask me for money, I silently begged. By this point I didn't have much of an idea what was happening in *Good Lord Bird.* But I kept my nose in my book to look busy.

Crazy asked where we were again.

"East Hennepin," said the newbie bus driver.

"Okay." Crazy continued talking, mentioning something about passing out on a bus. I had wondered how he had managed to get on the 825, the usual bastion of khakis and iPhones and solitude.

I shut my book and put on sunglasses. It was sunny, so I had a decent excuse for wearing them.

By the time we reached East Hennepin and Central, the faint strains of tinny music were really starting to annoy Crazy. "Miss, is that your phone?"

"No." I was ninety-nine percent sure it wasn't my phone, and I wasn't going to take it out and prove him right on the off chance that it was.

He got up to check out the situation. I flinched as he leaned toward me, listening for my phone. A girl across the aisle looked at me sympathetically.

"Sir, please take a seat," the bus driver said noncommittally.

"It's you, ain't it?" Crazy asked a woman a few seats back wearing headphones. "They're really loud, you know. Does that bother anyone else?"

We all stared at our shoes, or out the window, or at our books.

At the next stop, a woman got on the bus and sat between Crazy and me. Oh, you're going to regret that, I thought.

Crazy asked her, "Wanna hear a bad joke?"

"No, not today." She started flipping through apps on her blue 5c.

We drove across the Mississippi River in silence, until Crazy asked the bus driver, "Do I have a transfer left?"

"No, you don't."

"Can I get a free one?"

The driver didn't answer.

An 825 regular came up the aisle as we arrived downtown. He asked her for a transfer. "I'm sorry, I've got to use it myself," she replied.

"Oh, okay," he said.

"Say, are you from Michigan? You've got a Detroit hat on," she asked him.

"Oh." Crazy took off his hat and looked at it. "No, I'm from Green Bay. Actually, I usually look like this—" He pulled the binder out of his hair and shook it out. "I'm Native."

The bus stopped—my stop. I rose to get off. Crazy said to the woman, assuming she was leaving, "Well, you have a good day, ma'am."

"No, I've got two more stops to go. I just came up here to talk to you."

"Okay, well, sit down!" And she sat next to him.

I got off the bus.

I thought about Crazy and the woman who wanted to know who he really was the rest of the morning.

Battlefield: Ferguson

Andrew Orlebeke

Aᴜɢᴜsᴛ 2014 ᴡᴀs a terrible month for conflict resolution. The Syrian civil war continued unabated, minority sects were being hunted like animals in Iraq, Russia persisted in treating its neighbors like Risk territories and another Israel-Gaza cease-fire collapsed. As if that weren't enough, state brutality sparked another crisis that threatened to throw its region into open conflict. *Vox*'s Ezra Klein described it thusly:

> The crisis began in Ferguson, a remote village that has been a hotbed of sectarian tension. State security forces shot and killed an unarmed man, which regional analysts say has angered the local population by surfacing deep-seated sectarian grievances. Regime security forces cracked down brutally on largely peaceful protests, worsening the crisis.

This final example is the disaster of Ferguson, Missouri, where a police officer unloaded six rounds into an 18-year-old, unarmed teenager named Michael Brown. There are any number of cultural and social issues that the events in Ferguson have laid bare, not least among them the persistent, insidious, and disgraceful racial profiling of African Americans by law enforcement officers. For many, however, it is the militarization of our police forces that was the most shocking. Scenes from Ferguson—with Kevlar-coated paramilitary units roaming the streets and pointing their weapons at unarmed civilians—are associated with former Soviet republics, not the American Midwest. How did equipment which wouldn't look out of place on the streets of Kandahar end up in a small town in rural Missouri?

The reality is that the American law enforcement landscape has become exponentially more militarized in the past few decades, thanks largely to $35 *billion* in Departments of Defense and Homeland Security grants that were established for the war on drugs and proliferated after 9/11. Thousands and thousands of pieces of military materiel—guns, armored trucks, grenade launchers, and more—have been flowing into police departments nationwide. And those departments have not been shy about showing off their new toys: according to *The Economist*, Peter Kraska, a professor at the School of Justice Studies at Eastern Kentucky University, estimates that SWAT teams are now deployed around 50,000 times a year, compared to 3,000 per year in 1980.

SWAT teams, of course, do have a place. There are any number of situations—an armed gunman, a hostage-taker, a bomb, an actual terrorist threat—in which we want our police officers to be sufficiently outfitted. But is the gear really necessary when officers are—and these are actual examples—conducting arrests for illegal barbering, pursuing violators of copyright infringement, or patrolling the Keene, New Hampshire Pumpkin Festival? Maryland, one of the few states to document and measure its usage of paramilitary force, found that only six percent of the over 800 SWAT deployments over a six month period (that's over four a day, if you're counting) in late 2009 were for appropriate scenarios—barricades, hostage-takers, and other emergency situations. The remainder, according to *The Baltimore Sun*, were for simple searches and arrests.

If there is a silver lining to the tragedy of Ferguson, it is that official eyes have been opened to the dangers of police militarization. According to *USA Today*, the Department of Justice is planning a wholesale review of police tactics. In addition, and equally promising, advocates for law enforcement reform can be found on both sides of the ideological divide. The words "Rand Paul is right" were uttered by none other than Al Sharpton, MSNBC host and former Democratic presidential candidate. There is ground for both parties to stand on. This has not always or even frequently proved to be enough to effect change, but hope does exist that a consensus can be reached.

No one begrudges police officers their desire to be safe. But bulletproof vests are one thing, thirty-ton mine-resistant armored trucks quite another. As professor and former cop Thomas Nolan put it in *The Nation*, "when you dress up police like soldiers, they start thinking like soldiers. And soldiers engage an enemy." This is horribly dangerous, for a few reasons. First, police are not adequately trained in the usage of this new equipment, which makes tragic accidents far more likely. But just as importantly, citizens and officers are—or should be—on the same side. The wider the fissure in that alliance grows, the farther we creep along a path that ends in widespread violence and repression.

This issue affects everyone—police forces are a pillar of civilization which we rely on every day. However, it resonates especially for me—my grandpa and three of my uncles were police officers. It is a stressful, hazardous, and often thankless profession that is maligned, in many cases unfairly, by society. Precisely for that reason, it is imperative that a viable solution to the creeping militarization of law enforcement be found. As Mr. Nolan reminds us, military kit creates barriers between police officers and civilians far thicker and more impenetrable than two inches of reinforced steel.

A Simple Mistake

Paul Menn

Despair is for people who know, beyond any doubt, what the future is going to bring. Nobody is in that position. So despair is not only a kind of sin, theologically, but also a simple mistake, because nobody actually knows. In that sense, there is always hope.

—Patrick Curry, *Defending Middle-Earth*

WHEN YOU LOOK around the world, what do you see? When I look at the news, all I ever see are stories about wars, refugees fleeing their homelands, people being exploited, people struggling day-to-day just to survive, and on and on. There is a lot of pain, sorrow, and despair in the world. In our interconnected world, the endless feed of horrific and depressing images from all around the globe can lead you to think that there isn't a lot of hope.

I am currently in law school, and once every week or so, I volunteer at the Milwaukee Justice Center (MJC). It is a free clinic located in the courthouse basement staffed entirely by volunteers. It offers a few free basic legal services for those who can't afford to hire an attorney. Needless to say, every time I am there, the waiting room is packed.

And I see so much despair whenever I walk in at the start of my shift. I see it in the eyes of the young woman who has been abused by her boyfriend, but the police have done nothing to help her. I see it in the eyes of the father who just wants a few more hours a week to spend with his children, but his ex-wife is doing everything in her power to stop him. Single mothers working two or more jobs to support their children because the father doesn't pay his child support. The man who needs to reduce his child support because he was just laid off. The people who feel overwhelmed by the justice system, who don't feel like anyone will listen to them, and who don't know who to turn to. There's a lot of pain and despair in that basement room.

But do you know what else I see? I see students, paralegals, and attorneys who show up week after week to donate their time, even if just for a few hours, simply to help out those in need. Just to sit down with those who are overwhelmed and to try to ease the burden in whatever way they can. Five days a week, 8:30 a.m.–4 p.m., year-round (excluding holidays or when there is smoke damage from when a fire burns part of the courthouse), the MJC is open.

A lot of what I do at the MJC is just listening to people tell me their stories while trying to think of how I can help them. Most of the time, all I can do is help them fill out some paperwork, tell them the next steps in the (seemingly) endless legal process, and send them on their way. It really isn't all that much, but more often than not, people leave with less frustration and pain in their eyes. I don't know if I'd say that I gave them hope, but I maybe helped them back to the path to realizing that there is some hope in life. At the very least, I eased their burden for a little while.

Of course, there are bad days. Every single volunteer has had at least one person yell at them and/or storm off in a rage. But those are the exceptions. Most often the response is one the genuine appreciation. Appreciation that somebody took time out of their busy schedule to help them. That somebody cares enough to actually listen to whatever problem in life is dragging them down.

It is easy to despair. Likewise, it is easy to become so insulated from the world and wrapped up in our own busy complicated hectic stressful imperfect lives that we fail to see those around us who are truly despairing. Take time to inspire hope, in whatever small way you can, because the world has enough despair in it already.

Lessig

Andrew Orlebeke

IT IS LIKELY that the vast majority of people have never heard of Lawrence Lessig. He is not particularly famous, and he has not spent his life pandering to the lowest common denominator. He is, in many ways, the polar opposite of a politician. And yet in August of 2015, Lawrence Lessig announced that he would be seeking the Democratic nomination for president. He just may be the most interesting and, I would contend, most important candidate in either party, because the Lessig campaign is based on one thing and one thing only: leveling the voting playing field.

Professor Lessig, who teaches copyright law at Harvard, has long been a political activist. He came out strongly in favor of net neutrality and has been fighting corruption in politics for years. This is the first time, however, that he has decided to actually run for office, and he has done it in the most anti-establishment way possible: by crowdsourcing funds for his campaign. When he launched his campaign on August 11, Lessig announced that if one million dollars or more were contributed by Labor Day, he will run for president. Furthermore, he says, if he wins the election he will stay in office only long enough to pass the Citizen

Equality Act, a law which would curb gerrymandering, expand voter registration and access, and set new limits on campaign spending. After that, he says, he will step down and turn over the country to his vice president.

Why that issue, you ask? Why not education, or infrastructure, or economic inequality, or any of the other myriad issues which desperately need addressing? I would submit that voter equality is more important than all of them for the simple reason that it would give actual choice and electoral control back to the voters. No longer would our representatives be beholden only to mega-donors; no longer would they represent hyper-partisan districts carved out for them by hyper-partisan state legislatures. It would allow us, the voters, to vote for candidates who actually represent our interests and to actually hold them accountable if they don't.

Would it solve all our problems? Of course not. The Senate remains a woefully out-of-date institution and needs to be reformed and even with more voter equality, there is no guarantee that we could or would elect people who would make a difference. And perhaps more than anything, voters would still have to be informed and engage in the political process. But it would be a big step in the right direction.

Personally, I doubt that Lessig thinks he can actually win the nomination, let alone the presidency. But having someone like him—a candidate who would shine light on this devastatingly important issue—on a stage with people who actually could win the presidency would be an immense blessing to American democracy. We have already had a glimpse of it this campaign season, when in the Republican debate Donald Trump said for all to hear that he donates money to political officials on both sides of the aisle so that, when he wants something, they will be there for him.

I do not like Donald Trump. I do not like his personality and I do not respect his positions. But I liked that moment, and it provided a taste of what giving Lawrence Lessig his shot onstage could look like: shining the brightest spotlight our nation has to offer on an issue no one in power would touch with a ten foot pole.

Our democracy is badly distorted. The government "of the people, by the people, for the people," if it ever existed, is gone, replaced by officials beholden to corporate interests and big-money donors. But like it or not, it is *our* government, and fixing it is up to us. An outsider like Lawrence Lessig is exactly what is needed to reset the electoral process and, in the words of the Lessig campaign, to make democracy possible again.

Update: Due to limited ability to raise funds and a lack of national media attention, Lessig ended his campaign in November. The mantle of campaign finance was taken up by Bernie Sanders, who succeeded in including a section on reforming money in politics in the 2016 Democratic Party platform.

Earth Day and Weapons of Slow Violence

Robert Zandstra

APRIL 22 IS EARTH DAY, a day for environmental advocacy and for celebrating our relationship with the earth. The number of anniversaries of violent tragedies this past week is coincidental but not unconnected to Earth Day.

April 19, 1993: the fiery siege and attack by the FBI upon the Branch Davidian compound near Waco, Texas. Four government agents and eighty-seven Branch Davidians were killed.

April 19, 1995: the Oklahoma City bombing, which killed 168 and injured hundreds. The explosion measured 3.0 on the Richter scale.

April 20, 1999: the Columbine High School shooting. Fifteen killed.

April 16, 2007: the Virginia Tech shooting. Thirty-three killed.

April 15, 2013: the Boston Marathon bombing. Three killed, scores injured.

In each of these cases, the perpetrators were called "evil." Each time, several of the usual suspects were blamed—violent video games, religion, mental illness, guns or lax gun laws—but the focus was on the individual perpetrators. These actions were evil, no doubt, but I don't think it's right to identify individuals as "evil," as if the rest of us aren't. Certainly we can say they were sick, misguided, sinful, totally depraved even, but these terms apply to all of us, just as we are all created good and loved by God, and in need of redemption. It's easy to call someone else evil while overlooking the darkness in ourselves.

For example, people ignore that one of Timothy McVeigh's stated reasons for bombing a government building in Oklahoma City was retaliation for the unnecessarily deadly way the federal government handled its attack on the Branch Davidians. He intended by his violent actions to make visible the violence that the federal government committed near Waco and required of him as an Army soldier during the Gulf War on behalf of the American people. McVeigh's violence is deplorable, but systemic violence and our complicity in it should be visible.

The difference between us and these perpetrators is not in kind. Any difference in evildoing is only in degree. The more significant differences are disparities in privileges, stresses, circumstances, and graces.

Manhunts, vilification, and armchair psychoanalyzing unfortunately make for flashy news, whereas violence without directly intended victims doesn't. These unintentional victims are the collateral damage of a society that is more pervasively, if less visibly, violent.

For example, two days after the Boston Marathon bombing, the West Fertilizer Company facility (near Waco) caught fire and exploded (2.1 on the Richter scale). Fifteen people were killed, scores more injured, and many buildings destroyed. It's impossible to compare tragedies, but the coverage of this tragedy was lost in the coverage of the Boston manhunt.

The fertilizer—ammonium nitrate—was the same explosive used in the Oklahoma City bombing. No doubt lax safety codes and enforcement played a role, but this fertilizer explosion does not seem to have been intentionally criminal.

Anhydrous ammonia—used to make the fertilizer—is destructive stuff. It can violently explode and is dangerous to produce. But even worse is what it does to the land: soil sterility, erosion, hypertrophication, and aquatic dead zones due to runoff. Yet this is the nitrogen-adding fertilizer that is pervasively used in industrial agriculture.

The nitrogen cycle is one of earth's systems that humans depend on most directly. Yet the planetary nitrogen cycle is one of earth's systems (along with climate change and biodiversity loss) that humans have most perilously disrupted, largely due to fertilizer use.

After only a few generations of farming, the soil of the Midwest, one of the world's most fecund agricultural areas, is practically dead. Anhydrous ammonia fertilizer is chemically great for growing plants, but otherwise it is inhospitable to life. All those corn and soybeans are growing off the fertilizer (which comes from oil) put into the soil, not the living soil itself.

The soil of the very productive North China Plain had been kept and tended for hundreds of generations until it was overtaxed during the twentieth century. Sacrificing the soil was just another step in Mao's "war on nature" in the pursuit of industrial and economic progress.

The United States government is less overt about forsaking nature for power and financial gain. Nevertheless, people, places, and patterns of life are routinely sacrificed for profit. When value is primarily legible in abstract dollar amounts rather than as health, love, beauty, trust, or justice, too much is lost. Complex ecosystems and cultural systems are grossly simplified to be more easily controlled by governments and businesses to make money. The "economy," one of our worst idols, is expanded through ever more wasteful—that is, uneconomic—means (such as oil from tar sands).

This slow violence against the land is an unintended consequence of a great good: growing food. Yet it is far more destructive than any bomb. When the Deepwater Horizon oil rig operated by BP in the Gulf of Mexico exploded (on April 20, 2010), it killed eleven and caused the largest oil spill in United States history. But the death and ecological devastation of this disaster are dwarfed by similar tragedies in the "developing" world. And those in turn are dwarfed by the consequences of using the oil: climate change, toxic pollution, social inequality, cultural decay.

Growing up on a farm, I recognize the need for fertilizer and other potentially harmful practices, but I don't want to be blind to the victimization and violence they entail either. They should be visible.

Slow violence obscures the connection between victims and perpetrators of violence. The poor and marginalized are often the victims. The perpetrators are not only the corporate/government robber barons but probably everyone reading this as well. Perhaps we are all victims, too.

How should we think about violence that is done slowly and as a by-product of something good?

If I think of the clothes I'm wearing right now or the food I've eaten in the past day, and considered their past from fiber or food growth, extraction, processing, packaging, transportation, marketing, and so on, I know I would be appalled if I knew the injustices that took place in order to get them to me. But I don't know them. Our economic system renders the injustice invisible to those of us privileged enough to benefit from it. Slavery in the United States did the same for the Northerners privileged enough to oppose slavery on principle yet continue to reap its economic benefits. We might not have chattel slavery today, but we drive cars, fly on planes, eat genetically-modified high-fructose corn syrup, buy sweatshop-made clothing, surf the internet, and the list goes on.

No politician lasts long advocating for a steady-state economy or truly (socially or environmentally) sustainable policies. To paraphrase Wendell Berry, I am not optimistic about the state of things this Earth Day, but I'm not without hope. I want to consider what might be some steps in the right direction.

1 Practice Sabbath by resting periodically from participation in destructive systems. For example, try to relate to soil in non-destructive ways. The Bible from the beginning of Genesis makes abundantly clear that the drama of human life is inextricable from the life of the soil. Sabbath practices protect this relationship. I could use chemical fertilizer on my garden, but I use sheep manure and a cover crop of clover instead. Or read some poems about soil and spirituality (Two gems: "Calvinist Farming" by Sietze Buning and "Manifesto: The Mad Farmer Liberation Front" by Wendell Berry).

2 Recognize your own complicity in violence. We are still responsible even if we can afford to commit violence legally and indirectly. We as much as anyone are the violent of Matthew 11:12 who

attack the kingdom of heaven. "We repent of the evil we have done, the evil that enslaves us, and the evil done on our behalf."

3 Name violence when it is made visible, even in good things. Industrial food production, perhaps all industrial production, necessitates violence. So do climate change, globalization, resource extraction, genetic engineering, mass incarceration, and debt. Violence against the poor, against nature, against health, against community, against peaceful social conditions; violence against the laws through which God sustains the world. The Boston Marathon bomber was sentenced to death for using "weapons of mass destruction." The weapons of slow violence can be just as massively destructive.

4 Don't give up hope that love and life are stronger than all these weapons. Let's work toward God's kingdom in that hope. Let's not forget that Earth Day is also Easter season. Jesus Christ—God—took *all* violence, all death, whether inherent in creation or the result of sin, onto himself on the cross. And out of that comes resurrection and new creation.

Feminist Confessions

It's amazing how easy it is for life to pass a Bechdel test when there are so many named female characters.

Binders Full of Men

Mary Margaret Healy

I SIT IN MY CUBICLE, responding to emails and filling in some data, calling over the wall to the grant manager and answering her obscure grammar question. The grant manager is one of my favorite people at the office, in part because she asks me obscure grammar questions. As I sit talking to her, I am doing work for my supervisor, a severe woman who is simultaneously as cozy as a grandmother. She is my supervisor because I am filling in for a wonderful woman who is on maternity leave. As I sit with my emails and my data sheets, the CEO speedwalks down the hall to the program manager's office, and the two women talk loudly for a bit about the exorbitance of buying pizza for a hundred teenagers. Just at that moment, the CFO shouts profanities from the mini fridge because she spilled coffee on herself.

After a time, the four cups of tea I've had begin to take their toll, and I get up to go into the bathroom. We have a unisex bathroom here on the second floor, and when there are disgusting little flecks of pee on the rim, we know who put them there. There's only one person on our floor who is physically capable of such a thing. There are lovely smelling floral hand soaps on the sink, and someone left their mascara next to the extra toilet paper.

Later, I go to my class, my first and last of the day, and the first meeting of the semester. The professor takes roll, and when she comes to my name, I correct her: "I prefer Mary Margaret, actually." She makes a note. She comes to one name, a bit further down, and looks up.

"You must be Mason," she says, looking up at him. He sits near the middle of the room, towards the back.

"That's me," he says.

"I never have trouble remembering the guys' names," the professor says, and makes another note.

The next day, I arrive at my other job and say hi to my boss as I enter. He mumbles hi back as he sits with his eyes glued to his emails. I go to the front desk where the receptionist is already standing, putting something into the computer. She's pressing her hand firmly into her abdomen, and her face is contorted into a prolonged wince. "Everything okay?" I ask.

"Oh, just cramps," she said, returning her face to normal, but still typing with only her free hand.

"You too? I think half the staff is PMSing right now."

She nods in assent. "And the other half is either pregnant or praying that they're not."

I laugh. "Except Dave."

Finally, I have reached the pinnacle. This is what we have been waiting for for so long. A world without men. A world ruled by women. No longer under the thumb of the patriarchy, we are free to keep our floral soaps by the sink, stop for Starbucks on our way to our off-site meetings, and cry without reproach when the dog dies in the movie. It's amazing how easy it is for life to pass a Bechdel test when there are so many named female characters. And it's astonishing how quickly female solidarity falls away when it requires that you feel an intimate sisterhood with literally every other person you come into contact with in a day. This world is a little better smelling, a little better decorated, but other than it being a social worker's world, it's not that much different.

I sit back down in my cubicle and open up my emails and my data sheets again. As I go through the motions of my menial tasks, I hear the CEO talking to the outreach coordinator about the interviews they're about to start. "It's too bad there's not even a chance of getting a man," the outreach coordinator, the pee flecker himself, has the gall to say.

"I don't disagree with you," she says. Then she adds loudly, for the benefit of the entire second floor, "If I could, I would have binders full of men."

We all laugh before returning to our work. It was a funny joke.

But it wasn't a complete lie.

Because we don't love this world. We get along fine: we actually won agency of the year last year, so we must be doing something right. But there's something missing, and we know it.

And it matters.

Sorry

Cassie Westrate

I HAVE A BAD habit of saying "sorry."

I think I picked it up when I turned sixteen and landed a job as a banquet server for a local restaurant. I had heard terrible stories about the restaurant, including one in which the owner's goal every night was "to make a banquet server cry," but I couldn't find a job in retail, so one afternoon, I sat across from the manager, and the manager looked at me—slouched in a straight-back chair and shrunken-in with hunched shoulders as if I was perpetually asking *Who, me?*—and said, "Are you sure you want to work in food service?"

I wasn't, but I said "yes" anyway, and that was the beginning of hell.

(I'm joking. Kind of. It's difficult to love a job when a customer asks you for extra napkins, and you bring him a couple extra fancy cloth napkins, and he looks at you and says, "Oh, no. Paper ones, please. I have to blow my nose.")

As it turns out, I was terrible at the job. I was too shy and too afraid of my employers (and, admittedly, some of my co-workers) to excel in the position. Somewhere in those months, however, I equated being a lousy banquet server with being a worthless human being.

Always in the way. Always doing something wrong. Bringing cloth napkins instead of paper napkins. Too weak to carry the tray of mashed potatoes.

Sorry replaced *pardon me? Sorry* replaced *excuse me*, replaced *I have a question; I have something to say; I don't think this job is right for me.*

To be fair, I've had a lot to apologize for in my life. At the end of my first shift as a banquet server, I ran through the pouring rain to my car and promptly backed into another employee's SUV. I'm not immune to contributing to human tragedy. I've made mistakes. I've hurt people. There's a deep cry for justice out there warranting apologies from yours truly.

But there's a difference between apologizing to someone because I've wronged him and then chronically apologizing out of habit.

Recently, I came across a comic online titled, "If you want to say 'thank you,' don't say 'sorry,'" by Yao Xiao.

"Don't apologize for simply existing," Xiao writes, "because it's not wrong."

Somehow I believe that humans, rather than being the accident of a particle of dust spinning wildly out of control, are molded from clay by the hands of God, and yet, I walk around half-believing that my existence is a mistake. I can't completely shake the thought that I'm taking up space, taking up air, taking up time without giving enough in return.

"I'm sorry," I find myself telling my friends when I talk too much and too often about my job, about hopes, about worries, about frustrations and fears, about small successes and failures.

I'm so afraid of worthlessness and imperfections that I fail to appreciate the person in front of me who chose me for that moment, that day, that month. The manager who hired me. The friend who answered her phone late on a Monday night. Humans who, just like me, have neither a perfect existence nor existence perfected.

So lately I find myself trying, instead, to think less often about my insecurities and shortcomings, and to focus more on the person in front of me who is accepting me for who I am.

I want to change my "I'm sorry"s into "thank you"s.

Thank you for sitting in the passenger seat of my car with the heat blasting for hours on a Monday night because I don't want to be alone. Thank you for listening, listening, listening until I don't have anything more to say. Thank you for telling me what I need to hear and not what I want to hear. Thank you for making me feel like I'm worth something even when I feel like I'm worth nothing because life is trays of mashed potatoes, paper napkins, and terrible things in pouring rain. And yet, the beautiful thing about this mess of existence is that humans aren't created to live it alone.

A Time to Laugh

Sabrina Lee

WELL, IF IT'S a noun, then you really want to say "ass-scratcher," not "scratch your ass." I couldn't help but correct the wine merchant's translation. We—the Spanish assistant, the Indian assistant, and I—were sampling aperitifs, which were named with varying degrees of sexual innuendo. The vendor was having fun with his audience of three international girls, and we were expanding our French vocabularies, learning words our professors never taught us. *You've got to try this one,* he said, once we had finished the "gratte-cul" (ass-scratcher). *Everyone's got to try the chocolate blowjob.* A bit shocked by the name, we giggled, hesitated, and then held out our little plastic cups, *pourquoi pas?* Next was a "strawberry shag" (which I misunderstood as a strawberry shake and accepted way too eagerly), and then came a drink called "balls." When asked why the names were so sexual, the vendor, who was obviously more at ease with us than with an older, more serious couple, told us that the drinks used to be named after diseases, but that just didn't sell very well. It's true that we probably wouldn't have laughed had he offered us the measles.

I laughed, not because I particularly like that kind of humor in any objective sort of way, but because the exposition hall was bright and filled with colorful stands and because it was Friday and I was with my friends. I laughed and kept my feminist eyebrows from rising at the names' rather machismo bent because the protective distance of a wide counter separated the merchant and me and because he was one of the friendliest vendors there. I laughed at the absurdity and because it would have been absurd not to.

Laurent, whose crew cut is as severe as his perfectly sheared hedge, insists on paying me, even though I learn more French during our conversation sessions than he learns English. *I want to use you like a dictionary,* he explains, slapping down a crisp bill, *and if I treat you like an object, then I have to pay you. It will be like a hook up, but instead of having sex, we'll be doing language.* I can only laugh, half-disbelieving what I have just heard in the high school's small conference room, the one usually reserved for discreet parent-teacher meetings.

I am keenly aware of the situation: Laurent, as both a French man and an experienced teacher, is in a much more powerful position than I, the foreign, female assistant who looks no older than some of her students. He closes the door behind him. There are a few armchairs and a matching red couch. Rarely are we disturbed. And yet, his joke and these circumstances don't make me run because we know each other and because his humor is consistent whether we're having a conversation session, or visiting a castle with his wife, or chatting with the other teachers in the lounge. For example, at Chenonceau, Laurent turned to me and, using a colorful and distinctly British-flavored slang, described this majestic castle as a mere *boudoir* in which Henry II shagged his mistress, Diane de Poitiers. Laurent's wife didn't even bat an eyelash. And in the teachers' lounge, when I arrived one morning in a bright pink cardigan, Laurent poetically observed, *la sève qui monte*—the rising sap—and then asked what the English equivalent was. (I didn't—don't—know.) It took explanations from two female teachers who were also in the lounge at the time for me to understand that this tree metaphor is not a benign reference to springtime.

Perhaps these sorts of remarks are common in the United States, but I don't know. I am neither an expert in alcoholic beverages, nor am I an assistant in an American public high school, so I cannot say whether the sexualized streak in these conversations is more typical of French than American culture. I can say, however, that gone are my sheltered Christian school days. Which is okay. I get over my shock. And I choose to laugh rather than (de)cry, even though my education has definitely given me the tools to do just that. I could have lectured Laurent on the dangers of objectification, complete with a bibliography and citations. Or, instead of humoring the wine vendor, I could have curtly objected to the sexism and, then, underlined my point by refusing to taste his aperitifs. In short, I could have bared my carefully honed feminist fangs.

Or I could have taken a slightly different route. I could have tried to engage in a serious conversation and pointed out that this crudeness diminishes the dignity of not only women but men as well, that these jokes deprive sexuality—everyone's sexuality—of its worth and beauty, reducing it to a mere marketing ploy or a conversational ice-breaker.

But those seventeen years of school taught me more than just critical analysis and rhetorical flourishes: truth must be seasoned with love. And the love in those moments was to join with those men in laughter, recognizing their intentions to charm and amuse, to brighten the afternoon, not to embarrass or harm.

Don't get me wrong: there is a time when we should not—must not—laugh. Sexism and sexual harassment are serious issues and merit our most piercing censure. But then was not the time. In those moments, a critique may have corrected but would have also alienated, humiliating those men and setting me on a high and sanctimonious horse. There was only enough room for either judgment or grace, so I bit my tongue. I smiled, I laughed—happy to do so—and mentally filed away my cry for a different time, for a future paper or presentation.

Gray Matters

Wake up in the morning. Pick up the admittedly sharp-edged and scattered pieces of your life. Try again.

You're Okay

Katie Van Zanen

But that is what matters most in life, for all of us. The long obe-
dience in the same direction. Keeping at it. Finding honest hap-
piness in living within the contours of our choices. To wake up
another morning, beautifully bright as a summer day spreads its
warmth across the grass, or awfully cold as winter blows its way
over the high prairie, and stepping into the world again, taking
up the work that is ours, the life that is ours, with gladness and
singleness of heart, as the Book of Common Prayer *teaches us.*

—Steven Garber, *Visions of Vocation*

So. NOT TOO LONG ago, you graduated from college.
You decided, in a fit of principled, quasi-religious adventur-
ism, to move to another country for a year. People do it all the
time. People much less successful, thoughtful, independent, and/
or experienced than you are. *If they can do it, so can I,* you thought.

So here you are, in a dusty flat in one of the most populous
cities on earth, seven time zones from home, watching American
television streamed illegally over a mostly reliable wifi connection, which is probably exactly what you would be doing if you

were in the States, if you're honest. You have become one of those people who *watches TV*, and *actively reads Buzzfeed*, and *has a Pinterest wedding board*, and you are *almost broke* and *own too many books* and *drink too much coffee*, and you feel confused and lonely and tired, and you realize again that you are a colossal (millennial) cliché.

Go get yourself some chamomile tea.

Squash your skepticism about herbal remedies, turn your back firmly on the rabbit trail of ethical questions about *the influence of Enlightenment philosophy on Western medicine*, about *the limits of empiricism*, about *neo-imperialist appropriations of tribal wisdom*, and for once in your relatively short life, just drink the damn tea.

Do you feel better?

Yes. No. You're not sure. There are so many compounding factors and conditioned psychosomatic responses to ritual, and *correlation is not causation*, so who can say, really, if it's any medicinal property inherent in the tea itself—

Let's just move on.

The first thing you need to do is admit that you are scared. The second thing you need to do is tell yourself that *you will be okay*.

Yes, I know; yes, it is a strange and crippling thing to live in your own head, and that's why God ordained for you to have hilarious and tough-loving college roommates. Now, on your own in a strange country, you've figured out that it's not good for you to live alone. That's learning about yourself, which is one of the purposes of this whole ridiculous operation. And yes, you've learned that you need something that you can't have right now, and now you're learning about sitting in the slow ache of your longing, and that's good too. Things that are *good for you* often totally suck in reality, *building character* and evoking other nebulous benefits only apparent in hindsight. But you know you have to believe in that sort of goodness.

No one will congratulate you for your developing *maturity*. No one will give you a gold star for getting up without hitting the snooze button, for cleaning the bathroom, for staying on top of your email, for not burning the zucchini bread this time. If you're doing that out of some misplaced desire for external validation, you'll burn out fast. If you want to organize every cupboard in your apartment, do it. But don't ask for a prize. If you want to join the church choir, do it. But don't do it for applause. If you don't feel like you're doing enough to make the world better, take a look at your choices and change them.

No, unfortunately, adulthood doesn't come with a standardized evaluation mechanism to tell you how you're doing, but that's not an excuse to do less. You know that you wouldn't be happy doing less. It's you to whom you have to answer for your choices—God, ultimately, of course, but after that absolution, you have to make peace with yourself. Find an honest happiness with your choices, your standards. And don't give up when you don't meet them.

Because—be careful—you will flirt with Perfection, but Perfection will never love you. Don't spend too much time with him. And definitely, *definitely*, don't take him to the grocery store, because you really cannot keep having ethical + economic + emotional + existential crises in the cereal aisle. Pull yourself together, kid. Buy the imported German muesli and get out.

Go home. Unpack your backpack, or your reusable bags, or the plastic bags—whichever bags you have today. Pour yourself another cup of tea. Remember, no rabbit trails.

So no one is telling you you're doing a good job, and if they did, you wouldn't believe them. And doing a good job may not be, after all, the most important goal. If what you want is meaning and love, make it. Which doesn't mean every moment must be a symphony, or every acquaintance must become a bosom friend. You say you don't believe in averages. That's a defensible position, but maybe the best you can do is, in fact, a pattern of kindness. If you're going to make it in this life, you will have to believe that kindness figures larger than your failures, and that your efforts at obedience do, in fact, matter—to you and the world and a God who suffered the indignity of growing up, like you're attempting to do right now.

Wake up in the morning. Pick up the admittedly sharp-edged and scattered pieces of your life.

Try again.

You'll be okay.

Naked

Will Montei

The opposite of depression is not happiness, but vitality.

—Andrew Solomon, *Depression, the Secret We Share*

I'M OFTEN LEFT forcing my own feelings. I mean that I rarely feel the way that I want to feel, and I'm almost always thinking of how to just feel better. It never works. Most days slip by very quickly. At the end of the day I'm lying in bed feeling poor and stressed because I wasted all day not feeling correctly. I was too sad, too lonely, too indifferent.

These feelings carry into every single moment. The past few months look ideal on paper: I've climbed mountains, wandered new streets, met new people. Between the lines I feel as if I've done nothing—the white space is overwhelming. Which isn't to say I don't have feelings. I have an unreasonable amount of feelings; all hollow, all sadness, all unfulfilling. Now the year has ended, and I can only look back and reflect on how I didn't appreciate it enough. It will forever look like an empty, wasted year. Year piled on wasted year. I just want to feel some fullness, some goodness. I want to love the day. I'm not okay.

So I'm on a hike—I'm hiking up to Lake Colchuck. I'm with my friends Sam and Kevin. The land is beautiful. Mountains peek down at us through the trees. The sun is out, the sky is blue, we're young and we're active and I'm not fucking enjoying it and I can't figure out why.

When we get to the top of the trail, Lake Colchuck is a frozen and strange teal blue. The mountains are glorious, distant, snowy. Green pine trees cling to rocks. The sun is gleaming on the mountains so they look delicately painted. I'm frustrated to be surrounded by it all, not knowing what to do with it. I moved to Washington for these views—I want to feel them and love them, but I can't. So I walk down to the edge of the lake. It's well below freezing. I strip my clothes off and stand naked and red, looking around, trying to let the scene into my skin. It occurs to me that I might be depressed.

Hope feels like a distant memory. Hope in a well-lived life. I know how it should feel. God, I can remember those feelings. Sometimes I get so close to feeling okay, and my heart finally feels like it's lifting. Never all the way. That weight, so physical, is always there. I feel it now.

I had a dream once where I could see all my sadness suspended in my body like bright orbs. With my hands I reached in and pulled each one out. As I let each orb go, my heart actually lightened. When I woke I felt healed. I think I was, briefly. I knew it would all come back though, heavy, heavy, the same way we know the sun will rise. It's not weakness, knowing it would come back. The sun always rises.

I'm with my family on Christmas morning—mom, dad, brother, sister. I'm in love with my family, so it's odd to be with them and feel alone, like a viewer of a painting I want to enter. When we are all gathered in a room, the air itself is saturated with loveliness. I want to breathe it all in. I keep looking at my nieces squirming in my brother and his wife's lap, my nephew cuddled between my sister and her husband. I can see the separations of new families forming, future Christmases where I pick a family to be with. People have found my siblings. I wonder if it's my depression that keeps someone from finding me, me from finding them. I know it can make me jealous, quiet, bitter. I know.

God, it's a selfish state of mind. Christmas morning and I'm staring at walls, thinking about myself, mourning my love life like I do every other day. So I try to force feelings of contentment and togetherness so that I can be with my family just for a moment, be in the painting, breathe in their love. I can't.

Slowly

Griffin Paul Jackson

Wake up in the morning. Pick up the admittedly sharp-edged and scattered pieces of your life. Try again. You'll be okay.

—Katie Van Zanen, "You're Okay"

I just want to feel some fullness, some goodness. I want to love the day. I'm not okay.

—Will Montei, "Naked"

A FEELING SETTLES IN behind your eyes like heavy Michigan snowfall. Slowly, it floats down after an eruption in the sky of your psyche and fills every possible crevice. You can't even rearrange the thoughts in your head because the feeling covers everything too thickly, piling up in such a way that it keeps all your thoughts stagnant, cold, hard to reach.

The feeling is precisely this: right now, everything sucks.

You did not sign up for this, you think. You signed up for parties and spontaneity. You signed up for smiling uncertainly from opposite sides of the semi-crowded room.

You thought those Facebook likes would fulfill you. You thought OKCupid was *the answer*. Yeah, you did. You thought you had good lines. You are original, aren't you?

But what you got instead is a monster. A monster of biblical proportions. It comes up out of the sea to devour. Only, the sea is not a sea. It's a mix of neurons and soul—a concept you still don't really understand. And the monster is *in* you, may actually be you. It's a brutal thing.

At times, the monster makes you excited about *something new*—new town, new project, new relationship—only to drop you, flailing, from its shoulders. It makes you nervous to the point where you don't know if you are happy or scared.

Or both.

The monster goes in and out of view, like it's wearing a malfunctioning invisibility cloak, and so do its side effects. The monster you got is an idiot, and a mean one. This isn't any kind of Roald Dahl BFG; it's straight out of *The Witches*. It doesn't know you only signed up for the good parts of life. The memo didn't go through. The monster has no intention of inviting you to parties. It knows nothing of spontaneity or relishing small grins. It doesn't give a single schnozberry about liking your fake-ish Facebook life.

And—enough of these metaphors—some days the fear absolutely runs you.

But here's the thing:

You *are* original. You *do* go to parties (in your circles they are always called "get-togethers" and, for real, "extravaganzas"). You shoot glances. God knows, you shoot glances like you're the next American sniper. You remind yourself that buttons on social media *are only buttons on social media*.

Your life is not a cliché just because you did what your older brother did, or because your job title is *Project Manager*. No life is a cliché. Ever. Because you are *you* and no one else—and the fact that it's a cliché to say it doesn't make it a cliché to live it.

So, slowly, armed with a little forced excitement and the books your friends told you to read—Kant, Chan, Sedaris (because clichés can also be classics)—your new thought process mingles a very deliberate hopefulness with a smattering of epigraphs from your favorite authors.

And the feeling today is: right now, everything is fine.

You're going to write out what you're thinking. Process all that beautiful ash-heap. Or, maybe, don't write to *process*, but just for the fun of it. You're going to make your move, all JT-like, because what's the worst thing she could say? You're not even going to check Facebook today, like a boss.

And what was at the beginning of the day a deliberate hopefulness now becomes a more genuine, natural thing. You don't need to decide to be hopeful anymore. You don't need to be hopeful on purpose, because that's your native state of being. And those epigraphs you like aren't just cool strings of words, like posters hanging at the back of a classroom or in the back of your mind; they're real thoughts spoken by real people, and you're going to try to live them out instead of just saying them over and over in your head.

Some days, you just live.

Now, to keep it real, you don't know what tomorrow will bring. The monster might come out of the synaptic sea again, and you will want to lie down in the snow for a long time, as though it does not matter.

The feeling, the monster of regret about the past and worry about the future, will go positively *Assassin's Creed* all up on your life. It crosses your mind that, *Hey, I should not have gone abroad for a whole year, because I won't get married over here, and I won't make any money, and I'm going to miss out on all that millennial American Dream stuff my friends are doing.* The thought coats your cerebral cortex: I had a good thing going and I messed it up. Something, somewhere, whispers, *You're wasting away the possibilities for success, for love, for happiness.*

Alternatively, maybe you'll let a cliché not be just a cliché; you'll admit that today is an opportunity like any other—neutral, whatever you make it. You'll draw libraries to yourself, remembering in your drawing that all these angsty, pessimistic, postmodern novels you read in your *phase* are far outweighed by the classics you want to imitate and the theologies you want to live your life by.

You're going to try to figure out the difference between *emotion* and *mindset.* Between *psychology* and *spirituality.* Between *needs* and *desires.* You're going to get after it.

Here's what else you're going to do: you're going to wake up, *make your freaking bed*, and deny the world its cortisone shots so you can bring it to its knees.

You will risk something today. You will risk failure, in order that you might win the prize. You will risk prayer, in order that you might know peace in the will of God. You will risk going out into the world today. And the risk itself will make you better.

Because slowly, everything changes. Slowly, nothing is the same. Slowly, you see that "okay" is not a point, but a spectrum. Slowly, you realize that all of this is normal, and just believing that is itself a very great comfort.

Writing About Mental Illness While Mentally Ill

Mary Margaret Healy

MAYBE IT'S THE circles I run in. Maybe my friends and family ruin the curve. Whatever the reason, I've never felt particularly uneducated about depression and anxiety. I'm sure there was a time in my life when I didn't quite get it, but I think once I hit high school, someone explained it to me somewhere along the line, and it never got the chance to be scary.

Until I was diagnosed with it.

My family had always called me sensitive, dramatic even. I told myself I was just always nervous and that I took things too seriously. After Professor Vande Kopple died, though, things sort of spun out of control. I stopped being able to leave my house without help. I'd spend hours sitting on the floor doing nothing. I would tell myself I was going to apply for a job or go for a run or, hell, even take a shower, and then get too scared to do it. There were so many unknowns I couldn't control or explain, so I just avoided them. All of them. Everything. I avoided everything.

Two things saved me from my anxiety and depression that year: my fiancé and my dog. My fiancé because he pushed me past my comfort zone and got my brain out of the habit of being scared of everything. My dog because I knew if I didn't take her on a walk, if I didn't go to the store to buy her food, if I didn't get a job to pay for that food, that she would die, and I cared more about her than I did about me.

That's an important thing people like me—people who feel like they know about depression, but don't actually know about depression—probably don't realize. When you're depressed, you hate yourself. And you assume everyone else hates you, too. Not only do you have no interest in anything, not only do you have no energy, not only do you feel like your head is caught in some low-hanging cloud that keeps you from being able to focus or think or feel much of anything. On top of all that, you feel like you're stuck in an elevator all day with your nemesis. Yourself. Sometimes you can hear yourself, like a voice in your head, mocking yourself, asking rude questions like, "Why would you say that, idiot?" Sometimes your brain becomes the calendar-reminder app from hell, sending you a pop-up every ten minutes to remind you, "Don't forget, you're a loser, untalented, and nobody likes you!"

It was because of the hating myself that I never got help. When the bully is your own brain, you don't even know to tattle on it. I didn't realize I wasn't supposed to hate myself. I thought that I deserved it. And I believed me when I told myself that everyone hated me. So I didn't think a therapist or medication could help.

That all finally changed when I decided to become a social worker. One day, I was reading for a class on human development, and I got to the diagnostic criteria for major depressive disorder and read the words, "Feelings of worthlessness; excessive or inappropriate guilt." The little depression demon piped up and said "Ha! That's you, idiot! See, I told you! You're depressed. You can't help anyone." And I realized... I *was* depressed.

It still took months, a week of crisis, an evening in an emergency room, and the most supportive husband in the history of ever to finally get me into proper treatment. While I waited for the first appointment with the psychiatrist, I continued, dutifully, to go to my classes and do my homework. Things got a little weird when three of my four professors discussed crisis, trauma, and stress management in one day. Things got weirder when I was assigned to listen to podcasts describing in detail how to interact with a client who is suicidal. Things got especially weird when I sat through three consecutive lectures on the amygdala, and how, for people with anxiety, it is overactive and interprets social threats as physical threats. I had to study cognitive behavioral therapy to pass a quiz, but I also had to practice cognitive behavioral therapy to get through my day. It was surreal.

In the two months since my formal diagnosis and prescription, I've talked to several friends who are all going through the same thing as me and have been just as silent and self-isolating as I have been. I have read articles in *Chimes* urging the Calvin community to educate each other about mental illness and care for those among them who suffer and feel like they cannot ask for help. I have, myself, practiced telling my story, slowly, to people who love me and know me, and I have simultaneously practiced feeling shame and fear because some people aren't educated on the topic, and oh my god what will happen when I try to tell them? They will know I've been lying my whole life about who I am and how I feel. And they will hate me just like I hate me.

But the truth of the matter is that no one can educate you on depression, anxiety, OCD, bipolar disorder, schizophrenia, post-traumatic stress disorder better than someone who is currently living the nightmare. You can read all the DSMs you want,

Serenity at Some Point

Bethany Tap

For most of my life, I have been a go-getter, a self-starter, a leader.

When I was nine, I managed to con my friends into performing a play, under my direction, at my parents' house. It was an "American Girl" play, and we performed it on the stairway, an artistic decision symbolizing the "transience of life" or something.

In fourth grade, we did a project called "Reading Rendezvous," where kids got prizes for reading a certain number of books. I was determined to read more books than anyone else. I read forty-four chapter books in a matter of a few weeks. Another girl read forty-three. But I read forty-FOUR.

A few times, I dressed up my sister and her friends, making them go door to door, performing plays I wrote and in return, hoping for the neighbors to pity them enough to offer money (usually pennies).

Once, I organized all of my Barbies to form the chorus for the *Messiah* and played the entire recording, bringing forth the soloists and conducting the Barbie choir. My Princess Jasmine and Rosie O'Donnell Barbies were particularly enthusiastic about their performances.

These are some of the highlights of my eccentric childhood.

But at eighteen, my life changed drastically. I was diagnosed with major depressive disorder and I found myself, for the first time in my life, in the position to call myself a victim. I had grown up a privileged white girl with very few problems. Now that trouble had come knocking, I felt helpless and victimized. I cried and I wallowed. And I didn't know how to get out.

As is always the case with depression, "getting out" is not only difficult; it can be impossible. Lots of therapy and the right anti-depressant cocktail, along with incredibly supportive family and friends were what got me through the worst parts of it, a lengthy four-year struggle. Now, I have had to come to terms with the fact that I will be on medication for the rest of my life. But that doesn't make me a victim. I can still be a leader, a go-getter, and a self-starter.

This past year has been one of revelation. I graduated from Calvin last May, and while my time there was anything but a waste, I did find myself allowing events to happen to me, rather than taking initiative and control of my life. Shortly after graduating, I met my fiancée. The timing was not perfect. I was between jobs at the time and she was moving across the state. But we did long-distance for a year, got engaged in April, and are now living together in North Carolina, planning our wedding next June.

Life happens. I did not plan for half of the things that have happened to me this last year. I did not plan to meet Clarissa, and I certainly did not plan to get into one of my top choices for graduate school. How could I have known last May, walking in my cap and gown, that I would be here now?

A wise professor once told me that no one is simply a victim. Everyone is both a victim and an initiator. We don't have complete control of our lives, but we certainly have some.

Since moving to North Carolina, I've tried to be as involved as possible within my program. One of the first things I did was organize a workshop with a few other incoming students. I'm also excited to participate in the first reading of the year next week. Clarissa and I have hosted several events at our home already. I am determined to make a fresh start here, to overcome and not allow life to simply "happen."

Of course, there will be many events that happen which are completely out of my control. When those situations occur, the trick will be to let go while continuing to hold on.

It's like the serenity prayer by Reinhold Niebuhr, which has been adopted by AA groups:

> God, grant me the serenity to accept the things I cannot change,
> the courage to change the things I can,
> and wisdom to know the difference.

I remember my childhood self, the passion and exuberance I possessed then. And I ask God for wisdom as I move forward in this new chapter of my life.

Portrait of an Alcoholic

Paul Menn

"I THINK I HAVE a problem."

I was curled up on the bathroom floor, my face against the cool tile. The stench of sweat and vomit hung heavy in the air. I was coming down off a three- or four-day bender, and the withdrawal was hitting me like a freight train. It was in that desperate moment that I finally admitted what I had known for a long time—alcohol was ruining my life.

Ever since I was nineteen, I've been a drinker. It used to not be a problem. I could pass all my classes, make it to work on time, drink enough to get loosened up but not go overboard. Sure, there were times when I'd have a few too many and make an ass of myself or hear people say, "Oh yeah, you're the guy that drinks a lot." But I brushed it off—I was having fun, and it wasn't like I was going to live this way forever. I could stop whenever I wanted.

Until I couldn't.

Suddenly, what had been a weekend activity was creeping into the week. And I was starting earlier and earlier in the day. It was usually just whatever drink was leftover from last night to get me going in the morning. But then it became a few drinks to steady my nerves and prepare for a stressful, shitty day. Get back from school or work, have a couple drinks to unwind and de-stress. A few more at night either to go out and be social or simply to give me something to do.

Awake. Arise. Repeat.

It wasn't a problem; I only missed unimportant classes. I could make those up easily.

It wasn't a big deal; it was just a Nalgene of vodka and Red Bull—it was going to be a long night studying at the library, and I needed something to keep me going.

I didn't see why people were worried or pissed at me; sometimes I need some alone time, and that means ignoring every text, call, and email for a few days.

Of course I'm fine.

I'm getting married; this will help me get a handle on it. I wouldn't want to be the sort of husband with a drinking problem.

God, I wish she would just go to work so that I can be alone with the fifth I have stashed in my sock drawer.

It isn't that I am hiding anything, really; I just don't want her freaking out about my drinking because it isn't a big deal.

The anxiety is getting so bad; I just need a few drinks to feel calm again.

The panic attacks are happening so early; I need a few morning shots to function today.

Maybe I'll just stay in bed drinking. The world is so overwhelming; I need a day off to just dive into booze-soaked oblivion.

Suddenly, it is three or four days later, and I am on the bathroom floor. I don't even really remember how I got here, or what I've been doing for the past few days. I'm so sick, I can't even hold down water for more than fifteen minutes at a time. My stomach is in agony, and my heart feels like it is going to explode. I am shaking uncontrollably. I can't stop sweating, and the stench from the booze and toxins leaking out of my pores is sickening. The insomnia has made it so that not even sleeping pills work. There is no relief. No peace.

Tears in my eyes, I call my wife and choke out, "I think I have a problem."

That was roughly a year ago.

It has been a rough year. I've relapsed a number of times, but I am trying so hard to maintain sobriety and control. Each day is a challenge and a struggle.

Hi, my name is Paul, and I'm an alcoholic.

Small Talk

Calah Schlabach

I HAVE NEVER LIKED small talk, possibly because I have never been good at it. Over the past two years, however, I have developed something of a phobia regarding small talk, for a variety of reasons, of course, one of which being that small talk greatly ups the chance that I will be asked the following dreaded question:

"Do you have any siblings?"—or one of the many variations this question can take.

Seems quite unintimidating, doesn't it? I did not always hate this question, but now I do everything in my power (which, as I have discussed, is limited when it comes to small talk) to first, avoid the question, and second, if the question does arise, to limit the resultant discomfort.

This is how it usually goes:

"Do you have any siblings?"

Intentional Overly Pregnant Pause.

"Yes, one older brother."

If I volunteer the "older" part, sometimes it will head off the barrage of following questions. If I clip each word off quickly, avert my eyes, straighten my face—sometimes these do the trick too, making it clear that I. Do. Not. Want. To. Talk. About. This.

But, too often, it continues:

"What does he do?" or "Where does he live?" or "Is he married?"

Pause. Uncomfortable Look.

You have to do these things to soften the blow a bit, let them know something unexpected is coming.

"Um…. He passed away. Two years ago."

Sometimes, blissfully, it ends there. With an awkward condolence and a sympathetic look. After all, they don't want to be uncomfortable any more than I do.

But other times, they have to know. It makes sense—I am quite nosy myself. But more than sheer nosy-ness, the follow-up question is, I believe, a sort of reassurance. An uncontainable curiosity. They think, *She seems so normal, and this happened to her; does that mean it could happen to me?*

The question, too, takes various forms, of course:

"Was it expected?" or "Ohmygosh, how?!" or they just assume, "Cancer?"

And for some reason, this is where I stop trying to blunt the blow. Maybe it's because I hate euphemisms for their attempt to make something better that just isn't better than anything. Or maybe I don't want to soften for anyone what will always be sharp to me. Or maybe I think "suicide" is just too nice and neat a parcel to wrap the horror up in.

So I reply, "He killed himself."

I *could* be more harsh. I could say, "He hung himself." Or I could say, "He hanged himself," because I honestly don't know which is correct, and perhaps it is better I don't, for it would be unnecessary and perhaps cruel of me to go into too much detail.

For even barring all detail, when I say, "He killed himself," I see the thoughts whirring around in their heads. There is a change from *She seems so normal, and this happened to her; does that mean it could happen to me?* to *There must be something wrong with her or her family—that could never happen to me.*

I'm not saying it's universal. Many people have been very kind. Our close family and friends have showered us with immense love and support over the last two years. But when it comes to small talk and strangers, too often between "He died" and "He killed himself," there is a switch, and the person who, a second ago, looked like they wanted to embrace me has now scooted back to arm's length, as though I just coughed vigorously without covering my mouth.

In the months following Brock's death, my mom described the phenomenon quite well when she said, "I feel like a leper."

I'm sure the feeling is not entirely the others' fault. There is a stigma that comes with the dreaded word "suicide." I'm sure that, prior to two years ago, I might have given off a similar vibe if someone told me that a loved one had killed himself. I, too, thought it couldn't happen to me. I, too, would surely rather have pushed even the word from my mind for fear that even thinking about it might make it too real.

But if we don't think about suicide, or if we think of it as something foreign, only for the lower classes, or the higher classes, or the non-Christians, or those with lax morals, or those with a terrible home-life, or just those different from us or anyone we know—how will we ever prevent it? Because—guess what? It's becoming almost exponentially more common. And it happens to people like me, who aren't really so much different than you. Who went to Christian colleges and who had loving parents.

According to Thomas Joiner, a psychologist who has studied suicide at great depth, "Self-harm now takes more lives than war, murder, and natural disasters combined," but we don't like to talk about it. Why not? Why do we speak out against and do things to prevent war, murder, cancer, heart disease, and genocide, but avoid the most brutal killer in our midst?

Perhaps we avoid the subject of suicide because we have come to value political correctness above all—perhaps even above lives. We see people with signs and symptoms and hesitate to confront them because it is uncomfortable, or it's not our business—we are afraid to be perceived as nosy, or rude, or just plain wrong. Or we just can't understand why someone might do it, so we think it can't happen. Not to someone we know.

It *is* hard to understand why one might take her own life. Take my brother, for example. He had a history of depression, sure. He was tall and gangly and was bullied as a child. He struggled in school and seemed to have some trouble finding a life passion. But in some respects, he was at a high point in his life. He had finally gotten through college after having struggled academically his entire life. He was working the best job he'd ever had. And he had just welcomed a second beautiful child. Sure, he had some financial strain, but was it really that bad? I don't know; we will never know.

So what can we do? Well, for starters, I guess, people like me can stop fearing simple questions. I can swallow my discomfort and be willing to share—even if it makes other people think of me differently.

And what can we all do? I'm not encouraging you to run around asking all your loved ones if they have ever thought of taking their lives. Rather, I am encouraging this: ask questions, and set your phone down to really listen to the answers. Take an extra moment when you don't have time. Visit unexpectedly. Drop a note in the mail. Make a surprise phone call. Be a little intrusive into other people's lives.

Text START for Help

Abby Zwart

"IT SOUNDS LIKE you feel devastated because you've lost a best friend."

"So I'm hearing that you want to stop using drugs in order to take care of your family better."

"It must be exhausting to feel like you're not good enough for your parents."

"You're such a strong person for dealing with this depression and being able to ask for help."

"I'm impressed with how you handled that awkward situation."

I sometimes think of my bank of standard phrases as a Swiss Army knife. It's useful in all situations; you just have to choose the right tool.

When I log on to the Crisis Text Line platform on Wednesdays at 6 p.m., I whip out the knife and start looking around for the right tool to use with each texter. One with low self-esteem is going to need a lot of kind words and even some flattery—we call it "strength identification." Another who writes paragraphs before I can get a word in edgewise is just going to need me to shut up and listen without trying to problem-solve right away. A third who replies with two- or three-word answers to all my questions is going to need me to supply some language for their emotions. It's all just a matter of sensing who's on the other end of the phone.

Crisis Text Line is an organization offering a 24/7 hotline that anyone in the United States can text if they are in a crisis situation. They simply text START to 741-741, and a trained crisis counselor (maybe me!) will respond and help them through their crisis. "Crisis" is a broad term that encompasses any range of situations or emotional states. Sometimes a texter is being bullied at school and is feeling suicidal. Sometimes his wife passed away recently and he's tired of burdening his friends with his sadness. Sometimes her boyfriend changed the locks on the house and now she and the baby have nowhere to stay and no diapers. I've been volunteering with CTL for nine months now, and every week I get at least one situation I've never faced before. Common issues like depression, anxiety, work stress, or relationship/breakup drama come up often, but you really never know what you're going to get when you click that "Help another texter" button.

I started volunteering with CTL because I read about them in *The New Yorker*. There was this great article full of heartwarming, pathos-building anecdotes mixed with just the right amount of data science to pique my interest. *I could talk to people who are having a bad day and help them feel better. I'm a good listener. Or, I think I am. Maybe I'd learn to be better.*

I didn't exactly know what I was getting into when I applied to CTL. I was looking for a way to flex my latent social worker muscles (a teacher is part social worker, after all), and I thought texting was a really fresh service that we could offer to people who were too anxious to seek face-to-face counseling or to call a crisis phone line. What I got was so much more.

I spent several weeks going through an online training program that gave counselors-in-training a primer on the most common issues they'd face. I know more now about eating disorders and domestic abuse and depression than I ever have or will ever want to. I learned to put specific words to people's emotions, to show them I'm listening by rephrasing their issue and confirming it with them. I learned to encourage them by identifying their strengths and to use their names over and over and over again. I finished the training equipped with my Swiss Army knife of phrases and tactics and helpful reference websites. They're skills I've applied in a surprising number of situations—particularly in my classroom.

The number one thing I take away from every four-hour shift is a heightened sense of how universal pain and anger and loss are. The similarities among the texters I talk to are sometimes uncanny. One night I talked to a girl being bullied, and my very next texter was feeling guilty because her group of friends had started bullying someone at school. I've spoken with an incredibly diverse group of people—in age, gender, sexuality, race, religion, economic status, location, education level. But when you really get down to it, they're all feeling versions of the same things. In training, we were taught to give specific words to people's feelings, to say "devastating" instead of "sad" or "furious" instead of "angry." But those are just fancy words for the fairly small and basic set of emotions we face as humans. These people in crisis are sad or mad or jealous or worried. You don't need a thesaurus to see that.

The other universal thing I see is what people hope to get from a conversation with us. First and foremost, they just want someone to listen. I don't know if we do this enough in everyday life. In almost every conversation on the platform, I'll ask something like, "Have you been able to talk about this with someone you trust?" My aim is to expand their support network and help them see that they have options other than being stuck in their own heads. Sadly, very often their answer is something like, "Yeah, I told my mom but she didn't believe me," or, "My friends are tired of hearing about it." These people just need someone to listen. They don't want advice or platitudes. They don't want you to feel sorry for them. They don't always want a solution (though I'm trained to try my hardest to find one). All they want is to feel that their problem is important and merits attention. It's not a hard wish to grant.

I was fighting with a technology issue the other day and logged on to Apple's website to troubleshoot. I couldn't find the answer in any forums, so I clicked the "contact us" link, preparing myself to spend a long time on hold before talking to a technician. I was surprised to see that they offered a live chat service, and I decided to give it a try. Just moments after entering my serial number, I was talking with Heather, who was very concerned about my issue. "I'm hearing that your computer is not working as fast as it should. Is that right?" she asked. *What great service*, I thought, *making sure she understands the problem.* Then she said, "I understand your issue, Abby, and I can see how that must be frustrating. I'm so glad you contacted us for help. I'll do everything I can to resolve your issue."

Then I had one of those light bulb, semi-déjà vu moments. *She's crisis counseling me! She identified my problem, she used my name, she validated my feelings, and she vowed to come up with an action plan.* Even customer service has started to see the fruits of active and empathetic listening. Heather had her own Swiss Army knife of phrases that could walk someone through a crisis, albeit a different kind.

And it sort of made me think: what if I approached every conversation this way?

If you or someone you know is in crisis, Crisis Text Line is available 24/7 to bring you from a moment of panic to a place of calm. Text start to 741-741 to talk with a trained counselor.

If you or someone you know is interested in volunteering as a crisis counselor, CTL is always looking for new recruits. Learn how to join at crisistextline.org

Bread and Butter

Actually, I wish I wrote more like I cook.

Potato Salad Diaries

Cassie Westrate

August 12, 2014

TODAY, I RUINED 170 pounds of Chile Con Queso Dip.
I don't want to talk about it.

August 14, 2014

It was Potato Boy's last day.

We rarely spoke.

Aside from the passing comments, like the time he thanked me for picking that potato up off the floor for him and the time I was wearing a Calvin College T-shirt, and he asked me if I was going to be a freshman this year.

Didn't just graduate or anything.

August 15, 2014

I wish I could put "opened 486 cans" as an achievement on my resume, but I don't think employers would understand.

August 18, 2014

Today, the radio turned on by itself. Again.

That ghost we were joking about earlier doesn't seem so much like a joke anymore.

August 19, 2014
WZZM 13 filmed us for a "Made in Michigan" segment.
   I didn't agree to this.

August 20, 2014
It happened once before.
   And today, it happened again.
   The sealer didn't seal.
   Beet juice everywhere.

August 21, 2014
You know, when I was ten years old, I never imagined I would be shoveling potato salad. Life takes us crazy places.

August 28, 2014
Today, I scooped 550 pounds of Jalapeno Cheddar Potato Salad.
   Pardon my French, but: made it my bitch.
   I also ordered no-slip shoes.

September 2, 2014
Today, the radio turned on by itself again.
   And it wasn't plugged in.
   Just kidding. That didn't happen.

September 4, 2014
I wore my no-slip shoes for the first time today. Didn't slip once. I'm not sure why I'm surprised.

September 5, 2014
Today, my sock half came off in my shoe. I was too lazy to fix it. So I walked around like that all morning.

September 9, 2014
Liquid smoke, though. That stuff is potent.

September 10, 2014
Macaroni and Pasteurized Cheese Product.

September 17, 2014
"Hold it like you hold a bagpipe."

September 18, 2014
I can imagine the dinner conversation now: "Is it just me, or does this macaroni salad have more parsley in it than usual?"
My bad.

September 22, 2014
I can imagine the dinner conversation now: "Is it just me, or is this macaroni salad more yellow than it usually is?"
My bad.

September 23, 2014
We make nothing with fish. Nothing.
And yet, the place reeked.

September 28, 2014
Potato Boy is the new intern at church.
The world is small.
Too small.

September 30, 2014
"Smell this bucket."
I don't know what I was expecting.

October 2, 2014
Today, I accidentally flung Chile Con Queso Dip at my boss.
    I don't have good luck with that dip.

October 6, 2014
Dishwasher is on vacation, so I did the dishes for nine hours today.
    At least the sink is by the window.

October 7, 2014
MANAGER: We found a thirty-five-pound bucket of peanut butter in with the buckets of mayonnaise.
BOSS MAN: Cool.
MANAGER: What do you want to do with it?
BOSS MAN: Is it creamy or crunchy?
MANAGER: Creamy.
BOSS MAN: Shoot.

October 8, 2014
Brought home three pounds of peanut butter.
    Win.

October 16, 2014
Today, I learned something new.
    How to make cranberry relish.
STEP 1: Feed 760 pounds of frozen cranberries through a meat grinder.

October 23, 2014
Today, we had reviews. When Boss Man called me into the break room and told me to sit down, I didn't realize it was a review. So

when he asked me if I had any concerns, I asked him if he meant in life. Because I have a lot of concerns in life. But he clarified that he meant job concerns.

I'm worried that I'm going to get a hernia, but I didn't tell him that.

I Ate the Whole World

Abby Zwart

Έφαγα όλο τον κόσμο για να σε βρω[1]

I WENT TO PARIS and sat on the grass in a park outside the Tuileries. I ate cold, salty ham and creamy brie on a baguette that tasted like bread is supposed to taste. It was cliché and it was delicious. That French bread was so chewy, I had to spend twice my usual time on each bite, so I slowed down and admired the view. Hot chocolate that you'd convinced us to buy despite the warm sun was as thick as Hershey's syrup and so, so sweet. The bread cut the roof of my mouth and left a raw place there for the rest of the day. A sandwich echo.

I went to Grandma and Grandpa's house and ate hagelslag on a slice of buttered white bread for breakfast. Real butter, not margarine like we used at home. The bread was so bakery-case-infused that it tasted like doughnuts. You next to me, kneeling on the padded chair because there was no booster seat. Chocolate sprinkles skittered across the smooth wooden table.

I went to the dining hall and loaded up plate after plate at the salad bar. That lettuce, always too wet from washing, left behind

---

1 Greek idiom, literally: "I ate the whole world to find you."

puddles that diluted the peppery ranch dressing. Cranberries and sunflower seeds piled on boiled eggs and bacon until it hardly counted as a salad anymore. You followed suit, choosing chickpeas and carrots and cucumbers with a spoonful of peanut butter on the side for dipping. It always left me a little hungry and filling in the gaps with bowls of Cheerios and Cocoa Puffs.

I went to the brick house and your mom made bowls and bowls of kimchi and piles of rice. I sat on the stool in the kitchen and made awkward conversation while she dashed around tasting and stirring. There were mushrooms, which I didn't think I liked, cooked in something delicious that made them taste less like dirt. Everything was sour and spicy and so different than my childhood grilled chicken and potatoes. We ate it clumsily with chopsticks in the crowded living room. A feast among new friends.

I went to the amphitheater and sat in the hot sun with a cold beer. The picnic basket held chicken sandwiches and Marie's salads and the jewels of Michigan summer. Cherries so sweet they tasted false, like some candy-maker had developed a convincingly-real recipe. Raspberries that stained my fingers and blueberries a revelation. For dessert, a midnight chocolate bar.

I went to the mountain and was cold. Clumsy fingers unzipped tent flaps and fumbled unfamiliar boot laces. The tip of my nose like an ice cube. The little gas stove hissed as it worked to boil enough water for tea and oatmeal. You tore open those little brown waxed packets and poured the steaming water right in. Thick, hot, apple-y goodness sat like a glowing coal in my stomach. I never knew something so humble could be so soul filling.

I went to Concord and sat on the landing of a three-story bed and breakfast. We laughed and ate cinnamon-and-clove windmill cookies packed in my suitcase by my mother. On the tiny stove in my room, I boiled water for tea and sipped the vanilla caramel goodness that didn't even need sugar while we made terrible puns and talked about God and daydreamed about the future. Now, years later, I make a cup and breathe in. My face is suddenly hot, but not from the steam. Salty drops in my mug.

I ate the whole world to find you.

It turns out you were there the whole time.

Aquavitae:
My Life in Four Drinks

Andrew Steiner

Part One: Jägermeister

I think of drinks as elements that are entered, like bodies of water or locales.

—Lawrence Osborne, *The Wet and the Dry*

In the early nineteenth century, when Napoleon was scrounging the French countryside for young men to fill out his battalions, a young Alsatian named John Steiner was swept up in the wave of imperial conscription. A Mennonite and a pacifist, he was determined to escape, which he did, only to be quickly recaptured. But he gave it another try and this time managed to board a ship bound for Canada. There in the fertile fields of Ontario, he sired a family—a clan of farmer-preachers who made a slow migration over the generations into Ohio and Indiana. In the decades following World War II, as the national myth of that war solidified and their particular branch of Mennonitism was watered down with generic Evangelicalism, the Steiner commitment to pacifism softened, but its conviction that Jesus was Lord remained as strong as ever, and, nearly as strong, their abhorrence of alcohol.

In my childhood, I knew beer only as something sold by frogs on TV. It was the butt of jokes at family gatherings in the way that swear words are for elementary schoolers. Wine was something my mom's sisters drank once or twice a year at restaurants or an archaic term for the communion cup, a term of rite like fealty or canonization. Liquor was something unholy, a palatinate of dark spirits whose names were akin to those of Canaanite gods—whiskey, brandy, gin—the only conceivable purpose of which was the moral corruption of sad addicts.

I heard vague intimations that relatives on the Henry side were alcoholics, but these people were referred to only in the past tense, living or dead somewhere in New Jersey. My dad hinted about his college years, being transferred out of his small Christian school in central Indiana after freshman year for partying. Alcohol was something he had put behind him, along with convertibles and Steely Dan.

Gradually, inevitably, I became curious. The concept kept imposing itself on me. Sour applesauce in a buffet line. Blue cans in the canyon at McCormick's Creek. Stray Psalms and Proverbs, certain undeniable episodes in the life of Christ, Paul's instruction to Timothy about his stomach. My mom's glass of N/A red at a Carlson family gathering. The endless varieties on display on the shelves of restaurants and grocery stores.

I was working a wedding reception with my friend Brian and a couple other high schoolers. We were servers, carrying trays of bruschetta between the tables and out onto the veranda where the sun was bright on the lake and the bare shoulders of the bridesmaids. I was seventeen.

Carrying dishes back to the dish room, I caught glimpses of the chef toiling over the burners in his white smock, and as the night progressed, I grew increasingly curious about the bottles that seemed to gravitate towards him, sucked momentarily into his orbit before being slingshotted out into the dining room. This was something new for me. I was in the presence of a drinker, of someone who was in the process of getting drunk.

At the end of the night, he wobbled into the dish room to corral the wait staff. He addressed us, this stranger whose name I didn't know, as if we had served in combat together. I beheld him with soft wonder. He had four or five red Solo cups clawed together in his hands, and he passed them out to each of us. I looked in and saw a substance the color of engine oil hissing in the bottom of the cup. I took notice of a pair of Red Bull cans lying on their sides on the counter.

He raised his own cup and made a toast: "I just want to congratulate you guys on a hell of a job. This was a big-ass wedding. I couldn't ask for a better staff..." and so on until he trailed off, smiling at us. I don't know why—maybe it was the look in my eyes that drew his attention, or the simple fact of my height—but he turned that dumb, happy smile on me. The others, underage like me, had apparently noticed him noticing me because they were all looking at me as if for guidance. I sensed that we had come to a moment of truth. It was one of those rare instances when the pace of events slows and possibilities coalesce into a set of clear choices and demand that a decision be made.

I could do this. I'd seen it in movies. I raised the cup to my lips and threw it back.

It was remarkable. It was nothing. It tasted almost exactly like a fly I had swallowed once while riding my bike.

Walking down to the parking lot afterwards, I was filled with a strange lightness of step and buoyancy of mind. The evening sun looked beautiful and brassy. I got into the car with some trepidation and gripped the wheel firmly as I drove the twenty miles back to Holland, soaking in the wisdom that Brian, who had drunk Bacardi before and possibly beer, now felt free to impart. We stopped at a Family Fare two minutes from my house and drank chocolate milk in the deserted cafe until I felt the weight settle back into my shoes.

"That was a Jäger Bomb," Brian told me.

"Wow," I thought.

PART TWO: DALWHINNIE

Decus et Tutamen[1]

My first beer was a Rolling Rock, cracked at a Calvin house party when I was nineteen. I was prepared for the worst, but it was a soft landing, several degrees less sweet than Sprite, but nothing like the cross between prison bread and cat urine I'd been expecting. It was about a month before my flight to England and the beginning of my Wanderjahr, the bursting of the dam of temperance behind which I had been building little sandcastles for almost twenty years.

The York St. John Student Union. A pub on campus. Impossible but true, and every Monday and Saturday after nine was Pound a Pint Night. The president of the Union, during his orientation for the international students, must have explained

1 An ornament and a safeguard

its other functions—its open mic nights, homework help, student clubs, and I certainly remember the faculty advisor taking the floor at one point to make an unconvincing apologetic for the numerous activities on offer for non-drinkers—but once the import of that phrase had sunk in, the Calvin contingent, at least, heard nothing else. One British pint for one British pound. The price of a good sandwich was all we needed to get embarrassingly palookahed on Carlsberg or Red Stripe—or Diesels, the house specialty, a concoction of Fosters, Strongbow, and blackcurrant juice, as comforting and purple as a death embrace from Barney the Dinosaur.

I remember the feeling of those squat zinc coins heavy in my pocket, the portrait of Elizabeth II smooth under the thumb, the pleasing thunk they made on the bartop. Lubricated with the beer of the Union, we ran wild in the snickelways of the city where Constantine was crowned in search of more alcohol, and there we made discoveries:

The ales of Yorkshire with their deep malts that smelled like primeval rivers. The rites of handpull and cask. The shapely glasses wide enough to swim in. How conversations could open up and lead the speakers into regions they might never venture into sober. How laughter and anger and woundedness might sometimes be expressions of one emotion. How the night air tasted sweet in the throat like pipe tobacco or zante currants.

And, most precious of all, whisky.

Jon and I were eating curry at Bombay Spice on a Friday night, the two of us. We had been friends since *A Midsummer Night's Dream* my sophomore year when we both served on set crew. It was two weeks into our semester abroad, and this was the first real night we had spent together. Up until that point, we'd been wandering around buying phone plans and trying to find our classes. We talked well. There was a lot to say.

It was at that point that he told me he'd booked a flight back to Grand Rapids.

There was a girl. But more than that, the whole apparatus of his Calvin life, a scaffold suspended over the chasm between his love of English and his engineering major, had grown shaky. The more he thought about it, the less it made sense. He had already added a year onto his degree by trying to double-major. If he stayed in York through May, he'd add another semester at least. He had dreamed for most of his life about living in England, but now that he was here, he had to admit how ludicrous that dream really was.

We talked about it. I understood him. And then when we didn't know what else to say, we decided, screw it, we're here together now, and we're going to make it count.

We wound through town to the Three-Legged Mare and talked nonsense over pints of Centurion's Ghost and Wonky Donky. We laughed. We reminisced. We made fun of our friends back home. But something more was needed. This was a leave-taking, after all.

We opened the hard-backed drink menu and leafed through page after page of Scotch whiskies whose descriptions read like haikus and contained strange, exotic words like "phenolic" and "oloroso." Eventually we landed, as if by mutual inspiration, on Dalwhinnie. We ordered. It came. Subtle gold in the bottoms of the tumblers climbing the glass with viscous fingers. We looked at each other, we toasted to something, and then we knocked it back.

In that crystalline moment, I knew that I had discovered something totally new. I glimpsed landscapes. I couldn't speak. I just looked at Jon as my chest folded open with a glowing heat, not of fire but of sunlight waking a sleeper.

After the epiphany came the hunger, and we rambled off through the city until we found a sausage vendor in St. Sampson's Square, feeling even as we passed him our coins that we were on the downhill slope of a high point in our lives.

You can find parts three and four of Andrew Steiner's Aquavitae: My Life in Four Drinks *on thepostcalvin.com.*

How to Eat a Chicken

Amy (Allen) Frieson

L AST WEEK, MY FIANCÉ and I went searching for a chicken to
roast.

"All-vegetarian, cage-free, and 100 percent free of antibiotics," I
read from the green plastic packaging.

"Is it organic?"

"I don't know. It's grain-fed."

"But is it organic?"

We bought it and brought it home. I watched over Steven's
shoulder as he pulled out the plastic bag of innards. He washed
it under the faucet. He patted down the skin, looking for bits of
feather ("This is a really clean chicken. It must be organic.") and
peeling off bits of fat. Then he inserted pats of butter under its
skin, stuffed it with cloves of garlic and halved clementines, tied
its feet together, and put it into the oven. After its juices ran clear,
he carved it.

"I'm giving you some of this dark meat from the wing," he told
me. "I think you'll like it. And here's some white." He handed me
the plate with a little pile of chicken in the corner. I served up the
potatoes and green beans. And then I speared a bite of chicken
on my fork and put it into my mouth.

The crucial backstory here is that I've been a vegetarian for over ten years.

Roast chicken tasted exactly like I remembered. I chewed. I swallowed. I said, "Huh." I tried another bite. That texture, that taste. Nope. It hadn't changed.

I don't know what made me finally wonder if it was time to reassess my diet. Maybe that I always had a difficult time explaining to curious people why exactly I was a vegetarian—"I just don't like meat very much" always feels sort of lame to say. Maybe it was one too many times feeling limited in menu options. Maybe it was wondering if my constant tiredness was caused by a lack of vitamin B12, which is only found in animal-sourced foods, or if my frequent headaches were somehow related as well. Or, maybe it the fact that my friend group jokes about my supposed and fictional love of meats to the extent that one of them actually has me in his phone as "Amy Bacon."

Whatever the case, one day, I found myself surreptitiously Googling "I stopped being a vegetarian." And then I found myself saying to Steven one day, "Maybe I won't be a vegetarian forever." He didn't respond, but a couple of weeks later I overheard him telling the Amy Bacon friend that he didn't respond precisely because he didn't want to make a big deal out of it and scare me off. And then, when we had some friends over for a spaghetti-and-meatballs dinner party, I did it: I ate a meatball.

And I didn't die.

And it tasted really, really good.

The roast chicken was the last in a series of mouthfuls that have included chicken-fried steak, beef chili, prosciutto, and bacon. Some of these have tasted better than others. None has been a conversion experience.

Still, until now I hadn't told anyone other than Steven, who complicitly sneaks me forkfuls of his meals, that I am exploring a possible return to omnivorism. I'm kind of afraid of what the bacon people might say—of feeling judged. Which is dumb on my part. But if I didn't have a great reason for being a vegetarian, and I don't necessarily have a great, solid reason for stopping, it all seems kind of arbitrary.

And well, maybe it is.

I haven't stopped believing that the way I eat has an impact on the world. And there's a reason we spent all that time trying to figure out if the chicken was organic or not. I don't think I will ever be much of a meat eater, but I may choose chicken sometimes—especially if I visit someone's house and that's what they're serving—and I think that is okay. Even if I'm not yet at that point of decision-making. My reasons might not convince a lawyer, but they apparently have solidified enough to sway me.

We'll see what happens.

Some Garlic Sizzling in Oil

Jenn Langefeld

MONTHS BEFORE MY graduation from Calvin, I tossed my
neat plans for a sensible life. Instead, I took aim at full-
time writing. So I asked professors, fellow students, and strangers: Tell me what I need to know. How do I structure this writing
life? How can I not go crazy? What do full-time writers even do?

Several smart people told me: You can't just write and read all
the time. You need a non-verbal hobby. Something you're passionate about.

Well. You have to know this about me: I love food. As a student,
I sometimes read *Gourmet* magazine instead of doing homework,
daydreaming about recipes. I took frantic notes as a friend taught
me to make show-stopping curry; I baked pies and butterhorn
rolls in my apartment's dollhouse-sized oven.

A non-verbal hobby? Done.

And the advice is still good. When I run from my writing desk,
I run to the kitchen, where my world of food balances my world
of words.

Cooking has always been a release for me: if I'm tired, it wakes
me up. When my brain feels like slug fodder, a bit of sautéing
sparks me with inspiration. I dance while oil heats; I shimmy
while I chop. Cooking is a full-sense operation, the perfect anti-

dote to the numbness that settles in at my desk. I celebrate the sensations, even as I nick my fingers with the zester. I hold my face low over a pan to see if it's warm, I taste as I go, and I smell everything before it goes in, even the salt.

I have cried over good food (a goat cheese tart from Home Wine Kitchen in St. Louis, and it was perfect, and you would have cried too), and I have wept over bad. (A sweet potato risotto that took hours to make. I was starving, and it tasted like feet.)

But that's part of it: I value the risks in cooking. The hard-won successes. Some days my instincts repay me, and other days they're challenged and rewritten. There's the rush of emergency meals, the how-did-that-happen miracles. I rise to the challenge of complex, twenty-seven-step creations, but I also prize the simple. Like avocados on toast.

Or roasted beets. I'm smitten and surprised by beets. You pick clods of dirt off these whiskery, dimpled things, but cut the skin and they bleed purple-pink: they stained-glass dazzle. And the taste! If a potato went into a candy store, had an epiphany, and rethought its whole approach to life, it would become a beet. One part earth, one part sweet.

I know a lot of people who find God everywhere in nature. They see him in sunsets, woods, towering cumulus clouds. I see God in beets. He's right there: the creator made intimate, because I'm holding this beet in my hand, and we're the only two who have seen his perfect marbling work inside, pale white lines slipping through the pink. I see his work all through cooking; in every potato, bean, spice, there's his boundless creativity as he provides for us, giving me ingredients to transform into a simple supper.

This non-verbal hobby thing? This passion for the cooking process? It's worked out pretty well.

Actually, I wish I wrote more like I cook.

This has been a tough year with a lot of distractions, and frankly, I've lost my spark for the whole writing gig. I still love it—there's ink in my veins, words on my bones. I'm sure of it. But even this dutiful writing girl feels like she's been slogging through for a little too long. I don't want my writing to be the creative equivalent of "Ramen for dinner again!"

I want to steal some of that dizzy cooking passion. I want savory, sweet-hot. How can I drizzle salted caramel sauce all over my writing life?

What would that look like? Where is the cooking-writer me, who runs from the kitchen to the writing desk? Who mines for whiskery, dimpled stories, surrounded by dirt, the stories that bleed a little, but delight with brilliant marbled colors just under the skin? That taste a little like earth, but a little sweet?

I need to find a farmers' market for writers where I can pick up armfuls of raw paper, measure out markers and pens. Compare my techniques with that of the vendors, see if I can learn something, swap a recipe as we fan the flies away. Bring home the overflowing crates and get to work. I'll chop the paragraphs and dice adjectives (pick out the stray adverbs that fell in). Give the subplots a good scrub, then prick them all over with a fork and set them in a slow oven.

Maybe if I make this novel like I make a soup—start an idea like some garlic sizzling in oil—maybe if I savor every element that goes in the pot, maybe if I dance a bit as it simmers... maybe that will bring the excitement back.

Portrait Gallery

She teaches me how to see the world and live in it. She teaches me how to love.

Sydney

Sabrina Lee

M OM SAYS THAT SYDNEY tried to run before she could
walk—so intent was she on catching up with me. But, she
was always two years behind. In elementary school, her teachers
called her by my name and expected the same test results. If I
did something, she would follow: we both took classical guitar
lessons, attended the same summer art camps, and read the same
books. Oh, and her birthday is the day after mine.

As we've grown up, we've taken divergent paths: we've studied
different languages and cultures, worked different jobs, and lived
in different hemispheres. No matter where I have been, Sydney
has made a point to visit. Last weekend, though, it was my turn
to follow one of the twisting roads that she has already travelled
many times.

About eight hours and one time zone away from me, in eastern Kentucky, tucked between the steep, short mountains, there
is a small city with a population of around 7,000. Actually, this is
the largest city in the region. The outskirts are flanked by mobile
homes and *hollers*, narrow valleys that receive minimal amounts
of sunlight and have been home to generations of people seasoned and tried by the particular hardships of Appalachia. The

downtown area, built by revenue from coal, is charming with overflowing flower baskets and painted bear statues that boast notable aspects of the area. Some include: Miner Bear, Hillbilly Bear, and the Hatfield and McCoy Bears.

After dropping off my luggage at her apartment, I crossed two empty streets to the new pizza place where Sydney works her second job. I spotted her at the counter, chatting easily with strangers, making her customers feel special. Last year, I, too, worked in a restaurant, but rarely did I inspire as much laughter, rarely were my conversations as animated. As I watch my sister before she sees me, exhaustion heightens my admiration.

Of course, I'm tired from travelling, but I also know that Sydney worked eight hours before clocking in at the restaurant to work six more, and I don't know how she does it. During the day, she organizes summits and conferences to promote economic, educational, and health care development in an area where soda is cheaper than water, hepatitis C is running rampant, and the people—already struggling with unemployment—lost more than 10,000 coal jobs in the last year. Then, she spends her evenings with the locals who tell her all the small-town drama and warn her away from the mountain trails she shouldn't hike because she doesn't own a gun. She loves her little restaurant community, and the river gorges and scenic lookouts have captured her heart, but she also admits that she has never lived in a place so foreign— this coming from someone who has worked or studied in Hong Kong, China, Vietnam, and Cambodia.

Last weekend, I followed mountain roads all the way to my sister, but I realized that, really, I've been trying to follow her for a while. If I have to send a business-y sort of email, I run it by her first. An interview? I practice with her over Skype.

Fashion advice? She picks out my lipstick. What to think of a political issue? I trust her insight and judgement. Girl problems or boy problems or just people problems in general? Even with her overloaded workweeks, Sydney always finds time to console and counsel. Somehow, as we've grown up, we've switched places. Whereas my path has been (so far) more or less straightforward, Sydney has had to blaze new trails. She has navigated open doors that have slammed devastatingly shut and still done faithful work. So, I am assured that when the hairpin turns or the two-way, one-lane tunnels come, I will have an experienced and unswerving guide just ahead.

Texting with David

Andrew Knot

To my tale fin injoy.

—Spongebob Squarepants and my brother

AT 8:38 PM ONE JANUARY EVENING, my dad and brother were downstairs watching *Star Trek*, as is their custom. It goes like this: around 8:20, David approaches my dad, places a leading hand on his shoulder, and sighs hopefully. In a different situation, my dad might pause and ask David to articulate his thoughts. But *Star Trek* is liturgy, so the sigh is understood. My dad takes the cue, they go downstairs, and they beam themselves into a far-off galactic quadrant.

David can't—wait, doesn't—wait, *struggles* to communicate what he's feeling because he's diagnosed with *bilateral periventricular nodular heterotopias*. His mental mapping is different. This is why he can tell you that October 26, 1955 was a Wednesday, but he can't tell you the name of his math teacher. Some days I still can't understand this. *Who's your math teacher, David?* He sighs again, not hopefully, but angrily, huffing air through his nostrils and flailing his arms. You can't give the brain Alpine topography and ask it to traverse the Andes.

But TV is navigable. With my dad's prodding, David can recall complex plotlines, separate good guys from bad guys, and hoot at subtle and barely funny *Star Trek* humor.

Spongebob Squarepants is another staple in David's television canon. Rarely is he more engaged than when relaying the details of Spongebob's underwater undertakings. In his favorite episode, Spongebob gets a little self-absorbed after making a cameo in a Krusty Krab commercial. While on the job, he confuses a beckoning customer for a wide-eyed signature seeker. *And who am I making this bad boy out to?* Failing to detect the snark in the customer's rejoinder, Spongebob signs the autograph "To my tail fin." The customer swims off in disgust and leaves Spongebob, still oblivious, to hand the remaining autograph to the ever-cranky Squidward and say, "Enjoy." Each time he sees this, David cackles so gleefully that it makes me think for a second I'm just now understanding humor for the first time.

But evenings belong to *Star Trek*. This particular evening, they're watching "All Good Things." The episode hopscotches unannounced between past, present, and future to culminate in what my dad describes as "a kind of trial by ordeal to see if humanity has made enough progress to be allowed to go on." David could explain as much in his own words. I know because he's told me.

I've seen the episode before (David is very content with reruns) and, not being the Trekkie my dad and David are, I stay upstairs to watch The Taxslayer™ Bowl or some other corporately hijacked college sporting event.

It's not long before my dad has come upstairs looking for the Versed (ver · SED) because David is acting weird. Versed is a sedation and memory loss-inducing DIY anesthetic. We use it when

David shows signs of a seizure.

I run downstairs to see David on the couch. His skin is pallid, his arms are limp, and humanity is on trial before his eyes. I talk to him, ask him simple questions, and tell him to move his hands. I put my palm underneath his shaking jaw. He raises his arm, tries to open his hand but can't, and grazes my face with his knuckles. Everything he says is muffled.

We load the Versed into the syringe and shoot it up his nostrils. He breathes a little deeper and struggles to keep his eyes open. We're all down there—my mom, my dad, my sisters, even Millie, our dog—and we talk about David and his seizures, how this one isn't as bad as the one in November. David lies on the couch and sighs when he hears his name.

Last year, David started texting. His texts often mention Millie and always open or close with his favorite phrase: "To my tail fin, enjoy," or "To my tale fin injoy," as he prefers to spell it. His texts are occasionally comprehensible. Once I was hiking in Austria, and he texted me "Come home now to my tale fin injoy." But they are mostly baffling. I don't pretend to know the meaning of "To my tale fin injoy you sleep on the roof with Millie" any more than I pretend to follow most *Star Trek* plot turns.

Humanity survives in "All Good Things." Captain Picard successfully overcomes a discontinuity between past, present, and future to resolve a spatial anomaly in the space-time continuum. Q, the omnipotent Übermensch, then announces that past, present, and future have been reconciled.

We can be grateful humanity's not on trial. If we were, I suspect only memory loss could save us. And there's probably not enough Versed in the galaxy for that. So there are the memories that will always haunt us: David shaking on the couch, unable to say a word. But there are also the memories we hope for: David texting "To my tale fin injoy," laughing uncontrollably, and everything making sense.

Bea

Caroline Higgins

B Y OCTOBER I'VE LEARNED that Bea runs on apples and cig-
arettes. Dressed in pink-and-blue-patterned leggings, a tan
zip-up sweater, and Converse high-tops adorned with the Union
Jack, she power-walks around the school with more spunk than
colleagues who are half her age. She takes breaks only to excuse
herself to the school yard for the brief but regular smoke. Her
apples are eaten while walking or while giving direction to the
many colleagues who seek her aid. I, too, often stop her in the
hallway, "Where are the fifth graders today?" "Having an assembly in the gym. Just there." She points into the distance with a
hand that holds a half-eaten fruit.

By December I've learned that Bea, though she isn't the principal, essentially runs the school at which we both work. We are
sitting in the now-familiar staff room, except that tonight our
desks are laden with szalon cukor (a Hungarian Christmas candy),
midnight blue tablecloths, and glasses of champagne. Teachers
sit and chat while the scent of paprika and stuffed cabbage fills
the air and the principal distributes Christmas gifts—brand new
blue and red pens for everyone on staff, which are always appre-

ciated, as all official documentation and record-keeping is done with pen (*blue* pen) and paper in Hungary. I sit at a table with Bea, who can translate the principal's holiday message and the Christmas poem recitations with ease. When another teacher describes her favorite Christmas candy, the white chocolate and coconut Rafaello, Bea immediately reaches to open her desk drawer, where she just happens to have one for me to sample. I laugh, but no one else seems surprised at this Mary-Poppins-like readiness. When she leaves our table momentarily, her husband, Feri, who also works at the school and doesn't know a word of English, fills her champagne glass to the brim with the remainder of his own. Then he winks at me.

It's May—somehow it is May already—and by now I have learned that Bea doesn't stop giving. The eagerness and generosity with which she met us in August have not declined or decreased. My roommate Bekah and I are at Bea's house with Feri and their four-year-old daughter, Mira. In accordance with her character, Bea gives us a tour with an overall attitude of humility. "I know," she begins when we marvel at her neatly arranged flower garden, "but you see, we couldn't afford any of this if we didn't have my parents. And Feri made Mira's playground with leftover wood from the school desks!" Feri smiles proudly at his name and says something in Hungarian. Bea laughs and turns to Bekah and me, "He is always making me laugh. If you could understand him you would know he is very funny." We nod because we take Bea's word for everything, because we have been doing this all year, ever since we signed our lease and opened bank accounts with her guidance, scribbling our names on un-readable documents for days. Perhaps this is why she sometimes looks at me as though she is unsure of what I really think. Because I have never said no, the way you never say no to someone you not only depend on, but view with genuine respect and admiration. I worry that sometimes she doubts if I am truly happy and having a good time.

Later, in a sunlit attic, Bea's daughter is playing alternately with Bekah's and my hair. Frustrated by the fact that we spend our time speaking in a language she cannot understand, Mira imitates us. "Somebody, somebody, somebody" she says, trying to wind a hair elastic around my finished braid, "somebody, somebody..." I know that one day, Mira will speak excellent English, thanks to the influence of Bea, a self-proclaimed Anglophile. In the attic, we sit and pore over photos of a twenty-four-year-old Bea in London and listen to her stories of her young years there. It's strange to hear older adults rave about being the age you are now, and I am always unsure how to respond. A massage therapist I tutor recently told me, "Twenty-four was my best age. I wish I could always be twenty-four." Bea, similarly, remembers her nannying years in London with a far-off expression. "Even now, I can close my eyes and tell you how many steps it was to the end of my street." She explains how when she returned to Hungary, she got off the bus a stop away from her workplace, so as to give herself time to reminisce, often tearfully, about a life abroad that no one else could relate to or understand.

After a lunch of hearty stew and Hungarian fruit brandy, we hike up the hills behind Bea's house. Mira hangs cherries on her ears and belly-giggles. Feri winks at us, and Bea smiles, explaining again that the people with real money live farther up in the hills, and how she never thought she would be lucky enough to live here. I want to tell her I never thought I would be lucky enough to know someone like her, but I know my words will fall short, just as they fall short now, and decades from now, if I ever find myself explaining to someone why twenty-four was my best year.

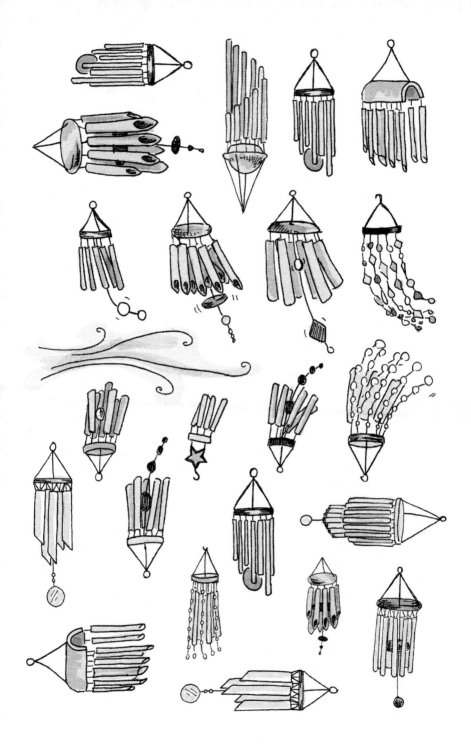

My Neighbor's Wind Chimes

Bart Tocci

IT MAKES ME LAUGH when people complain about their neighbor's wind chime, singular. What I would give for my neighbor to have only one wind chime.

Search for "my neighbor's wind chimes" on Google, and you get these results:

1 "Can I ask my neighbor to remove their wind chime?"
2 "Bad blood between neighbors keeps noisy wind chimes swinging"
3 "Franklin Hills Residents Suing Neighbor Over Wind Chimes"
4 The website where I ask most of life's tough questions, *Etiquette Hell*, answers "Are wind chimes rude?" with "If you have more than two, and they are near your neighbor's house, then they are probably rude." (TWO... HA! What a dream.)
5 "LORD GIVE ME STRENGTH! THE NEIGHBORS GOT A WIND CHIME!" This one, from twopeasinabucket.com, like all of the articles listed above, asks the question: can I ask the neighbors to take them down? Every question sparks a long thread, with a ten-to-one ratio—ten haters, near and dear to my heart, who think that wind chimes are the worst things invented. And one person who thinks you should wear earplugs because the sound is pleasant and they are insane.

6 "Can a neighbour put elastic bands round my wind chimes?" The first answer is undoubtedly from a fellow hater: "Sounds like they can and they have. So yes."

Wind chimes used to serve a purpose. In ancient Rome, you would hang them up on the patio, or the deck, or above your chariot garage, and they would keep evil spirits away because the evil spirits were so annoyed by the sound of the freaking chimes. In Eastern Asia, wind chimes were hung to keep away birds, which are bad, obviously, and more evil spirits. In current day United States, wind chimes are used to start legal wars between neighbors.

Imagine a deck. It's wood. It's a double-decker deck, which means that it starts on the second level of an apartment building and crawls up to the third. It's in the back. This is my neighbor's deck—she is a woman whom I don't know because we are in adjacent buildings. Remember how big cities have buildings that are about six inches apart? Remember that.

Deck furniture sits on top: three wicker chairs, a steel chair, and a mesh loveseat smaller than a two-person chairlift. (If there's one thing I know about loveseats, it's that two people in the heat of summer, with sweat pouring from their bodies, in bad moods, want to squeeze into a "two-person" summer chair together.) There are six clay flower pots on her stairs, all with the dish that goes *under* the pot *next* to the pot. *Infuriating*.

The whole deck has a new-age feel: a pizza-sized glass patio table sits in front of her loveseat, holding five other miniature clay flower pots with sanded-colored-glass chunks in them. They surround an elevated platter that holds a large blue shiny ball. It looks like a regulation-size bowling ball, or a regulation-size crystal ball. A little fortune-teller-y. I can get past that. But the wind chimes. Those chimes make the other objects sickening, like it's an elaborate spell-casting scheme.

"The spells! They only work when the wind is blowin' and the chimes are chimin'! *AHhhkkk, AHHHHKKK.*"

—Creepy hunched, shifty-eyed, phlegm-hawking neighbor, stirring a cauldron.

"Eyes of a snake! Toes of a rabbit! Teeth of a—" "—Grandma, rabbits have toes?"

(For all I know, she's a lovely lady who gets a wind chime every year for Christmas because she made the mistake of telling her grandchildren that she liked the *one* they brought back from Hawaii that one time.)

How many wind chimes would be considered reasonable? One, *maybe*. If it's nice-sounding, silent, and pretty to look at. Two are means for legal action. Guess how many she has. Go ahead. Say a number *out loud* that sounds reasonable. When people ask you why you've said a number out loud, ask them how many wind chimes are reasonable. I'll give you a second. How many did you say? Five? That's not too bad. You could probably be normal and have five wind chimes. *Ten?* Really, *ten?* That's a lot of wind chimes! A weirdo would have ten! Come on! Imagine all ten making noise! You could handle that? *Fifteen?! Wow! So many wind chimes—your friends might start to worry about you! HAHA!*

Child's play.

Try twenty-four. She has TWENTY-FOUR WIND CHIMES HANGING UP ON HER DECK! *TWENTY FOUR!* Her deck is smaller than a large area rug. My bedroom window looks onto her deck, and it's close enough for me to open the window and touch four of her chimes. It's about three feet away.

Why don't you close the window? Problem solved. I CAN'T! BECAUSE THE A/C BROKE AND IT'S EIGHTY-FIVE DEGREES AT NIGHT! It's getting fixed, but right now it's so hot and—IMAGINE SLEEPING WITH TWENTY-FOUR WIND CHIMES CHIMING THEIR FRICKIN HEADS OFF! I LIVE IN THE *WINDY CITY! THE NIGHT IS DARK AND FULL OF TERRORS!*

Twenty-four. "How many wind chimes? Oh I don't know, maybe two?" OH! OH?! Multiply that by *TWELVE. THAT* many wind chimes! Multiply anything by twelve, and you have a number so high, it's not even worth thinking about!

It can't be that bad.

First, I know that NO ONE would say, *it can't be that bad.* But to those with the audacity to *think* it, try this: hang up a wind chime in your room, in front of an oscillating fan. Go to bed. Tell me about it.

I wonder what this woman tells her guests—I know that it's hard to imagine that she interacts with other humans, but I saw two other people on the deck, so there must be others.

"Welcome to my home! You must be the Guinness World Record people! That's right—*twenty-four.* One for each hour that I drive my neighbors insane. Or, one for each member of a World Cup soccer team. Or, two for each month. Or, three for..." What's twenty-four divided by three? Just kidding. "Three for each deadly sin."

Or, "Good afternoon! You must be here for the wind chime convention!"

"No ma'am, just delivering the mail. There's no such thing as a wind chime convention, you old bat."

Or, "Come on in! Here's my kitchen and my living ro—Oh, forget it, you came to see my deck."

"Aunt Elsa, goodness gracious, where did you get all of these?

"I bought them all at once at a Christmas Tree Shop because I'm CRAAAZY!"

"Should we sit on the deck?"

"NO! IT'S NOT FOR SITTING. You'll go deaf out there! It's for keeping the neighbors away! See that window? That's a guy's bedroom! AHAHAA*aaakkk, Ahhhkkkk.* [Shifty eyes, stirring cauldron] Bones of a cat! Fingernails of a man! Basil!"

Sometimes you have to fight fire with fire, so I bought a huge country bell, the size of a watermelon, and I burned all of her wind chimes.

Nala

Stephen Mulder

THE DAY BEFORE my sister Lydia turned four, in the summer of 1995, my parents surprised the two of us with a cute, fluffy gray ball of fur with green eyes and white paws. She's still the best gift anyone's ever gotten me, even if, presumably, she really was meant to be more of a gift for my sister.

We named our new kitten Nala, after the lioness princess from Disney's *The Lion King*—VHS tapes of which were, at that time, still available in the "New Releases" section at Blockbuster. Admittedly an unimaginative choice, but it was 1995 and we were kids. I was a few months shy of eight years old.

Lydia and I initially weren't quite sure what to make of Nala, and Nala wasn't quite sure what to make of us. That first day, the three of us were bundles of nervous energy, following each other around, trying to play but not really sure how, or whether or not we could really trust one another.

It didn't take long, though, for Nala to win me over. Fortunately, Nala rather liked me as well, which was very good news because Nala was not always the easiest cat to deal with in her younger years. She did not get along with strangers; guests unlucky enough to cross her path could expect aggressive defensive action. More than once, I was called in to coax Nala off the stairs so some poor, unfortunate friend of Lydia's could pass through. Only family members could safely pet her without fear, and for a while I'm pretty sure I was the only one who felt safe enough trying to pick her up.

She was always trying to get outside, too, and if she succeeded, trying to reel her back in was a nightmare. I could sometimes manage, with patience, to coax her back in myself. For anyone else, a blanket, a pet carrier, an extra set of hands, and a first aid kit were the minimum standard recommendations.

But Nala could be very affectionate when she felt comfortable and secure, which is one reason why her more antisocial behaviours never much bothered me. Just about every afternoon after I got home from school, I would park myself on the couch, and Nala would show up about five minutes later. Sometimes she just sat next to me for a while. Sometimes she curled up on my lap. Once in a while, she would reach up and put her front paws on each side of my neck as I scratched between her ears and under her chin. Those are happy memories.

By the time I graduated from Calvin, got married, and moved out of the house in 2010, Nala was already beginning to slow down. But within the last year, her health began to deteriorate much more rapidly. Our family suspected (and later more or less confirmed) that her kidneys were failing. She was having trouble eating and lost more than half her body weight. (Mom kept trying different foods, a strategy that yielded only intermittent success.) She became feeble and frail, and she gradually lost her hearing, too, before eventually going completely deaf.

She wasn't in pain, as far as we could tell, and she had become as affectionate as she'd ever been in her life. She followed Mom around the house, asking for attention. For the first time, she was happy to let strangers pet her. She not only tolerated, but wanted to be picked up. You could even take her outside, if you wanted to—she was far too old and far too slow to get away or into much trouble. In some ways, she had never been a better, kinder, or more faithful pet than when she was dying, which only made it more difficult to accept what was happening.

Two weeks ago, Nala turned nineteen. The following Sunday, Mom made arrangements to put her to sleep.

I arrived at my parents' house a few hours before the vet's scheduled visit. Nala was curled up on the floor of the kitchen. I spent a few minutes petting her, but the experience was a little surreal. How strange to be aware, as your beloved pet simply goes about her day like any other, that in a matter of hours a stranger is going to stick a needle into her and stop her heart.

Suddenly I felt guilty, not only because of my participation in ending my friend's life, but also for not being there to visit her more during her dying months. I felt like, in ten minutes of scratching under her chin, I was somehow trying to make up for the last four years of only sporadic visits. Nala just purred.

The procedure went smoothly and quickly. We were told that it could take up to ten minutes for the tranquilizer to fully set in, but it knocked Nala out in under a minute. Mom and I barely had time to pet her before she had fallen out of consciousness for the last time. A second and final injection put her into cardiac arrest. Nala was gone.

After a few minutes talking with the veterinarian, I cradled my longtime friend and carried her out to the car. As I set her down for the last time, it occurred to me how much my final memory of Nala reminded me of my first. A cat wrapped in a blanket, her green eyes wide open. A boy, filled with nervous energy, not sure what to feel.

Costas

Elaine Schnabel

COSTAS IS A MAN with two stories. Two personal stories, that is; he tells others' stories for a living as a Greek tour guide specializing in New Testament history and the Classical Period around the Mediterranean. But I'm giving you the story that was told to me months before I met Costas. I was told he can remember everything he reads, that he knows more about the Holy Lands than the local tour guides, that he's the best guide in Greece—a savant with nothing but a bachelor's in business administration who is offered full-time history professorships by every American university that charters his Biblical history tour services in Greece, Turkey, and Jerusalem.

Then there's the story Costas tells about himself. Five years ago he found out he was dyslexic when he saw a special about it on TV. He had always struggled with reading and spelling, but his teachers said he was lazy. In fourth grade, his father gave him a choice: figure out how to pass his classes or learn his father's trade. Costas' father was a builder. At the time, the job was dangerous, requiring the dual skill sets of acrobat and weightlifter. Builders carried heavy buckets of cement five flights up rickety wooden planks, lifting and dumping them as needed.

Costas was nine years old and terrified. As he puts it, "I had to find some way to become a friend of the book." And he did. He became an accountant instead.

Costas is a short man with bright brown eyes, a salt-and-pepper beard. He dresses in long pants with a plaid button-up tucked into a high waistband. A faded and near shapeless ball cap to cover his bald head and shield his eyes. Sensible walking shoes. I can see him as an accountant hunched over numbers, quietly working through the rigmarole of tax season. He is mild.

The problem with accounting was that Greece revised its tax law in the seven years Costas ran an orphanage in Albania when the post-communist country opened up. He returned to Greece with an education so outdated as to be useless. He had nothing and no prospects. A friend suggested working as a tour guide, and the idea—along with the requisite three more years of schooling at the age of thirty-five—stuck. As Costas describes, he didn't have anything better to do at the time.

It's hard for me to believe he fell into his current career so haphazardly. His eyes and beard grinned with fierce joy when he told me about digging up a skeleton from the first century during an archeology internship he had at school. When I asked him how he combined the secular studies from his schooling with his Bible knowledge—the main component of the tour in Corinth I heard—he waved it away as nothing. Reading the original Greek is not much harder for him than modern, and he had been studying the Bible his entire life. As if that explained his in-depth explanation of who Erasmus was (a man whose name I'd never noted in the Bible), and the implications of the historically situated "bema" in Corinth, and how the word is used throughout the Bible.

Whether his is the story of the savant historian or the hard-working dyslexic, I don't know, and I don't want to perpetuate the wrong one. Nor do I want to be cliché. But Costas' trust-dive into tour-guiding gives me hope for whatever God gives to those who pursue him with dogged humility. Costas likes his job, and he shrugs off the near-weekly stress of not knowing if he'll get enough bookings to pay the bills as a chance to watch God provide for him, his wife, and three daughters. He likes his job, but fifty years into life, he still seems to be watching for whatever it is God has planned next.

The Sheep That Could

Ben Rietema

M
Y CAR DOOR CLANGED SHUT, and I ambled down to the stony beach. Mountains issued out of the lake in front of me as the clear winter sun cast everything in an early afternoon haze. A medium-sized RV was parked down on the gravel where a stodgy man with mussy hair, his wife, and his three daughters stared out at the lake. Hearing my approach, the girls turned to gawk at me, and one of them whispered something to the other.

"Hey," the man said as I approached. "There's a sheep out there. You can see him floating."

"No shit!" I exclaimed quite loudly, before remembering the little girls who stared up at me with wide eyes. I laughed nervously, then promptly shut my mouth and shaded my eyes to gaze for the sheep.

And there it was. A distant bobbing ball of white about a hundred yards or so offshore, frantically paddling this way and that.

"He just came tearing down here and cruised into the water," the man said.

"Well, I'll be...."

I stood there for several minutes and then politely excused myself to go eat my lunch. Maneuvering my way around a downed tree and a small cusp of gravel, I found a nice spot over-looking the bay and plopped down.

As I cranked open the top of a can of garbanzo beans—a precise art with my bargain can opener—I carefully charted the progress of the sheep. I mean, what else do you do? Calling emergency services seemed a bit too dire for the stupidity of the sheep, and there was no way I would swim out there to save this sucker. Yet as I watched the creature meander this way and that, I couldn't help but feel impressed.

Here was a sheep who somehow escaped the bounds of his home pasture, left his flock family, wandered across a road, saw a massive body of water, and decided to do what no other sheep had—*I'm going to swim that.* People may have questioned whether or not such a venture would lead this sheep to a top grass-eating career; some said it was impossible, that if God wanted sheep to swim, he would have given them flippers. But I'll be damned, that sheep was out there doing it.

Slowly, the sheep made his way to the shoreline and labored his heaving bulk up the shore about fifteen feet away from me. He stood there shaking, gasping short, labored breaths, looking like he had no recollection of where he was or what he was doing. He reminded me of a lot of Ironman contestants I have seen.

I prepared myself to get the blast out of there because if this sheep was crazy enough to swim, who knows what else he was capable of? This sheep may have been the pasture equivalent of a cracked-up New York hood rat and with a malevolent, skewed "baaahhhh," demanded my cash from me for its alfalfa addiction.

But this hoodrat sheep was exhausted. For another twenty minutes it stood there shaking. Every once in a while, he would try to shake himself like a dog, which only resulted in almost toppling over. Garnering up courage, I crept down the shoreline towards him, curiosity nearly bursting. I stopped some seven feet from him and bent over to his level. He stared at me. I stared at him.

I was there for a long time, hands on knees, head craned forward. I didn't know quite what to do. Should we vaunt this sheep among the echelons of the fluffy elite? Or was he mentally unstable? Did it matter?

It was such an elaborate feat, and only six people had witnessed it. At the end of marathons, we give people a medal, a free chocolate milk, and a silvery heat blanket; we cheer runners on and recognize that they have accomplished something of value. But this sheep left with nothing and came back with even less. This sheep was just wet and cold.

He gazed at me, seemingly serene yet still in obvious misery. Was he questioning his life? Was he brought closer to some meaning in his purposeless sheep existence? Do sheep go that deep? Probably not. Just wet and cold.

He shook and made a few faltering steps forward before stopping again. I took a photo, the sound of the iPhone's camera sounding harshly against the lightly lapping waves and the sheep's labored breathing. Later, I looked back on the photo. The sun shone brightly in the background, illuminating the sheep with sunlit rays. He almost looked deified as he stared at me, like the pure white sheep from the Bible you see on flannel church boards.

I put away my phone. I felt it was fitting to say something before I walked away, something to acknowledge that I saw, that I cared for this awesome act of the pasture, that the comeback

sheep, who was told he never could, swam in Lake Wanaka.
Someone had to do it.

I stared, silent.

"Well done, sheep."

Hi, My Name Is

Catherine Kramer

"**H**I, IT'S NICE TO MEET YOU. My name is…
…Catherine."

She is polite, she is professional. She has never met you before, and probably won't interact with you outside of a formal setting, or ever again. If you are a coworker or superior, you are probably older than her, and she wants you to take her seriously, so she uses her full name. She thinks her name is beautiful and regal, much befitting Catherine the Great and the Lady Catherines of yesteryear. She is flabbergasted that so many Katies are secretly Katherine/Kathryn/Katharines when they could be, you know, what they are. She was named after her grandmothers—her first name is one grandma's middle name, and her middle name is her other grandma's first name. Thus, quite literally, Catherine Joanne was born. If her parents had swapped which grandma's middle name would be her first name and which first name would be her middle name, her name would be Blanche Florence.

…Cathy."

She is young, and she is eager for you to like her. She doesn't feel like this name fits her particularly well, but she has watched enough peers struggle over the three-syllable hump that is Cath-er-ine to know that short and sweet is more likely to stick in your memory, and she would like to stick in your memory, because as previously mentioned, she is on the hunt for friends. It is most likely the first day of something, like a missions trip or tryouts or college, and whether you never talk to her again or become her closest confidante, you will likely call her this for the next 1–20 years, despite the fact that she doesn't like it very much. It will always remind her of that freshman feeling you get when you're new and eager to be liked, which is comforting, because if you are still using it, that means you like her and have continued to be friends with her and thus the initial goal was achieved. She will try to convince herself that this name is a good fit because Paul Simon once loved a woman named Cathy so now she has songs with her name in them. (Yes, indeed, she did walk down the aisle at her wedding to an acoustic version of "Cathy's Song," which is actually "Kathy's Song," but you'll never get her to admit that.)

...Cath."

She is core of this person before you. After all, you can't have Catherine or Cathy without Cath. Her family has always called her this and could never quite jive with the whole "Cathy" thing. In college, she discovered the designs of Cath Kidston and the song "Cath..." by Death Cab for Cutie. (This song, despite being about a wedding, was most certainly NOT featured at her nuptials.) These have inspired her to more earnestly strive to use this as her primary moniker. Her husband always introduces her as this and it is terribly confusing for most people, because they are not up on British fashion designers or Ben Gibbard songs from 2008. They are apt to callously remove the "h," but she can assure you she is not a feline, nor does she care for felines, and therefore does not want to watch a video of one doing purportedly hilarious things. Exactly two people have told her that they are uncomfortable calling her Cath because it reminds them of the word "catheter." (They were both Canadians. She refuses to believe that is a

Aunt Jackie

Brad Zwiers

AUNT JACKIE LOVES doctors and pastors.
Her memory warps her past so that any hospital visit she's had in the last years actually happened last week, and the highlight of her week almost always includes the sermon on Sunday, no matter who stands in the pulpit or what they say.

But it's more than that. For her birthday a few years ago, we went out to eat at Golden Corral, that bastion of American excess. As we pile-drived mounds of mashed potatoes and swirled ice cream two feet high on cake cones, my dad asked Aunt Jackie what she did for her birthday earlier in the week. She told us about a dinner with her sister (my grandma) and brother-in-law (my grandpa). And her favorite moment of the dinner?

"When Bob prayed."

Or Christmas day. Any Christmas day, really, not necessarily this year. We're all gathered in my grandparents' living room, and Grandpa hands out a litany he wrote to prayerfully enter into the festivities. Aunt Jackie's assigned reading is Luke 2, and she reads through the passage at a lightning pace and she's crying. The litany ends, and we sing a few carols. Aunt Jackie sings the loudest, and there's a kind of hope pulling at the corner of her voice that makes you think that everything, all of it, is true.

Sometimes when we're together, Aunt Jackie is asked to pray. I don't remember a prayer where her voice doesn't crack when she says the name "Jesus." Always when we're together, there's a small pause in conversation, and Aunt Jackie looks at someone and says, "I love you." This year, as she climbed out of a recliner, hips failing and feet shuffling, she looked at her mother (my great-grandmother) and said, "Can I have a hug? I love you."

Aunt Jackie loves so much. She loves our dog Rocket ("I love his fur; it's so soft!"), dolls, trips to the hospital ("I went to the hospital! I had pneumonia!"), sermons, pastors, deacons, prayers, chocolates, coffee, her sister. She loves little things in big ways. She loves God. She reads her Bible, prays, sings.

I don't love anything or anyone the way Aunt Jackie loves. She loves with precision and specificity, with faithfulness, power, pain, strength, hope, and eagerness. She loves full-bore.

There are a lot of things in this world that go unnoticed, and they slip silently away. I'm writing this because Aunt Jackie lets nothing slip away; the world is all right in front of her, full and bright. I'm writing this because I can't let Aunt Jackie slip away, not even for a moment. She teaches me how to see the world and live in it. She teaches me how to love.

What the Cat Dragged In

Jacob Schepers

"I HAVE A SURPRISE I'm bringing home :)"

Charis sent me this text a couple weeks ago. She was working an afternoon shift milking cows at the dairy farm, and, knowing well what she typically brought home—a few choice words for stubborn and kicking bovine—I was a little apprehensive.

"Uh oh, I'm nervous."

Three hours later, we gathered around a kiddie pool filled with cedar chips, water, a raggedy T-shirt for a bed, and some makeshift feeding bowls. In our hands was a timid, runty duckling. Liam was beside himself with glee, running around our three-season porch, and Oliver kept a fascinated, if wary, eye on the feathered stranger. A first family pet, unconventional as it may be.

"What should we name him, Liam?" asked Charis.

"Koonk." A fine name, indeed. Simple and zany and oh-so-Liam.

Charis had found the newly christened Koonk shuttered away in the corner of the milking parlor with no sign of how he got there. No quacks from a nearby mama, no siblings peeping in from the outside world, no pond on site to call home. Just a weak, trembling duckling. Our best guess was that one of the barn cats

had caught him somehow, separating him from all else, abandoning him for later use. So Charis scooped Koonk up in gloved and gentle hands to tend to him in whatever ways we could.

Koonk was with us for a short thirty hours. We knew from the start that Koonk faced a trying upstream paddle. Ruffled and matted feathers, glossy eyes, a lackluster appetite, and no poultry companion: he bore the telltale signs of an unkind life. And he had only us for some small version of comfort. For thirty hours, the four of us welcomed Koonk into our circle. Charis and I took turns holding him while we stroked his head until he drifted off to sleep. We nudged him toward his untouched food dish as Liam cheered on and Oliver waved clumsily. We provided him a heat lamp at night, and the boys checked in on him often by peering through the porch windows. Liam made sure we let him say goodnight to Koonk before hurrying off to bed. We did what we could and what we thought was best for our little duck. We consulted a family friend and vet for advice. And we watched as he kept slipping away.

Around 8 p.m. on a Sunday night, Charis came back from one of our routine checks and said Koonk had died. Since the boys were already asleep, the two of us stepped out onto the porch and viewed the duckling bobbing in the water, having fallen, lifeless, from his mound of fabric and cedar chips. I placed him in an empty coffee tin and buried him beneath the pines out front, fighting back mosquitoes and misty eyes.

When I sat back down on the couch next to Charis, we were both pushing down lumps in our throats, struck by how pronounced our attachments to the bundle of ebbed life had become in such a short time. I'll admit that later that night I straight-up ugly cried. Like Claire Danes in *Homeland*. Yeah. I'm still surprised at this reaction, which probably explains why I knew I had to write about Koonk this month. It's a way of sharing a life with you, a life that went largely ignored, brief and unimportant.

But it was important, silly and trivial as that may seem. Koonk was important to us as his misinformed, well-meaning, adoptive family. He was important to Charis, who couldn't shake the feeling that she could have or should have done more for him. He was important to Liam, who, even though we spared him the details and the harshness (those will surely come soon enough), still woke up a few days later in the middle of the night crying out that he misses his duck.

Far worthier and more pressing people and events deserve our cares and tears. This is fully realized and undisputed. Koonk was just a reminder of how even the smallest things can elicit strong affections and responses. It all started with a hungry bully of a cat and a rescue mission from trampling cow hooves. He was a lesson that whatever offerings of comfort we can give are no wasted efforts, a charge to do so more readily, more deliberately, and more often.

Tough World

Nard Choi

In May, I came back to Grand Rapids for the first time since graduating two years ago, and I've spent most of my time avoiding people my age and only seeking out my former professors in the English department. Once in a while, a few close friends managed to draw me out of hiding, saying, "What is this with you only hanging out with professors? We're your people!"

"I don't know," I would try to explain somewhat sheepishly. "I've always gravitated toward my teachers."

But this week, I've been trying to think through it more thoroughly, and I'm back to the time when I went to boarding school.

As someone already inclined to be highly anxious and hyper-conscious of the unnamed, always shifting, often cruel rules of school friendships, spending a good chunk of my childhood growing up in boarding school was an every-day, around-the-clock nightmare. The work of earning and maintaining the fragile threads of friendships didn't end at a bus stop in front of home but continued on at the dinner tables in the cafeteria, homework time in the dorms, secrets exchanged in bed, and even as an eleven-year-old, I became weary of this world that just would not let me be.

But it wasn't too long before I discovered my safe place in the presence of teachers at boarding school and every school afterward. I often found myself developing friendships with my teachers before my peers because they weren't complicated. When I was with a teacher, my churning mind relaxed a little. I could forget the popularity games outside the classroom door and find something sturdier in a teacher's friendship, which often started easily enough through my painstaking efforts in class. Perhaps it's from the set personal distance in a teacher-student relationship that I experienced the steadiness I didn't find with my peers. My teachers' willingness to spend time with me came from someplace entirely outside the realm of popularity status or if what I had to say was cool or funny, at least in my mind. When they didn't have time, I knew it was because of some kind of personal or professional obligation, and the next day or week they were still my teachers.

The more I think about it, I realize I got carried along quite far on childlike reasoning that teachers have to be nice to me because they're teachers and I'm their student. It's all I needed, though. Or maybe it's naïve trust, and I've just been lucky that I've never had to question it. Even when I look back over my time at Calvin, in almost every major turning point or period of growth, I've been guided and cared for attentively by a professor, starting with my freshman year when I put away my transfer applications after an English professor agreed to mentor me.

So when I returned to Grand Rapids this summer and was already feeling overwhelmed by the sudden influx of coffee dates in my schedule, I headed straight for the English department. The first person I ran into was Professor Vande Kopple. He swept me up in a hug, then held me at arms' length and roared, "What is this? Why was I not informed that you were coming today? And why have I heard rumors that a certain Vanden Bosch has been waiting for you this afternoon?" And so on we joked and insulted each other just like before. We made a bet about how Professor Vanden Bosch would react when he saw me. I cheated and won. And the last time I saw Professor Vande Kopple, he was swaggering out the office door, wagging his finger at me saying, "Now you take some time to prepare yourself. Then call me when you're ready for that lunch I owe you."

Then, a few days ago, my sister came to me, her face tense, telling me I should activate my Facebook. I did and immediately saw the first condolence posts, William J. Vande Kopple highlighted in blue. I barely registered the tears welling up. My sister asked me if I was okay and all I could say was, "We were supposed to have lunch. He was going to buy me lunch." And something inside me crumbled. For Professor Vande Kopple was one mighty bulwark of safety, laughter, and warmth in my life, even when he didn't get to know me so much as a brainy English student than as that cheeky girl who heaved snow into his truck and down his neck all the way through a writers' retreat. And as it is with all my teachers who have been such unchanging pillars of safety, friendship, and guidance in my life, I couldn't—I can't—imagine Professor Vande Kopple gone, not with his laughter still ringing in my ears.

I've been thinking about him every day since he passed away, mostly incoherent, childish thoughts, all of a sudden feeling so sorry about all the things I know I don't need to be sorry for. I want to ask him if he saw my affection through all my joking and cheek, if he knew that I only chose Vanden Bosch over him to make him laugh and hear him roar indignantly. I want to say thank you for making me feel so loved and part of something at Calvin and to say sorry that it took me so long to claim my lunch (which I know you offered me despite my cheating) when I would have sat down and maybe told you all these things, but now it's too late.

When I think of how he would respond to me, I can't help thinking of the writers' retreat when he read our poems out loud for the haiku competition. When one got voted out, he slapped it down on the floor and gave it a little kick away for good measure, saying, "Tough world, tough world." I find myself crying again and laughing at the same time, as only seems appropriate in remembering Professor Vande Kopple. I see him raising his eyebrows and giving me a droll smile, shrugging as he says, "Tough world, Nard. Tough world."

And I want to say back that it's all of a sudden too tough. But I remember when I went to him once before I graduated, already feeling a little lost in this big world, and he waited for me as I searched for something to say. "You make me happy," I finally blurted out. He just smiled and rubbed my arm warmly, and I knew that he knew I was ready, and that was enough. And today even as I still ache with this new emptiness inside, I know what he has given me—what he has given all of us—is still enough.

Afterword

Will Montei

L IKE SANDY COHEN AND U2, *the post calvin* is pro bono. It has been from the start and forever it shall be, until the day it peters out like a fire left alone through the night (which will preferably not happen in my lifetime). Aside from the small pleasures it provides for its readers and writers, there are no grand stakes for keeping it alive. Very little would be lost should Abby or Josh quit doing the work they've been voluntarily doing every single day for the past three years. They'll never receive an award for their efforts, never receive any wider recognition for their ingenuity, never be hailed as culture makers. Yet none of this has prevented them from tirelessly stoking the fire.

My own contribution of creating the Facebook page and sharing pieces daily is modest in comparison to what they do, but I'm glad they allow me on the team nonetheless. Josh and Abby are the editor, publisher, designer, IT department, web developer, and board of trustees contained within just two bodies. They are the platform on which our writers stand and the audience that cheers them on. They are the lifeblood of *the post calvin*. The only question remaining is "Why?" What makes *the post calvin* special enough to earn this kind of devotion?

Perhaps, now that you've enjoyed some of this book, you see the reason: *the post calvin* has a heart and a soul. Unbridled life fills these pages, as mundane, as revelatory, as off-kilter as a diary entry. The content is dictated entirely by what the writers choose to write about. This leaves *the post calvin* in a unique space where very few other publications exist: we have the talent of a literary journal, the output of a blog, and no cohesive vision. Thirty different lives all thinly connected but for the efforts of two people. If you were to ask them, Abby and Josh would tell you they are privileged to manage this community. They would tell you that this printed collection of essays is a gift.

I would agree. I love *the post calvin* because it is a home for unprofessional writers. It provides a spotlight on words that might otherwise remain in dark, unpublished realms. And what a shame that would be! I've found cozying up to the writing of my peers to be a rewarding daily routine. I like knowing what they're thinking about, what they're doing. I like seeing their sentiment and reflections crafted into words. There is a togetherness about this space, as both reader and writer, which most online communities don't have. We are all from Calvin College. We are all growing up.

And of course, *the post calvin* is defined as much by its writing as by Maria's artwork. While her pieces help illuminate the essays they are housed in, they are also essays in and of themselves. What began as me reaching out to a friend for help has ended in her becoming an indispensable part of the team. We couldn't be more grateful for everything she has given us.

Our hope isn't for this book to be compared to anything else—no other journals, blogs, or collections of writing in general—

if only because it is incomparable. That doesn't make it a vital piece of literature, but it does make it beloved. For that alone, Abby and Josh stoke the fire. Whatever modest warmth has been afforded here, I hope you have felt it.

About the Illustrations

Maria Smilde

I OFTEN PREFER TO look at my own drawings or paintings upside down. Something about the perspective shift allows me to forget some of the small mistakes and appreciate new details about the piece.

The writers of *the post calvin* all bring their own ideas, thoughts, and perspectives. Of equal importance, however, the readers come with their own views that affect how they interact with the piece. Rather than setting the scene for one particular interpretation, each illustration seeks to draw out elements from the essays and create layers and patterns that do not request to be viewed a certain way. There is no top or bottom to the drawings; the patterns can be viewed from any angle and allow the reader-viewer to respond to it in synchrony with the corresponding piece. With the opportunity to view pieces in new ways, I hope that both the readers and writers alike will find themselves able find new wonder in old favorites.

Contributors

ALISSA (GOUDSWAARD) ANDERSON ('10) 2013–2016

Alissa Anderson lives with her husband, Josh, in New York City, where she is earning her Master of Divinity at General Theological Seminary. Alissa enjoys binge-watching TV shows, singing in the shower, and perusing other peoples' bookshelves. For more, find her online at www.episcotheque. wordpress.com or tweet her @episcotheque.

NARD CHOI ('11) 2013–2014

Nard graduated from Calvin with a major in English and a minor in Latin. Currently, she is working on a PhD in Education and Children's Literature at Cambridge University.

JOSH DELACY ('13) 2013–2016

NPR called Josh deLacy "a modern-day Jack Kerouac" after he hitchhiked 7,000 miles across the United States, and a few dozen surprised drivers told him he didn't smell bad. Since that experience, he found homes in the Pacific Northwest, the Episcopal Church, and *the post calvin*. Josh deLacy's writing has appeared in places such as *The Emerson Review*, *Front Porch Review*, and *Perspectives*. His website: joshdelacy.com.

BEN DEVRIES ('15)

Ben DeVries graduated with degrees in literature and writing. He and his wife, Jes, another Calvin English grad, live in Champaign, Illinois, where Jes holds down a real-person job and Ben goes to school. He will maybe stop doing school in 2022 when he graduates with a PhD in American literature.

Miracle Drug   203

MELISSA (HAEGERT) DYKHUIS ('10)   2013–2014

Melissa lives in Lafayette, Colorado, with her husband Nathan, cat Sophie, and sons Matthew and Jonathan. She graduated from Calvin with a physics degree and then got a PhD in planetary science from the University of Arizona in 2015. After years of science, she's ready for science fiction again and is currently writing and editing young adult sci-fi novels.

Dr. Seuss, PhD   96

AMY (ALLEN) FRIESON ('10)   2013–2015

After graduating with an English degree, Amy moved to New York City and spent several years working in children's book publishing. Now, she works as a career consultant and has much more time for writing, reading, wandering the city, cooking non-vegetarian meals (a newer thing), dreaming about apartment renovations, and leading worship along with her husband at their NYC CRC.

DAVID GREENDONNER ('12)   2013–2014

David Greendonner is an MFA candidate at Western Michigan University where he teaches writing and is the managing editor of the literary magazine *Third Coast*.

GABE GUNNINK ('14) 2014–2016

Gabe Gunnink graduated Calvin with degrees in secondary education, Spanish, English, and writing. He is currently teaching our nation's youth how to say the colors in Spanish but hopes one day to relocate to York, England, where he will write poetry out of tea shops, go for lolloping runs through the British countryside, set the record for the most treacle cake consumed in a single sitting, and work part-time as a magical singing nanny with a knack for reminding families of the important things in life.

LAUREN (BOERSMA) HARRIS ('13) 2013–2016

Lauren is a spontaneous, idealistic, independent, fierce, over-thinking, damaged, adventurous, ordinary megalomaniac with a healthy sense of self-worth and a high word count. She has been a teacher both indoors and outdoors; she loves improvised comedy, backpacking, and writing, even when it's required.

MARY MARGARET HEALY ('13)   2013–2016

Mary Margaret is an English, history, and secondary education grad who currently works for Pennsylvania's Statewide Adoption and Permanency Network finding families for children and educating the masses about foster care, adoption, and permanency planning. She will graduate from the University of Pittsburgh in the spring of 2017 with a Master's in Social Work. Her major writing dream right now is to finish her science fiction novel that explores the concurrent futures of child welfare and artificial intelligence.

CAROLINE HIGGINS ('11)   2013–2016

Caroline Higgins lives in Brooklyn, New York, where she spends the vast majority of her time teaching English language arts to lively middle schoolers. She is consistently inspired by the energy and diversity of New York City and the beauty of that certain slant of light.

LAURA (BARDOLPH) HUBERS ('10)   2013–2015

Laura Bardolph Hubers is wife to Matt, mother to Samuel, and copywriter at Wm. B. Eerdmans Publishing Company. She counts the day the Chicago Cubs won the 2016 World Series as one of the happiest of her life.

MATT HUBERS ('12)   2013–2015

Matt lives with his wife, Laura, and young son, Samuel. He likes to spend his time playing board games, coaching high school forensics, and frolicking with alpacas. His dream is to write picture books.

GRIFFIN PAUL JACKSON ('11)   2013–2015

After a few years spent correcting grammatical errors and writing subtle, clever headlines in a Chicago newsroom, Griffin now does aid work with refugees in Lebanon. He writes about that, God, and, when the muse descends, Icelandic sheep. Read him here: griffinpauljackson.com.

MICHAEL KELLY ('14)   2014–2016

Michael Kelly graduated from Calvin College with a double major in psychology and writing. Shortly after graduating, he began his graduate level study of educational research, measurement, and evaluation at Boston College. When he is not studying learning and teaching, Michael learns and teaches through stories and writing—fiction and nonfiction, comedy and tragedy, and everything else in between.

GREG KIM ('14) 2014–2015

Greg graduated with a BA in history and international relations. He lived in Grand Rapids for a year and has since moved back to South Korea to fulfill his mandatory military service.

ANDREW KNOT ('11) 2013–2016

Andrew Knot lives and writes in Cologne, Germany.

CATHERINE KRAMER ('14)

Catherine Kramer has a degree in English and works in publishing. Her continued existence is made possible by grace, warm hugs, and iced chai lattes.

JENN LANGEFELD ('06)

Jenn Langefeld graduated from Calvin in 2006 and charged into a life of full-time novel writing. She is currently working on an exuberant, adventurous trilogy for middle grade readers. She writes under her great-grandmother's name, Lucy Flint, and blogs about making a lionhearted writing life at lucyflint.com.

GENEVA LANGELAND ('13)   2013–2016

Geneva survived graduate school with minimal blood loss, escaping with her MS in environmental policy and communication. She now works in Ann Arbor, Michigan, as the communications editor at Michigan Sea Grant. There, she gets to hang out with educators, researchers, and communicators who love the Great Lakes as much as she does.

SABRINA LEE ('13)   2013–2016

After graduating from Calvin with majors in English and French, Sabrina studied Italian for a month in Perugia, Italy and then moved to Tours, France to work as an English language assistant in a French high school. Currently, and for the foreseeable future, she is in the English MA/PhD program at the University of Illinois at Urbana-Champaign.

MATT MEDENDORP ('14) 2015–2016

Matt Medendorp graduated from Calvin in 2014 with a writing degree held together by duct tape and a few trips abroad. Currently he lives in Grand Rapids, works for Chaco, and claims to be producing a book of writing and photography from his time in Alaska.

REBEKAH (WILLIAMSON) MEDENDORP ('12) 2014–2016

Rebekah teaches English as a second language at Grand Rapids Community College. She does not drink coffee nor purchase Apple products.

NICK MEEKHOF ('15) 2015–2016

Nick graduated with a major in writing and a minor in geography. A farmer for the first twenty-three years of his life, Nick currently works for Mast Young Plants as a research and development specialist. When he's not engrossed in horticultural experiments, he can be found exploring the rivers, forests, and small towns all throughout the Great Lakes State. His current goals include kayaking one hundred Michigan rivers, swimming in Lake Michigan during every month of the year, and visiting as many Michigan breweries as possible.

PAUL MENN ('10) 2014–2016

Originally hailing from Wisconsin, Paul now lives in Grand Rapids with his wife, Emma ('10), and cat, Marco. When not working for a local hotel, he enjoys cuddling up on the couch with a good book, binge watching sci-fi shows, and taking long walks with his wife.

WILL MONTEI ('13) 2013–2016

Will Montei graduated with a major in writing and a minor in philosophy. He currently lives in Seattle, taking full advantage of the abundant local coffee and surrounding mountain hikes. He is an avid daydreamer, an old soul, and a creative potty mouth.

STEPHEN MULDER ('10) 2013–2014

Stephen Mulder is a copywriter, editor, account manager, husband, and member of two semi-professional choirs in West Michigan. He spent the majority of his college days inside the Chimes office, eventually serving as editor, web manager, and delivery-boy-in-chief in 2009–2010. He graduated with a degree in history.

ANDREW ORLEBEKE ('10) 2014–2016

After working in Washington, D.C., for two years, Andrew Orlebeke is in graduate school in Seattle, Washington, studying public policy. In addition to public service, he has a passion for traveling and an abiding love of sports.

KATERINA PARSONS ('15) 2015–2016

Katerina Parsons graduated from Calvin with a degree in English writing and international development. She lives in Tegucigalpa, Honduras, where she writes for a peace and justice organization, eats too many mangos, and is slowly perfecting her Spanglish.

DEBRA RIENSTRA 2013–2016

Debra Rienstra has published books on motherhood, Christian spirituality, and language in worship. She writes regularly about all sorts of topics for *The Twelve*, and she teaches literature and writing at Calvin College, where she has served on the faculty since 1996. Her website is debrarienstra.com.

BEN RIETEMA ('14) 2014–2016

After graduating with a major in writing, Ben Rietema has lived and worked in New Zealand and Australia. Besides spending time in the mountains, he makes a wicked hospital corner, digs a fine hole, and can whip up a batch of boiled eggs like no one else. He also writes stuff, which you can find at benrietema.wordpress.com.

JACOB SCHEPERS ('12)   2013–2016

Jacob Schepers is the author of *A Bundle of Careful Compromises* (2014), which won the 2013 Outriders Poetry Project competition. His writing, beyond *the post calvin*, can be found in *The Destroyer*, PANK, *The Common*, and *Verse*, among others. He holds an MA from the University at Buffalo and is currently in the English PhD program with a graduate minor in the history and philosophy of science at the University of Notre Dame.

CALAH SCHLABACH ('09)   2013–2014

Calah Schlabach is a Calvin graduate who—let's just be honest—majored in cross country and track while minoring in English and writing. After a year or so of global wandering, she discovered the sport of triathlon. Calah is currently working as a professional triathlete.

ELAINE SCHNABEL ('11)   2013–2016

Elaine Schnabel graduated from Calvin College with a BA in English and moved to South Korea for two years. Having most recently earned her MA in communication from Purdue University, she now studies theology at Fuller Theological Seminary with an interest in the intersection of organizational communication, power, and gender. She is married to board game aficionado Michael Stück, and they live with Lightsong, the fluffiest of cats.

MARIA SMILDE ('14)   2015–2016

Maria Smilde graduated with degrees in Spanish, studio art, and psychology, after which she moved out to Baltimore for a one-year AmeriCorps Community Arts program with an environmental justice non-profit organization. If that sounds like a lot of random interest areas, it is because she finds the world full of wonder and is constantly trying to make connections between its various facets of beauty.

ANDREW STEINER ('11)   2014

Andrew Steiner is a Grand Rapids native. He's a fiction writer with a day job at Feeding America West Michigan Food Bank. You can also find him working part-time for Ham Family Farm, pulling weeds, planting seeds, and slinging produce at the Fulton Street Farmer's Market.

Aquavitae: My Life in Four Drinks   298

LIBBY STILLE ('13)   2013–2014

Libby Stille lives in St. Paul and works in the marketing department of a children's publishing company in downtown Minneapolis. She recommends that everyone visit the Twin Cities, but only between June and October, unless you enjoy subzero windchills and slipping on ice.

Crazy   221

RYAN STRUYK ('14) 2015–2016

Ryan Struyk graduated from Calvin with majors in political science and mathematics. He currently covers the 2016 elections for ABC News in Washington. He's also done political polling in New York City and reported on the Idaho state legislature for the Associated Press in Boise. In his free time, Ryan enjoys talking about inferential statistics, music theory, and his beloved Detroit Tigers.

SARAH (VANDERMOLEN) SUNDT ('12) 2013–2014

A born-and-and-raised Grand Rapidian, Sarah is now a seventh grade language arts teacher in the Seattle area. She has been living there since the summer of 2015 with her music teacher husband, Mike. She loves reading, watching Netflix, playing games, watercolor, and walking at the off-leash dog park (even though she does not have a dog).

BETHANY TAP ('12)   2013–2014

Bethany Tap received her MFA in creative writing from the University of North Carolina Wilmington, where she also worked as the managing editor of *Chautauqua:* the literary journal of the Chautauqua Institution. She is currently working on her first novel. She lives in Wilmington, North Carolina, with her wife, Clarissa, and son, Alexander.

BART TOCCI ('11)   2013–2016

Bart Tocci lives in Boston where he write essays, performs at open mics, and threatens to start taco restaurants. He's been told that he looks like the kind of guy who stands up for what's right. And who goes to the store before the party. Read more here: barttocci.worpress.com

KATIE VAN ZANEN ('14)   2014–2016

After a year of travel and trial in Egypt, Katie Van Zanen is braving graduate school at Boston College. She reads and writes fiction, essays, blog posts, and letters from Lynn, Massachusetts. Follow her at kvanzanen.wordpress.com.

CASSIE WESTRATE ('14)   2014–2016

Cassie Westrate graduated with a double major in writing and international development studies. She works as a writer, poses as a barista, and approaches life one cup of coffee at a time.

ROBERT ZANDSTRA ('07) 2013–2015

Originally from a vegetable farm in northwest Indiana, Rob now lives with his wife, Hope, and daughter, Liefde, in Eugene, Oregon, as he pursues a PhD in English at the University of Oregon. He teaches undergraduate writing and literature courses and studies religion, secularization, and environment in nineteenth-century American literature. He graduated from Calvin in 2007 with a major in history of religion but returned the next year to complete the English major.

ABBY ZWART ('13) 2013–2016

Abby Zwart is a high school English teacher in Grand Rapids, Michigan. She spends her free time making lists of books she should read, cooking, and managing *the post calvin.*

BRAD ZWIERS ('12) 2013–2016

Brad Zwiers graduated from Calvin College in 2012 and Western Theological Seminary in 2015. He will not be graduating from any more schools. He often stares at books he wishes he could read but knows he will not finish and goes for long walks with his wife, Gwyn. Sometimes he plays basketball, and always he follows the greatest sporting club in the world, Liverpool F.C.

Permissions

This book was designed and formatted by Josh deLacy.
The text was typeset in 10.5/14 Adobe Caslon Pro and 16 Lustria.
All illustrations were created by Maria Smilde.

http://thepostcalvin.com